Revised edition

Revised edition

Elizabeth Manning Murphy JP DE

IPEd Distinguished Editor, BA Hons (Linguistics)
FCES FSBT (UK) AFIML

[Lacuna]
2019

# [Lacuna]

This completely revised edition published in 2019 by Lacuna Publishing
https://www.lacunapublishing.com

Lacuna is an imprint of Golden Orb Creative
PO Box 428, Armidale NSW 2350, Australia
https://www.goldenorbcreative.com

First edition published by Canberra Society of Editors, ACT, 2011

Copyright © Elizabeth Manning Murphy 2019

All rights reserved worldwide. No part of this publication may be reproduced, stored in a retrievals system, or transmitted in any form or by any means, electronic or mechanical, including photocopying, recording, scanning or otherwise, except under the terms of the Australian *Copyright Act 1968*, without the permission of the publisher. All permissions enquiries should be made to the publisher at email <general@lacunapublishing.com>.

Elizabeth Manning Murphy asserts the moral right to be identified as the author of this work. Everything in this book is the opinion of the author and not necessarily the opinion of anyone else, unless so attributed by the author.

Editing by Dr Linda Nix, IPEd Accredited Editor, BA Hons (English) PhD Grad Dip (Computing)
Cover and internal design by Linda Nix of Golden Orb Creative, based on concepts by Carina Manning (used with permission)
Photographs supplied by the author
Illustrations and figures by Linda Nix/Carina Manning based on originals by the author

Typeset in Times New Roman (text), Myriad Pro (headings) and Optima ('itchypencils').

A National Library of Australia Cataloguing-in-Publication has been created for this title
ISBN 9781922198365 (paperback)
ISBN 9781922198372 (ebook)

# Contents

| | | |
|---|---|---|
| Preface to the first edition | | viii |
| Preface to the revised edition | | x |
| *itchypencil 1*   Collective editors | | 1 |
| **Part 1**   **The craft of editing** | | 3 |
| | 1   Working words: the editor's job | 5 |
| | 2   Who exactly are you, editor? | 8 |
| | 3   Your friendly computer | 12 |
| | 4   On-screen editing | 14 |
| | 5   Variety in editing jobs | 18 |
| | 6   Seven deadly sins | 20 |
| | 7   Getting on with clients | 24 |
| *itchypencil 2*   Oops! False advertising? | | 28 |
| **Part 2**   **Editor beware: ethical and legal considerations** | | 29 |
| | 8   Courtesy, cribs and copyright | 31 |
| | 9   Disclaimers | 35 |
| | 10   Editing students' work | 38 |
| | 11   The ethics of editing | 41 |
| *itchypencil 3*   When 'brief' does not equal 'plain'! | | 46 |
| **Part 3**   **The business of editing** | | 47 |
| | 12   Project management | 49 |
| | 13   Project definition | 55 |
| | 14   Quoting: broad aspects | 59 |
| | 15   The proposal and quote | 61 |
| | 16   Invoicing | 64 |
| | 17   Office organisation | 67 |
| | 18   Editor, edit thyself | 70 |
| | 19   Editing on the move | 74 |
| | 20   Keeping in touch: emailing | 77 |
| | 21   A roundup | 80 |

*itchypencil 4*  A traveller's tale                                           82

**Part 4**  **Grammar: some basics**                                          85
    22  Why grammar?                                       87
    23  Rules, shmules!                                    90
    24  Parts of speech: some of the players               95
    25  Parts of speech: more of the players               99
    26  The arbitrating article                           101
    27  Relationships                                     105
    28  Verbs: some basics                                109
    29  Verbs: more basics                                112
    30  'Nerbs'                                           116
    31  One or more than one                              119

*itchypencil 5*  Distracting signs                                           122

**Part 5**  **Grammar: beyond the basics**                                   123
    32  Voice: active or passive?                         125
    33  Case: from Latin to modern English                127
    34  'That' pesky word                                 133
    35  Please allow my fancying possessives before gerunds  135
    36  Confusions                                        138
    37  More confusions                                   141
    38  Even more confusions                              144
    39  What is a sentence?                               147
    40  Stacking sentences                                151
    41  Shall we dance?                                   154
    42  May I? Might I?                                   157

*itchypencil 6*  Watch out! A roadside warning                               160

**Part 6**  **Punctuation: marks that matter**                               161
    43  Pausing with purpose                              163
    44  How much punctuation is necessary?                168
    45  What's the point?                                 173
    46  The powerful 'postrophe                           175
    47  Apostrophe do's and don'ts                        182
    48  The humble hyphen                                 187
    49  Dash it!                                          189

| | | | CONTENTS | vii |

*itchypencil 7*   *'Norf'k' – and the geese and cows*    192

**Part 7**    **What is style?**    195
     50   A reflection on 'style' from 1804    197
     51   Plain English is the style    200
     52   Strong, plain sentences    209
     53   How *not* to write    212
     54   Avoid style crampers    214
     55   Ambiguity, vagueness and other traps    217
     56   Sentence structure snares    221
     57   1 or 2 words about numbers    224
     58   Say what you mean – *in actual fact*    226
     59   Colloqualisms – colourful but *clunky*    228

*itchypencil 8*    *Only in Melbourne!*    231

**Part 8**    **The future of working words**    233
     60   Inclusiveness: who is 's/he'?    235
     61   International English    239
     62   Editing ESL writing    242
     63   Whither grammar and plain English?    246

**References**    249

**Index**    251

# Preface to the first edition

A lot has been written about English grammar, editing, plain English, effective writing, the business aspects of working from home as a freelance editor, writer and mentor, and so on. There are formal reference works on all of these topics, and this book does not seek to compete with any of them. Rather, it is a companion to all of them, to be picked up and dipped into at random for a somewhat lighter approach to these topics. It is dedicated to everyone who loves the English language and wants to make words work in their own writing and wants to help other writers to present their words to best effect.

I am a descriptive linguist – not a prescriptive grammarian. I have been editing as well as teaching, coaching and mentoring students of business English, academic writing and linguistics from a variety of cultures and language backgrounds since the 1970s. My work has included editing government, business and academic writing during this time. This has taught me that, while there are some conventions we need to follow in order to be understood, there are also new ideas, new technologies and changing fashions, all of which cause changes in those conventions and in the English language as a whole. I have, therefore, a flexible approach to the application of the 'rules' of English grammar in the workplace and in academic and other forms of writing. I tend to 'go with the flow'. The words have to work. If they don't, the whole document fails. Despite a grammar book's insistence on a certain preposition with a certain adjective, for instance, it is clear that our living language will make today's usage look 'old hat' in a few years, so it is often better to go for readability than to stick rigidly to a rule that was drawn up by prescriptive grammarians fifty or a hundred years ago.

*Working words* is based on the articles I wrote for the newsletter of the Canberra Society of Editors over a period of ten years. It is divided into eight parts, and the individual 'chats' (my word for chapters written in a chatty style) are grouped according to subject matter. The book first looks at what makes an editor and the craft of editing; and then some legal and ethical considerations. These are followed by the business side of working from home as an editor or writer. Several parts are devoted to aspects of English grammar, including some of the confusions that need demystifying, and punctuation. There's a word or two about style in writing, and finally a look at what the future holds for communication in English. And there are some little surprise packages in between the parts which look at some of the oddities I have observed in the use of English as I've travelled – 'itchypencils'.

My work these days is largely in editing, and this is a strong influence on the content and style of the chats. However, I hope the book will find a place, alongside the dictionaries and the more formal texts, on the bookshelves of editors, writers, teachers and anyone interested in making words work.

## Acknowledgements

My first thanks go to the Canberra Society of Editors in whose newsletter, *The Canberra editor*, the originals of these chats appeared, for agreeing to my basing this book on those articles and for joining me in this adventure. And thanks to the Society for Editors and Proofreaders for interest in the project in the UK.

A book like *Working words* doesn't just happen. My sincere gratitude goes to Ara Nalbandian, who has pulled together the material into themes and edited the resulting chats. Thanks also to the rest of the Canberra Society of Editors publication team: Cathy Nicoll, Edwin Briggs, Virginia Wilton, Martin Blaszczyk and Tracy Harwood; and a very big 'thank you' to Carina Manning, designer.

I also acknowledge the public authorities and others who put up the roadside and other signs that I had fun writing about as I travelled. I took all of the photographs in the book.

I couldn't have done all this without the love and encouragement of my family and friends, in Australia and England, who put up with me in writing mode for many months. I appreciate everyone's interest in the project. Special thanks are due to my sister Judy Angus for reading drafts.

*Elizabeth Manning Murphy JP DE*
Canberra, 2011

# Preface to the revised edition

This has been an interesting new adventure. Several of the original newsletter articles were written as long ago as 2003, so some rethinking was necessary. Most of what I wrote in the 2011 first edition still stands, but the English language has moved on and the way we express ourselves has become increasingly informal, even in formal writing. I have tried to reflect this in this revision while keeping to the basic premise that good grammar makes for good communication, and that good principles of ethics and other aspects of writing, editing and running a freelance business never change. I hope you enjoy dipping into the 'chats' in this revised *Working words* whether you are an editor, a writer or just interested in how words work.

## Acknowledgements

My sincere thanks go to Dr Linda Nix AE of Golden Orb Creative and Lacuna for her expert editing and our really productive interchanges on editorial matters. Thanks to Linda also for her friendship as well as her design and publishing advice and all her assistance in the production of this revision of *Working words*. Thanks to Carina Manning for allowing the continued use of elements of her original cover design and other artwork for this revision. Thanks also to editing colleagues and friends for helping me to think through some revisions, particularly Dr Jon Rosalky whose advice on some areas of grammar was invaluable and Dr Scott Nichol for much helpful discussion about the changing usage of words. And I would like to reiterate my thanks to all the members of the Canberra Society of Editors publication team who helped me put together the 2011 edition – the overall structure of the book is unchanged, including all of the 'chats' in their original order, and a lot of the text that you helped me to craft has been kept. Particular thanks to Ara Nalbandian for his structural editing and for a number of examples that remain in this revision.

May your words continue to work for you, dear reader.

*Elizabeth Manning Murphy JP DE*
Canberra, 2019
BA Hons (Linguistics) FCES FSBT AFIML
Honorary Life Member of the Canberra Society of Editors
and the Institute of Professional Editors
Member of the Society for Editors and Proofreaders (UK)
Member of the Australian Society of Authors
Website: www.emwords.info

*itchypencil 1*

## Collective editors

**Have you ever stood** on the outskirts of a gathering of people and wondered how to refer to them all at once? I found myself wondering just that at an editors' conference I attended some years ago. There they were: such a huge ......... of editors – a *bunch* of editors? No, a bunch of flowers. A *collection* of editors? No, a collection of antiques. An *amalgam* – no, that's dentists. What is the collective noun for editors? Well, why not ask them? So I sent out an SOS on various email lists, and this is what came back (with acknowledgements where I know them):

Carol in Indiana said 'Depending on the size of the group, it could be a *ream*, *galley*, or *proof* of editors. Or, perhaps you are referring to the more classic and always correct *punctilio* of editors'. Sara in Boston said 'I don't know the "official" word, but how about a *nitpick*?' Dwight in Florida suggested that 'a *delusion* of editors sounds almost as good as a *screed* of editors'. John Bangsund in Melbourne suggested a *barrage* was appropriate, and Rishi in India recommended a *column*.

The suggestions also included a *stroke*, a *pedantry*, a *colophon*, an *appendix*, a *bracket*, a *quire*, or a *chapter* of editors. Going down the path of generic names like hoover for all vacuum cleaners, Kat in Rochester, NY, recommended a *fowler* or a *strunk* of editors. And another New Yorker, Eli, put a bit of a lid on it for a while by saying he was 'starting to get board [sic] of editors' (pun entirely intended)!

An individual editor was described as an *itchypencil* (from Al in California) and from that comes the disease that afflicts all editors: *itchypencilitis*.

This suggestion was what gave me the idea for a title for the little light-hearted moments that appear between the parts of this book. Haven't you often spotted something on a signpost and thought 'Oh for a pencil to write that down'? That's *itchypencilitis*. So these moments are called *itchypencils* – how I wish for a handy pencil when these moments occur!

Martha in Boston suggested an *emendment* of editors while Ginny in Seattle thought an *opinion* of editors was appropriate.

Some suggestions I would blush to include in a serious journal, let alone a book, so I'll stop here with a contribution from my friend Gerry in Ottawa: 'According to *An Exaltation of Larks* by James Lipton, there are actually four collective nouns for editors – a *mangle* of copy editors, a *caprice* of assignment editors, a *dyspepsia* of city editors and an *ultimatum* of executive editors. For what it's worth, there's also a *scoop* of reporters, a *platitude* of sports writers and a *query* of checkers'.

# Part 1
## The craft of editing

# 1  Working words: the editor's job

WELCOME TO MY WORLD OF WORKING WORDS. Do you like reading, and do you find yourself noticing how words don't always work as well as they might? Editors help writers to make their words work, and it's an absorbing occupation. Most of what an editor does is to see that the words in a document really work to get the author's message across. But it's not just dealing with words. Editing is a multifaceted occupation, involving all aspects of the publishing industry, working with others in specialist areas, having confidence in your own understanding of acceptable English grammar, and so on. And it's great fun.

Well, just what is the editor's regular job? Where does the editor's job end and someone else's begin? Is an editor supposed to get involved in design work, or indexing, or making decisions about how documents should be presented?

Why not? Some might contend that indexing is not an editor's job. Designers might feel that they are the best qualified to advise on the look and feel of a book – and so they probably are in most cases. Some publishers restrict the editor to working on the text and not interfering with any other aspect of the publication. Others welcome the editor's suggestions.

Often we editors are asked 'Oh, by the way, would you have a look at the cover too, and while you're about it, could you do an index?' Now, if I didn't have some design skills, or know something about indexing, or have a feel for the whole document and not just the words, nobody would ask me. But I do, and they do ask.

It's like plain English. Many people think of plain English as just readable text, but that's only half the battle. Text can be perfectly correct, straightforward, easy to read, yet miss the mark because it's set in uncomfortable surroundings.

Anyone editing for plain English needs to consider white space, paragraph length, type size, readability of font, placement of graphics, and so on. Without consideration of all these, the text might as well be gibberish.

So editors have a wide-ranging role to play, if they want it. They can be part text editor, part designer, part indexer, part writer, even English grammar tutor or mentor, all at once. Or they can stick to the narrow path of, say, copy-editing or proofreading on certain jobs. Editing jobs are as varied as that, and the work is the more enjoyable when that variety challenges all of our skills at different times.

However, all of the above is only the editing part of the job – the words. How about other things that must be considered, such as explaining your recommendations to your client, following through to see that the document reads well and expresses the author's intentions clearly, and checking that any instructions to designers and printers are carried out? Let's look at each of these.

While you might not be a teacher in the accepted sense, you still have an explaining role as an editor. Your written comments on the text or your comment notes in Track Changes or your verbal explanations must all be clear. For example, there's no point telling the client that they ought to use active voice instead of the passive construction that's in the text if they don't understand the difference between active and passive. You need to be confident that you can explain that difference and show the client how much better the material would be if they followed your recommendation.

You need, at the same time, to have respect for the client. It won't help them if you write a stream of negative comment notes – this will only demoralise and discourage them. If you find yourself with material that will not get to publication without major restructuring, your responsibility is to help the client understand the value of good structure – achievable by means of a few short examples from an early part of the document and a word of praise for the ideas they are trying to get across. Having understood that your recommendations have merit, the client is likely to be in a frame of mind to accept that much more of the same is going to be required throughout the document, and that you are willing to help. At this point, they may well ask for guidance in English grammar, or whatever the problem area is. Great! You've won a friend and a convert to good writing.

Leaving the document after the initial edit is not always a good idea. You may have only one opportunity to work with the author (as perhaps with an academic thesis), but if you can follow through (as perhaps with a novel), all the way to final proof or pre-press stage of the document, do so. A book often has to go through many stages before it is ready to go to the printer. Try to stay in control throughout.

Some jobs include illustrations, photographs with captions, complex design issues and so on. It is the editor's responsibility to get the document to publication; therefore you as editor need to liaise with designers and anyone else involved, so that you can keep control of all these aspects that impinge on the effectiveness of the words that you have carefully edited. This doesn't mean that you need to have design qualifications, or be an indexer or an artist, but such people need to keep you informed and you have to be happy with the work that they produce, or the document will be a failure. If you have agreed to take the project right through to printing, you then need to liaise closely with the chosen printer to make sure that you all agree on the stock (the paper) to be used, the colours for the cover and any illustrations, the print run (and nowadays how it will appear in ebook formats).

The editor's job is as big or small as you want to make it. Having an interest in all aspects of the process of getting ideas into print makes the actual editing all the more interesting and satisfying.

# 2 Who exactly are you, editor?

OBVIOUSLY WHAT FOLLOWS IS MY PERSONAL VIEW of the editing profession, professionalism in editing, the responsibilities of an editor and the skills an editor ought to possess – in my opinion, that is.

## What exactly do we mean by the term 'editor'?

For the purposes of this book, let's think of an 'editor' as being a member of one of the branches of IPEd or societies of editors around Australia. We do not usually mean a newspaper or magazine editor. That person's job is to select material for publication, to cull stories that can't be included and to decide just how much of any particular story will make it to the publication and on which page, in all likelihood.

Such an editor doesn't always have a great deal to do with checking spelling, grammar, punctuation, style and so on, but is very likely to have more to do with restructuring and even refocusing stories to bring the meat of a story to the most prominent position so that it will 'sell' the publication. There are often subeditors to do the detailed checking.

What we generally mean, thinking of the editors who are accredited, or currently seeking accreditation, as professional editors, is a text editor. As text editors we work at various levels of edit, and, if we're wise, we don't quote for editing anything until we've looked at what level of edit is required for the job. The client frequently has no idea. A common question to me is: 'What do you charge for editing?' Well, you can imagine my response. It goes something like this: 'That depends on what is to be edited, the complexity of the document, the level of edit required, and perhaps whether I've done editing for you in the past, among many considerations'.

Mind you, there are magazine editors who also edit text (this would describe me in one of my roles) – they have to because their organisations are small and can't afford two separate people for the two aspects of the editorial function. However, a lot of our training and interest is in text editing. Perhaps our professional societies should broaden their horizons and include magazine and newspaper editors, and provide more topics at meetings that would interest such people too.

## Professionalism

Professionalism and accreditation go hand in hand but are not joined at the hip. Editors can be totally professional and not bother about accreditation because they already have a good reputation around town as meticulous editors with professional standards. Accreditation alone can't make you a better person. It can't make you more professional in outlook. Your personal standing among your peers is still a good gauge of a professional approach to the job.

Having said that, there is a great deal to be said in favour of accreditation of editors as a necessary step towards full professionalism in editing. It will be the norm in years to come – it will become increasingly difficult to get editing work without accreditation at some level or other. My earnest hope is that accreditation will be a rite of passage from 'learning to be a professional editor' to 'being a professional editor'. But remember that accreditation can't teach you professionalism – it's something, like adulthood, that you grow into.

## Responsibilities

Much has also been said and written about the responsibilities of an editor. To me, one responsibility is paramount: to make the author's work look as good as possible. Now, that assumes that you know something about the author, the audience, the subject, and have at least a nodding acquaintance with the author's reasons for writing the document in the first place. Squiggles in margins or Track Changes can be assumed – as text editors we ought to be able to use any form of editing that the author can relate to – after all, the author needs to understand the changes you are recommending. There are many styles for many purposes. They range from very sophisticated house styles through various professional styles to simple everyday words that clearly tell the author (or printer or publisher or designer) what you recommend. If you work where a particular style of editing is required, it is your responsibility to learn that style and use it.

One responsibility doesn't get much of a mention – being a teacher. What is the use of all the squiggles and marks if the author has no idea what they mean and therefore ignores them and sends your version off to the printer without question? That author will go away and make all the same mistakes again. If an editor is doing something to someone else's written work, it seems reasonable to expect that the editor tell them why it's being done. It's no good waffling on in esoteric terminology that the client doesn't follow. They need to know, at their own level of understanding of English grammar and syntax, just what each squiggle means and what was wrong with their original and why the editor's version is likely to be better for their document. These days, with the benefit of Track Changes, it is easy to include comment notes that explain the changes you are recommending – I have undertaken this 'teaching' role alongside the editing job many times.

Of course, you can't teach unless you are also teachable. The seminars and other teaching aids available to editors ought to be snapped up and devoured by all of us. Over time, we learn new ways of performing our craft; we absorb the basics of editing skills and the grammar, and other aspects of effective writing that support those skills; we also grow in confidence in our own understanding of what we're doing. Gradually we become better and better equipped to pass on tips to authors and to explain to authors why we are recommending certain changes in their work.

How about this as a catchcry for editors: 'Be teachable in order to be able to teach. Learn and then go out and teach what you have been taught and are practising'?

And this leads to another, related, responsibility – being a mentor. What's the difference between a teacher and a mentor? Plenty, but we all have our own ideas about where teaching ends and mentoring begins. To me, a mentor guides and encourages a person and allows them to develop along their own lines. A mentor needs to be able to see beyond the present situation to where the person being mentored (the 'mentee', according to the Macquarie Dictionary) is heading in their career. It is the mentor's role to help the mentee to see stumbling blocks and get over them, to help them develop skills by seeking training, to help them evaluate their own level of expertise by posing insightful questions, and so on – but never by actually doing work for them that they ought to be able to do for themselves.

Mentoring in the editing business is a challenge, an extension of teaching, and perhaps not for everyone. Indeed, a mentor may not even be a highly skilled practitioner – but a mentor will certainly have 'people skills'. A good mentor knows when to let go and allow the mentee to take off on their own. Teaching, in contrast, means passing on specific skills, actively helping the learner to acquire a set of skills, testing them on their understanding, and making sure that they are competent to use those skills. Of course, teaching can include the philosophy and theory behind whatever practical activity we can think of, but I've kept my comments here to what's mostly required to get a new editor up to speed.

If, as a novice editor, you can find a mentor to guide you while you gain experience and build editing skills, so much the better, but a mentor won't do the work for you – that's up to you. There are senior editors in all societies of editors – they are generally very approachable and happy to mentor new editors while they find their feet.

## Skills

As in many walks of life, there are some standards in editing practice. We need to adhere to them, but we also need to be flexible. Just exactly what is copyediting, for instance? To me, the term relates to a blurry area on a continuum – I don't think we can divide up the editing role into three, or four, or five, or fifteen levels of edit clearly, though we have tried to specify three – there are huge areas of overlap; see the Canberra Society of Editors' *Commissioning checklist* at <http://www.editorscanberra.org/wp-content/uploads/checklist.pdf>. It takes time and the development of skills all along the continuum to be able to say that a document requires a copyedit or a substantive edit or a proofread. We need to take advantage of every opportunity to learn all the skills necessary to edit anything, and to find out who or what to refer to when we don't know something ourselves. Very basic skills should be a given – such skills as understanding the requirements of the *Australian standards for editing practice*, being very familiar with the conventions of English grammar, knowing at least the most common proofreading symbols, and knowing how to use something like Track Changes so that the author understands our comments. We build on those skills over time.

\*

So – who are we? How do we want to appear to the general public? How do we get there? Are we thinking sufficiently far ahead to take into account changes in what others think of as 'an editor'? A great deal has been written and spoken about differences among the generations. For a senior editor like me, contact with Gen Y and 'Millennials' can be quite an experience – we all need to learn respect for each other's views on work and life. To many of us in the editing profession, particularly the seniors among us, 'editor' means one thing: to Gen Y and later generations it may mean something quite different. We need to ask them and take their views on board – they live in the world of smart phones and message apps, and have a totally different view of how to achieve their needs from that of their elders. It can only be good for a profession if it grows as the generations grow and as technology extends into every aspect of life. And it can only be good for a profession if older and younger, more experienced and less experienced editors learn from each other and learn respect for the fundamental values of their profession.

# 3   Your friendly computer

THERE ARE TIMES WHEN WE'D ALL LIKE to heave the computer through the nearest window. But there are times when the computer is so clever that you wonder what you ever did without it. Here are a few things you can do with your computer to save money, paper, ink, and keep the environment happy.

A good motto is *Think before you ink*. Don't print out unless it's necessary. The computer age was hailed as the age of the paperless office, but we're still waiting for that to eventuate. If anything, computers have generated more and more use of paper as we all write draft after draft after draft and print them all out to check. Many of us haven't learnt yet to read on screen very well.

It's a good idea to design forms that stay inside the computer and never get printed out. I have invoice forms, a range of letterheads for different purposes, several envelope return addresses, application forms for training and other purposes, nomination forms for membership of committees, fax cover sheets, advertising material. All of these require updating every so often, but there is no need to print them out. And there's certainly no need to spend money on printed forms.

Business cards are easy to design and print. There are various design programs that do an adequate job. You can customise them to suit yourself, and print them out on fairly substantial card. I have been printing mine out for years, and they are quite acceptable – they certainly save a lot of money and can be altered quickly.

A sideline of my business includes doing a lot of printing for a voluntary organisation. This includes brochures, forms, newsletters and so on. These are printed 'on demand' only, so that there is no stock of any of these hard copies. Once the document is designed or updated, it is only necessary to press the Print button and let the printer do the rest. Setting this up takes very little time, and paid work can continue while the printing proceeds. So the voluntary organisation benefits as they only get charged for paper and ink cartridges.

The friendly computer can help us to be organised too. For those new to computers (believe it or not, I know of some, even within editorial ranks), there are facilities for putting material in specific folders, so that all the work for one client can be gathered together in one place, for instance. This gets rid of clutter, particularly in your email Inbox. And what do you do with this clutter? If it's important, it should be saved, and all business material needs to be backed up somewhere other than on your main hard drive. In the event of a computer crash, you don't want to lose important material – business documents, photos, personal memories and so on. These can all be backed up onto your computer's little helpers: external drives, flashdrives or 'the cloud'. I have used flashdrives (otherwise known as memory sticks and several other names) a lot because I could take them round the world with me, slung on a lanyard around my neck. Things have changed: I would rely more on 'the cloud' now.

For editing, you will have Track Changes or some other editing tool. It is helpful in that you can keep track of the alterations you make to a document, and allow the client to see exactly what you recommend cutting out or altering, whereupon they can choose to accept or reject your recommendations. While you're working you can save various versions of the document, retrieve material from previous versions, change your mind about alterations you make, rearrange the placement of illustrations on pages (such as graphs, tables, photographs, text quotes from elsewhere), change colours of fonts and backgrounds – the choices are seemingly endless.

If you have a lot of spreadsheets to do, there's Excel. And PowerPoint is a great tool for designing conference slide-show presentations.

And don't forget multi-tasking. You can interrupt whatever you are doing and do something else – open and answer mail while in the middle of writing a report, redesign your company logo if you want to, as a break from editing an annual report, and so on. You can help this along by investing in a wide enough monitor that will allow you to have two versions of a document on screen at once, both of which you can manipulate, or be working on two completely different tasks at once. And with broadband, everything can be achieved so much more quickly than was possible with dial-up internet access.

Please don't heave the computer through the window just yet – it can help a lot, but do remember to keep it up to date and then learn how to use the updates yourself.

# 4   On-screen editing

Here is the answer to how to use Microsoft Word's Track Changes, Find and Replace, Styles and other editing tools. It was delightful to find Michele Sabto's very handy little book called *The on-screen editing handbook* (see 'References'). The book is not new – it was published by Tertiary Press in Victoria in 2003 – but the information is so clearly set out that I would recommend it to anyone taking up on-screen editing for the first time, or wanting to brush up on some of the topics in the book. It's very compact: 89 A5 pages, crammed with screen images or 'dumps' to illustrate points, and full of step-by-step instructions for doing just about everything. Although it's based on a much older version of Word (Word 2000), many aspects of Word's functionality are much the same. I have since moved on to Word 2007 with no difficulty, and would not expect any problem transferring to a later incarnation of Word.

For newcomers to on-screen editing, the first thing you need to know is that the built-in spelling and grammar check facilities are next to useless. The spelling check, for instance, will happily allow *there*, *their* and *they're* in situations where only one of those is correct. Why? Spellcheck can only spell – it can't tell the difference between those words contextually. It will recommend *who's* as a replacement for *whose* when *whose* was correct in the first place. Spellcheck will pick up a 'spelling error' in the expression *mind your p's and q's* and suggest changing *p's* to any one of a number of options like: *pHs, ape's, pass, pes, puss*. It doesn't like *q's* either but can only come up with one suggestion: *EQ's*.

The grammar check will pull me up at the sentence in the paragraph above: *The book is not new – it was published by Tertiary Press in Victoria in 2003 – but the information* ... It doesn't like the passive and wants to change it to *Tertiary Press in Victoria published it in 2003*. Fair enough, but any competent editor knows that it's just as silly to cram a document with active voice as with passive voice – variety is the spice of effective writing. These devices have their uses merely as checks for typos or to help in your thinking about a grammatical construction that may be unwieldy. They should not be used as the sole editing tools, and a client should understand that using these tools will not obviate the need for an editor.

The book is divided into six chapters, starting with Chapter 1 'Managing files'. This is an aspect of on-screen editing that a lot of people don't think about until they find they have a mess of files scattered throughout their emails and other Word documents, in 'My documents', 'My briefcase', and perhaps even in a file labelled with the client's name. But logically, file management should come first, as it does in this book. A simple procedure is suggested, based on the blindingly obvious: new job – new folder. Then the reader is warned about the dangers of not filing absolutely everything – files can easily get lost. It was gratifying to discover that my filing methods are pretty close to the recommendation – first make a copy of whatever the client sends you and keep one version untouched as a reference and use the other as the first working version. Keep that pattern of behaviour up, and you should arrive at the end of the job with a complete progressive picture of how the job proceeded, right up to and including a final version ready for the printer.

I remember once being asked by a regular client whether I'd kept a complete file of all stages of the edit, as they had lost their files in some sort of catastrophe. Yes, they were all stored safely, and the missing documents could be sent to the client to restore their own files to what they should have been. That was a lesson to all – it was impressed upon me to be meticulous about keeping files complete and always up to date. At the end of every job, my practice is to transfer everything in that folder – all stages of the edit, correspondence, copies of invoices and other files – to a CD. Usually, it is then possible to shred paper records and delete the files from the computer, but even those are kept for a while – just in case of another catastrophe. (It would be nice to be able to say the same for my hard-copy personal filing system, which currently needs a bulldozer through it!)

Chapter 2 of the book deals with 'Removing redundant spacing' – like what? Well, to start with, extra spaces after punctuation: many authors were taught (as I was) to type two spaces after end punctuation and one elsewhere, but the norm today is one space after all punctuation, both to keep it simple and to avoid problems when full justification is used (huge spaces can appear after full stops as text is dragged across to the right-hand margin). This is where the Find and Replace feature comes in handy: if you haven't found it yet, it's in the Edit menu, Home tab or Navigation pane. Select Replace and position the cursor in the Find What textbox – if we're changing double spacing after just full stops, for example, type a full stop followed by two spaces. Now place the cursor in the Replace With textbox and type a full stop followed by one space. Now click the Replace All button, and watch the magic happen before your eyes. A message will tell you how many times the alteration was made in the document. You can use this feature for all manner of global alterations, such as changing all double quotes to single quotes, one kind of dash to another, all spellings of an unfamiliar name from the wrong spelling to the correct spelling, and so on.

The matter of 'styles' in on-screen editing preparatory to publication was always a bit of a mystery to me in my early days of editing. Sometimes sorting out styles is forced on you when you receive an editing job that has already been gone over by someone else who has set certain styles that seem inappropriate, or that are haphazard. Some publishers have templates of styles that you must adhere to, but more often than not, you need to set your own. Chapter 3 'Creating and applying styles' sets out clearly how to go about it. For those who are new to this, there is a hierarchy of styles – put very simply, you might want all main side headings to appear in Arial bold 14pt, all subheadings in Times New Roman italic 12pt, and body text in Times New Roman regular 12pt, like this:

## Main side heading

*Subheading*

Body text which burbles on and on about something ...

You can set all this in Styles, which is in the Format menu, the Home tab or the Styles pane. Michele Sabto goes into a lot of helpful detail about formatting styles of all kinds, including bullet-point lists and tables – it's well worth careful study.

When you edit in hard copy, your alterations are there for all to see – textual marks, marginal marks and notations, and probably extra pages of explanations. You can do all that, and more, using Track Changes in Word, or the equivalent in other programs. Chapter 4 is entitled 'Editing with track changes and comments'. The Track Changes feature in Word displays the changes you make as you make them. If you delete something, it changes colour, or is moved to a side balloon, and may be marked with a strikethrough. If you add something, it is added in a different colour. You can highlight text that you want to make a long comment about; and you can write comment notes right at any point in the text.

The material on this topic in the book is very well set out in easy steps, and covers much more than is outlined here, including 'accepting' and 'rejecting' changes, altering or deleting comment notes, printing with and without revision marks or comments showing and so on. A word of warning: it is perilously easy to forget to save the version with all your revision marks – use Save As to save versions and give them suitable names and pop them into that job folder.

The remaining chapters of the book, Chapter 5 'Working with authors' and Chapter 6 'Other Word features', are very short but valuable. We sometimes forget that editing isn't just a matter of putting little marks on documents – there's a client out there who is perhaps also the author; we need to develop a pattern of dealing in a businesslike and helpful way with these people from quote to invoice. Depending on the type of work you are editing, you may need to know about inserting footnotes and endnotes, preparing a table of contents, creating templates to standardise the look of a large document over all its parts, and creating macros to save you the effort of repeating the same chores (such as Find and Replace actions) – all set out in the final chapter.

This little book is a good guide for anyone new to on-screen editing. It won't replace training courses and it won't replace on-the-job experience but it will enhance both. Word has now moved on to 2016 and beyond. An upgrade is not on my agenda at the moment, but a bit of advice is appropriate here: this book is still excellent for its general principles – just be aware that some of the facilities get moved to different places with each incarnation of Word.

# 5   Variety in editing jobs

VARIETY IS THE SPICE OF LIFE, THEY SAY. Well, there has certainly been variety in the editing jobs that have come my way during my career. Let me share a few of them with you.

Think of me in the same category as a GP: no specialisation in any particular genre but enjoyment to be had from working in almost all – 'almost all' because there are a couple of exceptions. Documents that consist almost entirely of columns of figures, or statistics, or scientific material containing huge quantities of numbers are not my favourites – my preference is to stick mostly to words with just occasional tables and other figures. Getting bogged down in massive tomes isn't my idea of fun, so don't ask me to edit *The rise and fall of the Roman Empire* or *Gone with the wind* or the Macquarie Dictionary, however fascinating they all may be – short and sweet provides my kind of variety.

Just looking through my records reveals a wide variety of editing jobs. Let's start with the material for the 2001 Census – certainly a massive job, but consisting of many small and very interesting documents, ranging from contract documents through guides for collectors (including a fascinating and charmingly illustrated one for Indigenous collectors) to the forms you (or your parents) all completed in August 2001. That job included a great deal of tuition in points of grammar and plain English.

Then there was a set of leaflets setting out guidelines for procuring materials for building purposes. The challenge here was to make the words clear to people from a non-English-speaking background. Another small 'leaflet' job was a newsletter put out by a musical group in Canberra – here it was helpful to have a musical background and know that foreign performers' names need to be checked for spelling and that Mozart, and not Beethoven, wrote a particular symphony.

A fun one was a delightful booklet about the gardens around Parliament House in Canberra, written by the gardeners themselves and illustrated with drawings of some of the plants and birds that thrive in the gardens.

A difficult job was one concerning taxation. When has taxation ever been easy, you ask? This was about persuading industry that it was a good thing to comply with taxation requirements, and showing them how to do it, relatively painlessly. That job required all the diplomatic skills available to me.

Another job that taxed my personal resources was a massive one undertaken with a number of other editors – project management skills were needed to manage a team of editors in Canberra and Melbourne.

My favourite job for several years was a military service annual. That consisted of many short articles written by serving men and women – all interesting. It could be done anywhere (and was, even while travelling around Australia and overseas). That job required me to think about the whole collection of very varied contributions, their grouping into sets, their placement so that they followed reasonably well on each other – all this apart from the editing, which needed a sense of overall design with text wrapping around photographs and so on. It was a challenge to make sure that the words would look good in the finished book.

A recent editing job has been a really interesting collaboration with an author in another state on behalf of a government department – a bit like the eternal triangle, and sometimes just as touchy. However, it all worked out, a couple of nice little booklets on a topic of concern to teachers and parents being the eventual outcome.

Editing jobs have included poetry, teaching materials, advertising flyers and brochures; books, manuals and leaflets; material written by people with English as a second language, as well as by native speakers of English; and documents ranging from the warnings on cigarette packets about the hazards of smoking to learned treatises such as PhD theses and articles for scholarly journals.

So, there's been variety aplenty: straight editing, tuition, project management, design, diplomacy, large and small jobs, solo and team efforts, government and private sector documents. And that's not counting the several writing and editing jobs that have been added to the mix just because they were really enjoyable to do – my monthly column for *The Canberra editor*, a series for *Stylewise* and a long-time commitment to the text and editing of the email newsletter and the website of a voluntary organisation.

Variety at work prevents boredom and makes you a more interesting person. More academic editing than anything else is coming my way as the years go by, but always interspersed with challenges of other sorts – like a short thriller novel that's about to go to the printer. This variety is what keeps my brain ticking over!

# 6   Seven deadly sins

THERE ARE MORE THAN SEVEN, OF COURSE, in editing as in life, but these are some that seem to me to be pretty deadly and worth avoiding if you want to be regarded as a competent editor. Try making your own list.

## Sin No 1: Writing a slapdash EOI or quote

If you're asked for an expression of interest (EOI), you give just that, no more: your interest in the job, your qualifications to do it, an understanding of what's required, and not much more. You can't provide precise hourly rates until you see a sample of the manuscript. The tone needs to be friendly without giving too much away – don't commit yourself until you write the quote. The EOI is an important piece of writing – it's the client's first impression of you. I saw a four-line EOI recently that was rejected because the editor concerned had not checked for spelling and grammar errors, had quoted an hourly rate before reading any of the manuscript, had used a peremptory tone and didn't refer specifically to the job (see Chat 18 'Editor, edit thyself'). No client will employ an editor who writes in a slapdash style and doesn't proofread their own emails.

Plenty has been written about quoting for editing jobs. There is no need to say more here except to advise being clear about the time required (after checking a sample), what you need to charge for the level of edit required and to cover expenses, your planned approach to the job and what the client can expect and when. The quote is a definitive document: the EOI is indicative. There's much more to writing quotes – please refer to Chats 14 and 15, respectively 'Quoting: broad aspects' and 'The proposal and quote'.

## Sin No 2: Not owning and using standard reference books

An editor needs to have at least the following immediately available:

- a good, up-to-date dictionary – in Australia, generally the Macquarie (latest edition or the online version), which gives Australian-preferred spellings first; in-house editors may need other dictionaries as dictated by house style

- *Style manual: for authors, editors and printers* (latest edition); editors of academic material may also need the *Chicago manual of style* or the *Publication manual of the American Psychological Association* for material to be published in the United States
- a thesaurus such as *Roget's thesaurus of English words and phrases*
- a good grammar book – nobody can 'know it all' and everyone can be confused by 'creative' grammar in a manuscript.

In addition, my bookshelves contain classics by authors including Strunk and White, Gowers, Fowler and the like; editing handbooks (such as those by Butcher; Flann, Hill and Wang; Mackenzie; and others – see 'References'); and grammar and style books. This doesn't mean that the beginning editor should go on a shopping spree, but do own the essentials and do refer to them while editing. The best editors are meticulous about grammar and keep up to date with stylistic and idiomatic changes.

## Sin No 3: Losing your copy of the *Standards*

You aren't meant to commit the *Australian standards for editing practice* (*Standards*) to memory, but have a copy handy. Print it out from the Canberra Society of Editors website <http://www.editorscanberra.org> or the Institute of Professional Editors Limited (IPEd) website <http://www.iped-editors.org>. You do need to know what your role as an editor is and what a client expects of an editor. It's all set out in the *Standards*. Print out the *Commissioning checklist* at the same time.

## Sin No 4: Thinking you can compete in a highly technological world with antique technology

Computers date very quickly. If your editing is all hard copy, you won't have this problem, but on-screen editors need to be able to offer quick turnaround, editing with Track Changes, formatting that is acceptable to printers and so on. If you need to get broadband to cope more speedily with large downloads, do it. There are no prizes for second best – only the best will do in editing. Build the costs into your quotes over a period.

## Sin No 5: Resting on your laurels

Editing, like anything to do with language, moves on. Qualifications acquired years ago are probably not sufficient anymore – get up to date with postgraduate courses and with training provided by the branches of IPEd and other associations of editors. Read *The Canberra editor*, and read other journals, manuals and handbooks on editing and style.

Learn what's available on your computer and use it. Grab any opportunity to network with other editors. This is where you learn more about editing than almost anywhere else, and all associations of editors welcome visitors from other similar groups to their meetings, training sessions, conferences, and other gatherings.

Learn something about our allied professions – indexing, technical writing, graphic design, publishing. There are often joint events, and these are wonderful opportunities for updating knowledge of the whole publishing industry.

## Sin No 6: Not being meticulous and crystal clear in your editing work

The client has every right to expect pernickety editing – that's what you're supposed to be good at. Manual mark-ups should follow standard guidelines and symbols for proof correction; electronic mark-ups (whether or not using Track Changes) should include comment notes where explanation is necessary.

I was once asked to re-edit another editor's work because the client wasn't satisfied. The first editor had done a 'broad brush' edit which was not what the client had asked for, not what the document needed, and not clear in its recommendations. The client had every right to expect more from a competent editor. This was a little embarrassing, but it was good to be asked to do it because the reputation of our profession was at stake.

## And the seventh deadly sin? Sloth

Sitting back and doing nothing. With accreditation here to stay, we all need to lift our game. Very broadly, accreditation of editors means telling the world that such editors have met stringent criteria set by our professional association in Australia, IPEd, in much the same way that accountants, doctors and other professionals are accredited by their professional bodies. In Australia, accreditation examinations seek to find out whether the candidate is competent according to the *Australian standards for editing practice*. The *Standards* are revised periodically to bring them up to date, and accreditation management will develop to accommodate the needs of the profession.

But there's no point in any of the hard work being put into all this progress towards greater professionalism and recognition for our profession if we don't take advantage of it and indulge in some self-improvement. Many will prefer not to seek accreditation – that is their choice. We all, however, do need to hone our skills and keep learning how we can do better. For some, this may mean first looking at what we're typing in an expression of interest and making sure that our 'first impression' is our best impression.

# 7   Getting on with clients

MY FORMER HAIRDRESSER WAS COMPLAINING that new young hairdressers often have no idea how to communicate with their clients – 'client relations' isn't taught in their courses, and they apparently don't learn these basic human skills at home. The result is that she won't take on an apprentice. She feels she can't be there every minute of the day to supervise and to make sure that apprentices have the communication skills to provide the niceties that her clients expect. What's it like in other trades and professions?

In the editing profession, we have to deal with clients all the time, and it isn't just a matter of dealing with text – it includes dealing with people, of all ages and all walks of life and all levels of education. This chat is addressed directly to new editors.

You've got your first client – what next? Much has been written about client relations, and the late Janet Mackenzie's book *The editor's companion*, second edition, is a good place to start learning about some of the more technical aspects, including contracts – you do have a written agreement with your client, don't you?

Here are a few of the strategies for getting on with clients that have helped me over the years and that seem to have paid off – you'll develop your own, but here are my 'starter' thoughts.

## Listen

Listening to what your client wants or needs is important in any business relationship. Your client may have no idea at all about editing, or may know a lot, or anything in between. Nevertheless, listen patiently and don't be judgemental in your response. The client comes first – try to formulate your response based on what the client is telling you. For example, they may say 'It needs a quick check for spelling and grammar, and that's all', but your assessment of the manuscript shows that it needs a restructure as well if it's going to be an interesting and logically formulated piece of writing. You will need to agree with the client about the spelling and grammar and ease gently into the need for restructuring. Or they may say 'I need help with the things I get wrong because my native language is "x" – can you show me how to fix this?' If you know the ins and outs of 'first language interference' and their effect on written English, you can use comment notes in Track Changes or, better, face-to-face consultations, to teach the client how to overcome whatever the problem is (for example, lack of appropriate articles – the, a, an) and suggest they try to fix the omissions themselves before the edit starts.

## Keep in touch

Keep the client informed on a regular basis during a long job. Develop a practice of reporting to the client every week at least. Clients tend to get edgy if they don't have contact with their editor at predictable intervals.

This practice of keeping in touch has a side benefit – it helps to keep you organised. As you plan the project, it helps to know that a particular day of the week is the day for reporting to a particular client. You can organise your work so that you will have something to report – keeping you on the ball and keeping the client happy, knowing that you're beavering away.

## Use plain English

Don't use technical jargon when explaining editing recommendations to a client – you could only confuse them. Even a client who is in the same line of business appreciates explanations in plain terms. For example, if you have to recommend cutting down sentence length by making new sentences of subordinate clauses, try showing the client the main 'sentence' (without using the term 'main or independent clause'), and then show them how the other string of words can be turned into a proper sentence – making two easy-to-read shorter sentences to replace the one complex and wordy sentence. Your client may be confused if you talk glibly about independent and subordinate clauses. They will appreciate simpler terminology, and may actually ask for more help as a result.

## Smile!

Yes, even when you write to your client. Try to look and sound relaxed, enjoying the job, keen to get the client's message across to the target audience.

Your personality and attitude can shine through even in a phone call. I once heard a client say to their editor, whom they'd never met, 'You must be very beautiful – you are so caring over the phone'. The editor wasn't physically beautiful, but her voice gave that impression, and this was the important thing for the client. How do you do that? Literally put a smile on your face while you write or talk to your client – it will show!

## Don't assume

Don't read into an email request from a stranger anything that isn't there. We all make mistakes. We spot a typo in the email and assume that this represents the standard of writing in the document we are being asked to edit, though we haven't yet seen the document. We see a particular type of grammatical error a couple of times in the sample sent for assessment and assume that this means an overall culture-specific writing problem that will require quite a lot of time to fix in the edit. This is not fair. Don't jump to conclusions.

Equally, don't assume a role for yourself as editor that is not yours to assume. Once a book of mine was edited by someone who thought he liked certain words and grammatical structures better than mine, so changed a lot of mine to suit his preference. Unfortunately, the grammatical structures were wrong and the choice of words put a totally different, and rather pompous, tone on the book. The publisher dealt with the matter by having me fly to another city to sort it out with the editor. Stick to being an editor, perhaps with some added help in indexing, design and even English grammar tuition if you feel up to it. But remember it's the client's work – not yours.

## Be patient

Rome wasn't built in a day, they say. And a book wasn't put together in a day either. As the author of a number of books, I have been in awe of the patience of my various editors on most occasions. The editor of the first edition of this volume, for instance, Ara Nalbandian, was patience personified as he gradually winkled out of me what he needed to make the book's structure work for you, the reader – a structure retained for this revised edition. For my part, I have learnt to be patient with clients too, particularly the students who write PhD theses and whose entire careers depend on how well their thesis is received by their examiners. Many of them have never learnt English grammar thoroughly; many of them have heaps to say about their topic but it tumbles out in a verbal roller-coaster; most of them have never had to write anything as long as a PhD thesis and find the whole thing daunting. Helping students through this trying time for them, and making sure that the work remains theirs, with no hint of my help visible, is a really enjoyable challenge. It certainly requires patience.

## Finally, be honest

Say what you can do and don't pretend to be more clever than you are. As a new editor, you can't expect to have accumulated the wisdom of years of experience – it will come. Know what your limitations are and acknowledge them. Any editor ought to be able to undertake most of the general copyediting requirements as set out in the *Australian standards for editing practice*, but not necessarily all the specialised aspects of it. If you need help, seek it from an experienced editor. Likewise, if you need help in preparing a quote for editing, or anything else to do with the business of editing, there are people in the associations of editors around Australia ready and willing to help. You are not alone.

\*

You're on your way in the editing arena – enjoy your relationship with your clients!

*itchypencil 2*

## Oops! False advertising?

I was in Sydney one day and couldn't help noticing this sign above a shop:

> **REMANUFACTURED PRINTER**
> Sales & Service of Office Equipment    T

Well, a quick glance made me wonder whether the local printer had become remanufactured and was now selling and servicing office equipment, having given up the printing business! My linguist's curiosity about weird language then made me ponder whether the shop might be selling remanufactured printers, and was also servicing office equipment of all sorts. I didn't bother to go into the shop, reasoning that if their signwriting was so ambiguous, it might not be quite the place I wanted to do business with. Look at the different meanings you can get from this sign:

1. We have here a remanufactured person who has been in the printing business but who has now switched to selling and servicing office equipment.
2. We have someone who remanufactures printers and sells and services them – hiccup! We're stuck with 'of Office Equipment' left over, so that can't be right!
3. Perhaps they remanufacture printers and sell them. In addition, they service office equipment.

Any more ideas? To be fair, it looks as if a chunk of the sign is missing – some guesswork might provide clues as to what sort of office equipment they service – **T** might be the start of 'Typewriters', for instance. And the top line might have nothing to do with office equipment at all – it could be that the whole line once referred to remanufactured printer cartridges.

Next time I'm in Sydney, I'll find out whether or not the signwriter has been back to repair the sign. Meanwhile, it serves to remind us to avoid ambiguity of expression and to eradicate it in the work we edit.

# Part 2

## Editor beware: ethical and legal considerations

# 8 Courtesy, cribs and copyright

I WAS BROUGHT UP TO SAY *PLEASE* AND *THANK YOU* – for everything, no exceptions. At home, it was common courtesy to say: 'Please may I have a drink?' 'Thank you for having me at your party.' 'May my friend borrow your book, please?' 'Please, is it OK for me to quote from your thesis?' As I grew older, the *thank yous* extended to the courtesy of acknowledging authorship of quoted bits and pieces in essays, theses, journal articles and the like. Parents and schoolteachers saw to it that I learnt to do my own thinking, certainly drawing in part on other people's theories and experiences, but expressed in my own words as far as possible, in academic pursuits and elsewhere.

In some cultures that are known to me personally, it has been common practice to copy the words of teachers and fellow students when it comes to answering examination questions. It's not called 'cheating': it's called 'helping each other'. This is not the Australian way, however. While I was president of an independent examining body in commercial subjects, there were many occasions when the body had to work out a strategy for overcoming the 'helping' that was rife in some of the countries in which we examined. Students were desperate to get an Australian qualification by any means available. It took years of visiting these countries, but we finally succeeded, and students from those countries are now at the top of the list for receiving prizes for excellence in examinations – and not a hint of 'helping' anymore. Students excel on their own merit – not by copying from others without saying 'thank you'.

If you're old enough, you might remember what were called *crib sheets* – explanations of Shakespearean plays to help one understand the significance of the language or the intricacies of plots. We all used them and were grateful for them – but only as additional reference material, to be acknowledged in essays. There were 'crib sheets' in many school and university subjects.

'Crib' is a multi-defined word – the Macquarie Dictionary gives more than twenty meanings. In 2005 the meaning was '*Colloquial* to pilfer or steal, as a passage from an author'.\* The *Macquarie dictionary online*'s update to this definition in 2019 is 'Colloquial to steal or plagiarise (a piece of writing etc.)'. The word 'crib' even made it into Kel Richards's *Word of the day* on the

---

\*   *Macquarie dictionary*, 4th edn, Macquarie University NSW, 2005.

ABC's Classic FM Breakfast on 6 June 2002: '*Cribbing* meant "an act of petty theft; or anything *cribbed* or taken without acknowledgment" from another's work (plagiarism, in other words)'. See also Chat 10 'Editing students' work'.

Ah, there it is again – the 'p' word. So what really is plagiarism? A good definition and explanation used to appear on the website of the Presbyterian Ladies' College (PLC), Melbourne, describing plagiarism as 'using other peoples' [sic] words and ideas without clearly acknowledging the source of the information'. The University of New South Wales goes further:

> Plagiarism ... is using the words or ideas of others and passing them off as your own. Plagiarism is a type of intellectual theft.
>
> [It] can take many forms, from deliberate cheating to accidentally copying from a source without acknowledgement.*

In that last definition lies an important point: 'accidentally copying'. It is perfectly possible for someone to have read something somewhere, absorbed it over time, and then included it in their own writing, as though it were their own. And the author can firmly believe that the writing truly is their own and that no acknowledgement is therefore necessary. I would have to say, however, that this could only possibly be true for short passages – maybe a phrase or a sentence.

Once, while tutoring at a university in Canberra and reading a student assignment on an aspect of linguistics, I was struck by how knowledgeable the student was on a certain point, until it dawned on me that the writing was my own! The student had copied, word for word, without acknowledgement, a passage of several paragraphs from my own thesis on the subject. The student was expelled from the course as this was the punishment for plagiarism at the time, regardless of how flattering it was to me to be quoted so freely.

Plagiarism on the grand scale has been made more and more tempting and easy for lazy students by people who provide whole essays on all manner of subjects on the web. Teachers and supervisors have to be more vigilant than ever to make sure that they are reading their students' own work and not that of others. Plagiarism at academic levels can take many forms. The PLC Melbourne website used to list these examples:

- buying a paper or essay from a research service or online paper-mill
- handing in another person's work with or without the author's or creator's knowledge

---

\*  'What is Plagiarism?' <https://student.unsw.edu.au/what-plagiarism> (accessed 14 January 2019).

- copying an entire source and presenting it as your own
- copying sections from a source without appropriate acknowledgement
- paraphrasing material from a source without appropriate acknowledgement.

PLC offered teachers various ways of trying to prevent plagiarism, largely by being vigilant and prepared – visiting some of the sites where such material is available; including discussion of plagiarism in student study sessions; encouraging correct citation, rigorous research methods, and inclusion of a number of different resources in writing tasks.

In recent times, software has been developed to help students avoid accidental plagiarism and to help teachers and lecturers spot plagiarism in essays, theses and other academic assignments. I have no experience of using any of them, but suggest searching for 'detecting plagiarism' on your favourite search engine. Some programs cost money but some are free.

Of course, plagiarism is not restricted to students or academia. It can occur anywhere. However, it is possible to encourage good habits at student level, and this was my own practice in the Study Skills Unit at the Signadou (Canberra) campus of the Australian Catholic University in the mid 1990s. The aim was to prepare students for professional and commercial writing, and not just for university requirements. See more on plagiarism in Chat 10 'Editing students' work'.

I have encountered confusion in the minds of some people recently about what is and is not in the 'public domain' and what that term means anyway. Unfortunately, there are people – including friends with lengthy academic, writing and even editing experience – who think it is OK to pass on emails to third parties without the permission of the author. The reason they have given has been: 'It's an email, therefore it's in the public domain'. That is not true. An email is no more public in its intent than a letter written on paper and mailed through the post. And even material such as government information papers, while publicly available for free, still needs to be acknowledged if quoted. The same people have told me that they believe it is all right to print out and make multiple copies of fact sheets from websites. No it isn't. If you read the fine print carefully, you will usually find a privacy statement, copyright information or other material that prevents copying more than once for personal reference purposes only.

This brings me to copyright. There are some excellent information sheets on the web, put out by the Australian Copyright Council and updated from time to time. The two main ones are:

- 'An Introduction to Copyright in Australia':
  <https://www.copyright.org.au/ACC_Prod/ACC/Information_Sheets/An_Introduction_to_Copyright_in_Australia.aspx>
- 'Duration of Copyright':
  <https://www.copyright.org.au/ACC_Prod/ACC/Information_Sheets/Duration_of_Copyright.aspx>.

But there are many more, and you should consult them if you are in any doubt as to what copyright is all about. A good rule of thumb is to assume that someone owns the copyright on anything written, and that it's not freely available until at least seventy years after the death of the author. Before that period is over, you have to seek the permission of the owner of the copyright before using anything, wherever in the world it has been written. In Australia, this all comes under the *Copyright Act 1968*. When copyright has expired, a work can be said to be 'in the public domain', not requiring permission to use it, but usually not until then.

So who owns copyright? Usually the author, and it's automatic – as soon as something is written down or recorded, it is protected under the Act. It doesn't have to be published, and you don't have to use the word 'Copyright' or the symbol ©, though these are helpful if you need to let people know just who owns the copyright and that the material is protected. Sometimes, work is written as part of employment: in that case the employer owns the copyright. At other times it's difficult to tell who owns the copyright: I own the copyright in all of the articles I have written for *The Canberra editor*, but when I wanted to republish adaptations of them in this collection of chats, it seemed to me to be courteous to seek the permission of the Canberra Society of Editors to do so and to acknowledge this permission in the book. Some of the original articles have been republished in other editing newsletters, such as *Blue pencil* in New South Wales and *Book worm* in Western Australia. Invariably, the editors of these newsletters have sought permission from me as author as well as from the editor of *The Canberra editor*. It's just common courtesy.

So we're back to courtesy – and really that's what it's all about. If you want to use other people's writing, illustrations, website material, sound recordings, films – indeed, anything that doesn't belong to you – just ask and then acknowledge the source in the text or in a bibliography or footnotes, using any clear method of citation or referencing. It's easy to do. It's no more difficult than saying 'please' and 'thank you'.

# 9   Disclaimers

Should my quote contain a disclaimer? It's a frequent question. So let me share with you some disclaimers I've used in quotes for editing and writing jobs, and, for comparison, some website and email disclaimers I have been involved in preparing. It won't answer all the questions, but may stimulate discussion and help you to start thinking about writing a disclaimer in your next quote.

## Why have a disclaimer at all?

You need to protect yourself, as far as you can, from legal action arising out of the material you work on, and from the possibility that some information may be out of date or inaccurate, through no fault of your own. You need to be clear about where your liability ends and becomes someone else's responsibility.

For anything more than a very simple disclaimer, it is probably a good idea to get legal advice. However, even a lawyer will tell you that a disclaimer will not protect you from determined legal action – it is only a deterrent.

The following simple disclaimer goes with my quotes for most straightforward, enjoyable editing jobs, where the client is well known to me:

> I should emphasise that my editing is my recommendation only.
>
> [The client] is free to accept or reject my recommendations, and I do not assume any liability for what may ensue from [the client's] acceptance or rejection of my recommendations.

It is by no means legally binding, but is a help in getting my point of view across.

Editing scripts for oral delivery is a different ball game. The person recording the script could misread a word or could put the emphasis in the wrong place. I don't want to be responsible for what might ensue as a result of an actor's poor performance. Mind you, my editing is backed by a lot of experience in radio script writing, so I know what will work and what won't. Here is the disclaimer that has been used several times for that sort of job:

> As usual, I have to emphasise that all editing I do is my recommendation only. It is up to you [project manager] and [client] to accept or reject any of my suggested alterations to the text, and I cannot be held responsible for any

misunderstandings that may occur as a result of what finally appears in the recording.

A newsletter that I prepare has a section called 'Diary Dates'. Information for this section is gathered from many sources – personal communication, websites, other newsletters, and so on – and this is the disclaimer:

> Diary Dates information comes from a variety of sources. No liability for the accuracy of dates or other content is assumed. For details, please refer to the respective contact organisations or persons.

It is very important that websites carry disclaimers. At the time of writing the article on which this chat is based, the Australian Government Culture and Recreation Portal recommended that:

> if your website carries information which may influence the behaviour or activities of others, which makes any claims, or is sensitive in some way, then it may be worth getting legal advice from experts about what exactly you should include in your site's disclaimer.

Although this portal has closed and has not been replaced, the advice is still valid. It is vital in the case of voluntary organisations that do not have the money for hefty insurance premiums but want to protect themselves as well as they can.

Here is part of the disclaimer that appeared on the website of a voluntary group that was based in Canberra:

> We try at all times to present accurate information and to recommend reliable links. At all times we will act in good faith to provide the information sought. However, we depend on information given to us by both the communities seeking the information or advice and the potential providers of the information or advice.
>
> …
>
> … the onus of assessing the accuracy and relevance of the information or advice provided by [the group] must lie with the community seeking assistance from [the group]. It is strongly recommended that if the community is in doubt about the quality of advice or assistance offered, they should seek other advice.

The full disclaimer was the result of lengthy consultation with a lawyer.

## What sort of message is a disclaimer trying to get across?

A disclaimer:

- alerts readers to the fact that, while we do our best to make sure that everything is accurate and up to date, we cannot guarantee that accuracy
- warns readers that information is intended for the correct recipient and may contain confidential material
- puts the onus on readers to check for viruses and defects in attachments.

Here is an example of the second kind of disclaimer, about confidentiality:
> Material in this email is intended for the person or persons to whom it is addressed. It may not be passed on to anyone without permission from [name of organisation]. If you believe you have received this email (including attachment/s if any) in error, please contact the writer and immediately trash the email.

Disclaimers go some way towards protecting both editors (or writers) and their clients. In the sort of work we do, often something very simple like one of the examples above may be sufficient, but if in doubt, seek legal advice.

# 10   Editing students' work

IN MY SCHOOL AND UNIVERSITY DAYS it was expected that every word written in an essay or assignment was my own – that nobody helped me with it at all. The only exception was that I could show a draft to my tutor, who would check my thinking and guide me to the research tools available in the libraries. School essays would be shown to Mum and Dad, but only if my work had been awarded A or had 'Excellent' written on them by the teacher – otherwise they'd be hidden away out of sight!

My university assignments and theses grew out of a deep interest in a particular field of study. My practice was to choose topics that would stretch my knowledge or even break through the existing boundaries of knowledge. They were personal things, nurtured through draft after draft and nourished with the results of extensive reading and thinking. They were tested in the muddy waters of fieldwork, written with words chosen carefully to give meaning and impact to the arguments propounded, then checked and double-checked for spelling, grammar, typos, layout. Finally, they were bound lovingly in sober academic garb of neat plastic binders or handed over, with trepidation, to book binders who treated them with infinite respect and clothed them in rich cloth with gold letters sparkling from the spine.

Never did anything written by me at school or university ever get into the hands of an editor. Just as well I had fussy parents and brilliant teachers. It's different now. Many students have come through a school system that has neglected to teach them how to think critically or how to write. They have ideas, but their ideas are tumbling over themselves for expression. They have no idea of order or of reason or of logical presentation of material in writing. They don't know how to plan an essay. They don't know what terms like *discuss, analyse, compare* or *critically examine* mean. An *argument* is a row with a mate at work. Reading the *literature* means finding a book, any book, and looking for any reference to the topic under review. They don't know how to spell or put a complete sentence together – and they often don't care about these details. It is so bad that university lecturers in leading MBA courses have been heard to say: 'We have given up – we have to award marks for content and ignore the way it's presented, or nobody would pass'. Perhaps that's what's needed – for nobody to pass.

Instead, editors have come to the rescue. Is this right? My feeling is that the student's work should be identifiably the student's work, including the writing. I have no hesitation in helping a student to structure an assignment – from outline through several drafts – that's tutoring, not editing.

When the assignment is 'finished', however, I baulk at restructuring or rewriting whole slabs of text because the fundamentals of planning, emphasis, appropriate citation and coverage of the question still haven't been addressed. For students who are familiar with English, it should not be necessary to do more than proofread and suggest improvements at such a late stage in the production of an assignment. Students whose English is a second or third language, and students visiting from other cultures, need special assistance. It isn't fair to compare the two.

Should we edit at all? Should we edit selectively? Should we combine editing with tutoring/mentoring in the necessary thinking and writing skills? How should such assistance be acknowledged?

Yes, I think we should edit students' work, but we should be careful to tell the student how much we are prepared to do while ensuring that the student retains ownership of the writing. Yes, if we're competent to do so, we should guide the student in the skills that will help them to do better next time – but we're not all teachers, so if this isn't one of your competencies, don't attempt it.

Acknowledgement is important. When I was running a Study Skills Unit in Canberra, I devised a statement that all students were obliged to include on the cover sheets of their submissions if they received editorial help. It read something like 'I acknowledge that I received editorial assistance from XX (name and phone or other contact for the editor)'. The lecturer was then able, if necessary, to contact the editor to ask just how much assistance was given to the student. (This was in the days before the societies of editors and the universities had agreed on guidelines for the editing of academic work, including theses.)

While it is perfectly possible to advise a student on how to overcome thinking and writing problems, it would not be proper to change the substance significantly if what's written is what the student finally *means* to say. It's a fine line and sometimes difficult to draw.

As discussed earlier in Chat 8 'Courtesy, cribs and copyright', plagiarism is another difficult problem to deal with. Should an editor check a student's work for plagiarism? Plagiarism can be difficult to detect, and if the editor is not familiar with the literature surrounding a particular thesis topic, for example, they are unlikely to recognise a passage as plagiarism. Be suspicious of passages of text that are exceptionally well written – that is, of a much higher standard of writing and content than the rest of the document. My inclination would be to ask the student to tell me the origin of such a passage, and point out to them the penalties for plagiarism. That should be sufficient to make the student think carefully before quoting from a source and failing to acknowledge it. Having said that, is it really the editor's job to check for plagiarism (for example, by scanning it with software programs that are now available)? We could debate whether this properly comes under the heading of 'content' and therefore more appropriately in the province of the student's supervisory panel.

In the end, the student has to be responsible for the content of the work. It will not profit them if a paper is written in a slapdash manner, with woolly thinking, or if bits have been 'borrowed' from other sources and passed off as the student's own work. There is only so much the editor can do – largely restricted to copyediting to make the text as readable as possible. The guidelines for editing academic theses, agreed between the universities around Australia and the Institute of Professional Editors (IPEd), have been revised to allow for on-screen editing, with material being returned to the student in PDF form, for preference. (For more on this aspect of editing, see Chat 11 'The ethics of editing'.) It is possible that agreement could be reached between professional editors and universities about the use of programs that scan for plagiarism. However, the ultimate responsibility for content should always remain with the student, the student's supervisory panel and the university concerned.

All of that having been said, there is nothing more rewarding to me than working with students who are pushing the boundaries of knowledge in their chosen fields. Academic editing is a challenge, but a great experience, and very much to be recommended as a branch of professional editing.

# 11   The ethics of editing

And so to what could be considered one of the most important aspects of editing – ethics. As editors we have a duty to behave in a way that upholds the profession. We need to be totally trustworthy; we need to think carefully about whether or not to accept jobs that may be outside our comfort zone; we need to be reliable about meeting deadlines; and we need to be honest about our own ability to undertake jobs. Unethical behaviour is soon spotted and dealt with.

Ethics is a serious matter, and unethical behaviour by just a few people can undermine the whole editing profession.

Some aspects of ethics are fundamental and are included here. However, every profession, industry or trade has its own behavioural standards that may need to be considered. Think about further ethical considerations in your own area.

The Macquarie Dictionary provides three definitions of ethics: 'a system of moral principles, by which human actions and proposals may be judged good or bad or right or wrong'; 'the rules of conduct recognised in respect of a particular class of human actions'; and 'moral principles, as of an individual'.

Ethical principles are laid down in many organisations and professions, and members are expected to adhere to them. They may be called codes of behaviour, ethical guidelines, or standards of conduct. They all boil down to a set of principles to help members do the right thing by their clients and fellow professionals – and in some cases for the 'public good'.

In the editing profession, there are many such principles – some written and some just 'understood' as 'the decent thing'.

## Ethics in academic editing

In Australia, we have special obligations when editing students' papers and theses. These are set out in the 'Guidelines for editing research theses'. The main principles are as follows:

- We may edit on hard copy or on screen; however, if we edit on screen, we must return the marked work in such a way that the student cannot blindly 'accept' alterations suggested by the editor. The student needs to decide whether the alterations are appropriate in the context or not. One way to ensure this is to send the work back to the student as a PDF file.

- We may not perform structural edits, but must stick to what is covered by Standards D ('Language and illustrations') and E ('Completeness and consistency') in the *Australian standards for editing practice*. Structural edits, apart from broad recommendations for attention, are the province of the student and the student's academic supervisor.

- The student must acknowledge the editing and the editor in case the examiners wish to check the extent of editing performed. It is possible that the quality of the student's work could be greatly affected by the editor's efforts, and we need to remember that it is the student's original work that is being examined.

These principles are available in full from the Institute of Professional Editors (IPEd) at <http://iped-editors.org/About_editing/Editing_theses.aspx>.

If you are asked to edit papers for students of overseas universities, it is important to find out what degree of editing is allowable in the particular institution. See also Chat 10 'Editing students' work'.

## General editing ethics

Some editors set out their ethical stance on their websites or in their expressions of interest in a job. This usually amounts to a short statement about confidentiality and privacy issues, work standards, policy on accepting or not accepting jobs, and perhaps their proposed action in the event of a conflict of interest or other difficulty. It helps the client to get a full picture of the sense of professionalism of the editor.

### Confidentiality

It should be obvious that an editor who is a member of a respected professional society of editors would be trustworthy. However, authors are often understandably nervous about handing over manuscripts to total strangers. They need to be assured that you are not going to discuss their work with anyone other than the team working on it, and that if you don't want to undertake the work or don't get the contract, you will return or securely trash all the material sent to you.

Clients are also entitled to know that you don't pass on their details to anyone else for any reason. There are people who pass on such information, including mailing lists, without authorisation, and who think it is all right to discuss current jobs with other clients. This is not only unethical gossip but may also be a breach of privacy laws.

**Work standards**

It is not possible to be skilled in all areas of editing, and your client is entitled to know that you have the necessary skills for the job under consideration. It is unprofessional to pretend to a client that you have a level of skill, or very specific skills, that you do not have. Own up, and be willing to develop skills on the job, but only if the client is agreeable.

**Accepting or not accepting jobs**

There are some jobs that are just not for you. If you are asked to quote for a job that you know you will hate or that you don't have time for or that you honestly don't know how to do, forget it.

If the potential client has asked you to 'just cast an eye over this for typos' and you find that the document needs a major rewrite, be honest in your appraisal. You can't do a substantive edit on a proofreading budget. And it would be unethical to do merely the requested check for typos when you know that the manuscript will fall in a heap at the next hurdle – publication.

You may decide to accept a job, in good faith, and find later that there is a conflict of interest. For example, editors are often asked to edit material that conflicts with their own views on a subject. It is not our business to try to 'correct' the client's views while correcting their grammar or their writing style. If you can't distance yourself from your own views, don't take the job on. The ethical thing to do is to immediately inform the client and offer to withdraw from the contract.

**Meeting deadlines**

Don't promise to keep deadlines that are not achievable for you. If you fall behind, you cause the whole publication process to fall behind. The ethical editor, faced with an honest delay because of sickness or a private emergency, will contact the client immediately, apologise, and offer to withdraw.

## Other forms of unacceptable behaviour

Apart from the points above that could be addressed in a statement of your ethical stance, there are other examples of behaviour that are, to me, unacceptable:

- **Taking on work at a level at which you are not either qualified or sufficiently experienced**. We all have to start somewhere, but it is bad for the whole profession when you take on work which you have no hope of doing at a satisfactory level of competence. The client will be unhappy, and is quite likely to complain to the editing organisation to which the editor belongs.

- **Claiming expertise that you don't have**. Bluff will get you nowhere in the long run. We all have to learn our craft the hard way – through training in editing; through working with a mentor until we are confident; and through years of practice, working up from simple jobs to huge complex jobs. Clients can see through bluff.

- **Actually working on a document and charging a fee for a job that you know is not up to scratch**. This is downright dishonest, but it happens. Clients have brought documents to me for re-editing after an 'amateur editor' has failed to find even obvious grammatical errors, spelling errors, typos and so on, and has not given any advice on plainly necessary restructuring, page layout and placement of illustrations. That level of slapdash behaviour really bothers me.

- **Quoting a very low fee (or even no fee) just to get a job**. This is equally dishonest. It downgrades the value of editing as a whole. The only 'freebies' should be for your favourite local charity that has no money anyway. Everything else should be paid for at a businesslike rate. This includes editing student theses and dissertations. These days, funds are often available to graduate students to help them pay for professional editing – you should charge your regular fee. If you don't know what to charge, ask a senior editor for guidance and then work out what your effort is worth. Don't undersell yourself – most freelance editors undercharge, but it is possible to gauge the 'going rate' for various jobs and various levels of edit.

The late Janet Mackenzie set out a number of additional areas of concern that editors ought to be aware of, including that the editor has 'a three-way responsibility to the publisher, the author and the reader' (*The editor's companion*, 2nd edn, p 41). It is sometimes difficult to meet everyone's needs, but you need to try to keep a sense of balance throughout a job.

Ethics is an enormous subject. This introduction to it may provide something to think about next time you are asked to quote for an editing job that is a bit out of your comfort zone.

# itchypencil 3
## When 'brief' does not equal 'plain'!

At the height of the drought in Canberra, I spotted this sign attached to a letterbox post outside a private home:

The day was hot, the sun was beating down, the bark chips around the letterbox were as dry as dust. And yet, the sign proclaimed that rainwater was in use. Sorry, there wasn't any rainwater being used at the time. Wouldn't it have been better to let the water police know that rainwater collected in a tank at the back of the house is all that is used for watering the garden?

Brevity is good, but it can also be less than plain English.

How about 'Only rainwater used in garden'? You might think of something briefer, more meaningful and certainly not ambiguous.

# Part 3

## The business of editing

# 12  Project management*

Editing isn't always just sitting at a computer and manipulating words. The project management aspect of the editing task often forces editors to cope with the totally unforeseen, and, increasingly in this uncertain world, they need to know how to cope with sudden changes in circumstances.

When you first receive a request to do an editing job, you need to find out quite a bit about the job: the size and complexity of the publication, its target audience, its purpose, what level of edit is appropriate, and so on – indeed everything you need to know before you can submit a quote. This is **project definition**, and you need to go through this process every time, whether you get the job or not.

Once your quote has been accepted and you've agreed to do the job, you then need to organise your work and possibly that of others on your team, schedule tasks, set deadlines, assemble resources, work out a budget and see that you and your colleagues get paid. That's all in addition to actually editing the document (which is your real skill).

It doesn't matter how large or small the project is – if it's a real project, it needs **project management**.

Here I'll touch on the major stages of the project cycle and the steps the editor can take to make sure that the project meets some management criteria. But first—

## What is a project?

- A project has a definite beginning and a definite end. An example would be getting your organisation's next newsletter out. A project is not a process – a process is ongoing, and an example would be administering the personnel section in a company.

- A project has direction – it's goal-oriented. Once you've decided on the objective for the project, stick to it.

---

\*   The information in this chat is based in part on notes for a workshop presentation on project management by the author, in association with Roger Green, Shirley Purchase and Loma Snooks in November 1993 – part of the Canberra Society of Editors *Levels of edit* training workshop.

- A project is made up of connected or interrelated activities or tasks – everything that has to be completed before you can say that the project is finished and satisfactory. These can be grouped into main sections such as initial negotiations with the author, the designer and the printer; the first read to find out the extent and level of edit required; doing the actual edit; and other sections as appropriate. Major projects need to be broken down and grouped like this so that the whole project doesn't appear daunting. Dealing with lots of mini projects is much easier than trying to cope with the whole thing in one gulp.
- A project is unique – there's no other project exactly the same. Even if you churn out a newsletter every month, each newsletter is a separate and unique project. The principles of project management remain the same for every project, large or small, but the components change every time, so each new project is a different ball game.

## What is project management?

Project management brings together and makes best use of all the resources needed to complete the project. These include people skills and effort, facilities and equipment, technical know-how and money. I don't think you can do this in your head – the components needs to be written down and preferably charted along a time line. A lot of factors have to be considered, such as budget, time constraints and variability of team members' skills. Time for pencil and paper!

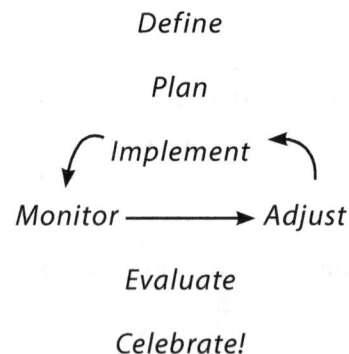

## CHAT 12 PROJECT MANAGEMENT 51

**Defining** the project is a major part of the whole editing process. It includes identifying what the job is about, who will read the finished version and what its purpose is. Does the job require a straightforward copyedit or does the whole structure need rethinking in order to be effective? How far can I go, given time and budget constraints? Are my current skills good enough for what's required? What is the aim – to clean up or to clear up?

**Planning** is essential. There are a couple of sayings that have more than a grain of wisdom in them: 'Failing to plan is planning to fail' and 'Plan your work, then work your plan'. It's always a good idea to brainstorm: to scribble down quickly all the tasks you can think of, in any order, that you'll need to attend to. Then use arrows to indicate sequence. You might end up with something like this:

> Go!
> Read
> Check spelling, punctuation, grammar, paras
> & correct
> Who? ID audience
> Style check
> See author
> File to printer
> Done!

Convert this list to a task sheet, with the name of the task and its identifying number, an indication of what must precede a particular task (predecessor), and an estimate of the duration of each task, as shown over the page. (There are many more tasks in most projects, but this will serve to illustrate how you can set out a task sheet.)

| ID | Name of task | Predecessor | Duration |
|---|---|---|---|
| 1 | Start | N/A | 0d (day) |
| 2 | Identify audience in order to set appropriate style and level of language | 1 | 1d |
| 3 | Read document file | 1 | 1d |
| 4 | Check spelling, punctuation and other basic grammar and paragraph construction | 3 | 1d |
| 5 | Correct errors in these | 3, 4 | 1d |
| 6 | Check for consistency of writing style | 3 | 0.5d |
| 7 | Send copy of marked-up document to author (or liaise some other way) – reach agreement | 6 | 1d |
| 8 | Send document to designer or printer | 7 | 0.5d |
| 9 | End project | 8 | 0d |

Having scheduled the tasks involved in this project, consider the triple constraints of project management: time, budget and performance. Try to answer the following questions:

- What is the *project deadline*? The job has to be completed by 5 pm next Friday. How can time be allocated? Have you the time to do the whole job yourself in between other jobs, or will you need to enlist help?

- Is the *budget* constraint already set? Perhaps it's limited to your salary, or perhaps you know what the client can afford to pay, or some other consideration.

- The *performance* constraint is determined by you and the client or publishing house – how much effort can you put into it, given the time and budget available? Is quality or speed more important?

Remember that project management is not editing: it's part of the business side of the job, and would be much the same whether for a small editing job or for planning the construction of a multistorey office block. Very small projects can be kept under control by doing as much as I've outlined above, but when you have several editing jobs running at once, or when the project is large and involves other people besides you, a means of tracking progress is essential. Even a small project benefits from being charted clearly, and I recommend using a Gantt chart because it's very easy to see how the sequence of activities affects the progress of the project, and shows you where you might have some slack time to catch up other jobs or to liaise with the author perhaps.

Below is a simple Gantt chart for the job above. The thick black lines represent estimated time required for each task. The dotted lines represent estimated slack time.

| ID | Task name | Mon | Tues | Wed | Thurs | Fri |
|---|---|---|---|---|---|---|
| 1 | Start | ♦ | | | | |
| 2 | Identify audience → set style, level of language | — | | | | |
| 3 | Read document file | —— | | | | |
| 4 | Check spelling, punctuation, grammar, paragraphs | | —— | | | |
| 5 | Correct errors in these areas | | —— | | | |
| 6 | Check for consistency of writing style | | | ——··· | | |
| 7 | Marked-up document to author – reach agreement | | | | —— | |
| 8 | Send document to designer or printer | | | | | ···—— |
| 9 | End project | | | | | ♦ |

You can also show resources, critical paths, task dependencies and other factors. Blank Gantt charts and help wizards can be found by searching the internet for 'Gantt chart'.

The next phase is **implementing** the plan, and this means:

- proceeding with the edit
- liaising as necessary with author, publisher, designer, printer, etc
- maintaining quality control throughout.

In this phase, you need to keep everything under control and to make alterations to timing, personnel, budget allocation and other factors relevant to your project, as required. That means:

- *monitoring* – keeping an eye on your chart and controlling resource use and expenditure

- *adjusting* – dealing with glitches such as scheduling conflicts, project running behind schedule and so on.

The last major phase in any project is **evaluation**. Of course, you constantly evaluate progress, but at the end of the project, you check that quality, time and budget aims have all been met, and whether the management techniques you used on this project have worked or need revising for next time.

And let's not forget the last leg of the project, when the document has gone to the printer and everyone is happy with the outcome – celebrate! You might be the only person working on this project – give yourself a pat on the back for completing it without losing your sanity.

# 13   Project definition

DEFINING THE PROJECT IS A VITAL FIRST STEP IN PROJECT MANAGEMENT. You can read in the *Australian standards for editing practice* and in the *Commissioning checklist* (see 'References') comprehensive lists of things that the editor should consider before submitting a quote for an editing job. Here, let's run through a typical project definition routine as it happens in my own business. For many years, my work consisted mostly of editing government documents. You might edit fiction, annual reports or scientific material – your criteria for defining the project and deciding whether or not to submit a quote will vary accordingly. Quoting is another difficult part of the job, and I discuss that in Chats 14 and 15, respectively 'Quoting: broad aspects' and 'The proposal and quote'.

Project definition really takes some concentration. At the end of it, you might decide not to quote at all because you realise that the job isn't your cup of tea. Or you may quote but not get the job. You still have to go through the routine every time, and gradually you hone your project definition skills to the point where you find yourself getting the jobs more often than not.

So what's my routine? There are several, but here's a straightforward one.

## Responding to the invitation to quote

Before even thinking of looking at the project, it helps to know several things, not necessarily in this order:

- What sort of job is it? Non-fiction or fiction (which might rule it out straightaway because fiction isn't generally what I like to work on)? A topic that I'm familiar with or a topic that might require time for research?

- What is the client's deadline?

- How long will the job take? These last two together might rule the job out if the client wants it done by 'yesterday' or it's massive and can't be fitted into my schedule.

- Who is the target audience? Either you like working on material for 12-year-olds or maths students, or you don't – there's no point in continuing if you can't relate to the target audience.

- How technical is it? Are there tables, diagrams, scientific or mathematical formulae and so on that need checking?
- What level of edit does the client think it needs? Very few clients really know what the document needs, but they mostly offer their opinions, and it can be useful to take their views on board.
- Are there budget constraints? You may have to work within a set budget, so it is necessary to know if you can do the job in the time to make the pay realistic.
- Can you do it alone, or do you need a team?
- Is it to be a hard-copy or on-screen edit? Many academic papers and theses need special treatment to comply with the agreement that professional editors, through their editing organisations and IPEd, have with the universities around Australia. (For current details, go to the IPEd website <http://iped-editors.org>.)

It's a good idea to ask the client about all these matters on the phone or in emails before proceeding.

## Assessing the task from a sample

You need to see at least a representative sample of the job – a whole chapter, or about ten per cent of the text – or even the whole document if it's short. If you make an extra copy, you can scrawl lots of possible alterations over it in pencil, write calculations of time taken to read easy versus more complex sections, and note costings here and there on it. The copy that I work on looks very messy indeed when I've finished with it. A fresh, clean copy is needed for working on later for real.

Here are some of the things to look for – by no means an exhaustive list, but a good basis on which to build:

- readability – does the order of the information flow logically; are sentences of a reasonable length; are words going to be clear to the reader and not drive them to a dictionary; is grammar going to have to be worked on?
- plain English – look at sentence length, use of active versus passive constructions, parallel structure, use of familiar words, use of technical jargon and clichés
- spelling and punctuation – a quick check of the sample pages should give an indication of the level of command the author has of spelling and punctuation (correcting poor spelling and punctuation is very time-consuming)

- illustrations – photos, graphs, tables and so on: are they positioned as near to the relevant text as possible, and are they set out clearly and accurately?
- special considerations – for example: fixing the writing errors made by an author who has English as a second language; switching to a different set of rules for editing a document for publication in another country.

Also, time yourself actually editing the sample. Select several five- or ten-page sections to work on, for a spread of the different types of material in the document. The outcome is a page rate that is easily converted to an hourly rate. Then add time for non-editing factors like consultations, travel and photocopying.

All this added together is project definition – getting clear in your mind just what is involved in the job and what extras you might have to allow for.

## A sample assessment

Here is part of an actual task assessment for a job where I was asked to do a substantive edit of a document intended for researchers, teachers and other academics, written by an experienced author. You will see that I have commented on the level of edit.

My reading so far indicates a need for the following:

- Layout/design: suggestions concerning heading hierarchy, line justification and consistency of bullet-point formatting need to be made (and fixed where appropriate)
- Consistency of style: small items such as single/double quotes, use of numbers, use of underscore/italics need attention
- Sentence/paragraph structure: plain English principles need to be applied as far as possible to avoid a surfeit of passives and long, convoluted sentences; some grammatical structures need attention; punctuation needs attention
- Copyedit: a substantive edit is not necessary, in my opinion, as the author has structured the material well; copyedit level is all that is required in the text (apart from the design aspects mentioned above).

I won the job, and the client agreed with my assessment of the necessary level of edit.

*

Most project definition will be more detailed in all areas than this. Let me finish with a word about the scope of a project. To me, this means how far you can go (or need to go) in an editing job, given budget and time constraints. It may mean the difference between a quick check for typos (a proofreading exercise) and a full copyedit. It may mean taking on team management, or parallel services Always identify the scope of the task. Know your limitations – if a project is not for you, walk away, and maintain your professional integrity.

# 14  Quoting: broad aspects

AS EDITORS WE HAVE ALL BEEN ASKED: 'Would you give me a quote for editing this, please?' So perhaps a look at quoting won't go amiss. If we all worked in offices and employed staff and were members of a union, perhaps our hourly rates would be pretty much determined for us. But we don't, and we aren't. Some of us have high overheads to consider, families and homes to maintain, staff including graphic artists, office workers, other editors and so on to think of and budget for. The vast majority of us, however, work at home, alone, often in a corner of the living room, sometimes sharing the family computer with children doing homework – maybe the house is paid off, maybe there's another breadwinner, maybe this is more of a hobby than a career, occasional rather than full time.

None of that is anyone's business but our own. Whatever our situation, we are all expected to have professional standards and maintain a professional image in the eyes of our clients – in Canberra that means largely the federal public service but in other places clients may be a mixture of state government, local government and the private sector.

So how do we arrive at a reasonable fee for the work we are about to do? In my early editing days, phoning around a group of editors working on documents similar to those I was editing, and chatting with them about fees, gave me a rough idea of where fees were at the start of that particular year. As time has gone on, and I have gained experience and a clientele, my basic fee has moved up to a point that seems fair for the job and doesn't seriously undercut people who have much bigger overheads than I have.

But there should be a formula for arriving at a fee for any job. Can we devise one by trying to answer these, and probably other, questions?

- What level of edit is the job?
- What other responsibilities go with the job (eg project management, indexing)?
- What proportion of the document can you winkle out of the client for assessment? Is the sample representative of the whole document and sufficient to assess the level of edit required, the time needed for the job and the fee you need to charge?
- Is the job purely editing, or is some tuition or explanation expected on the side?

- How well qualified or experienced are you as an editor?
- Can you work confidently alone, or do you need help or mentoring?
- Can you work on-screen or is hard copy required?
- Can you meet all of the criteria set down by the client?

The lead article by Helena Bond in the October 2001 edition of *Offpress*, newsletter of the then Society of Editors (Queensland) (now Editors Queensland, a branch of IPEd), raised a number of issues related to quoting – ones that certainly are still valid – and ended with the experienced quoter's solution:

> I've trimmed my quoting time down enormously. I kept detailed statistics until I could see patterns emerging, then I analysed those figures to understand how many words I do an hour for each service.
>
> So when I'm asked to quote, I get a word count, then check my rate and speed for the service required. After that it's just simple arithmetic to get the hours for my schedule and the dollars for my quote. Add any standard extras, like a loading for jobs with extra-tight timelines, allowances for meetings, a quick reality check on a sample of the document, and hey presto, the quote's ready.

That approach is easy for me to relate to – I use it myself. But is it as simple as that for the new editor? I don't think so. New editors worry over whether something is really just a proofread, or rather a proofread with a bit of copyediting thrown in, and if so, should they charge at the copyediting rate or what? And anyway, what's the copyediting rate this week for people with not much experience yet, and heck, what's 'substantive editing' anyway? If you have to turn a sentence upside down for it to make sense, is that substantive editing? Or only when you have to rewrite whole slabs? And how many meetings can you charge for? And who pays for the depreciation on your computer and other equipment, not to mention the horrendous insurance you have to carry these days?

And let us not forget a formal letter that sets out what has been agreed to (in public service editing, this will be a contract that you can have amended if need be). And at any time during the assignment, there must be more formal letters setting out any variations that have occurred and confirming phone conversations and so on.

The questions are seemingly endless, but I suggest that it ought to be possible to come up with a formula to help all professional editors when it comes to dealing with that most difficult part of editing – quoting.

# 15   The proposal and quote

GROAN!!! Yes, this is probably one of the most difficult tasks that an editor has to deal with. I wrote broadly about quoting in Chat 14 'Quoting: broad aspects', so here is a sort of running order based on a number of my own quotes.

Where to begin? First, **read the request for an editor carefully** (this may be in an email inquiry or notice or an actual job advertisement), or listen carefully if it's a phone call with the prospective client. Watch for indications of what level of skill is required, what they think the document requires to make it readable and publishable. If there are actual **selection criteria** in the request, make sure you can address every one of them confidently and succinctly. You may have to send for the selection criteria.

**What if there are no selection criteria?** This is often the case with private-sector organisations. In that case, get clues from the request, and contact the organisation for further details.

Is it a government job? Government departments often, but not always, ask you to sign a standard **government contract**. These are 'one size fits all' so a lot of what's in them does not apply to editors. Most government departments will listen to reason – put up a case for varying the clauses in the contract to suit you and the editing job, and they are likely to go along with you. These contracts also often include a demand that you take out **massive insurance**. Again, if this seems unreasonable to you, put up a case for reducing the amount or cutting out the requirement altogether. I have done this on many occasions, and have found government departments and agencies very reasonable. If there is no contract, it is in your own interests to make sure that you get **agreement in writing** to your proposal for tackling the assignment. Then, if things go wrong, or if the job changes along the way, you have your proposal and their agreement to refer to when you need to write a supplementary quote. This is particularly important when working for friends – keep business on a businesslike footing.

Now it's time to put in an **expression of interest**. This can be a quite general document – often just an email saying little more than that you are interested and why (perhaps because the material is in your own field), and offering to quote for the job after you have been sent a representative sample of the document. Never quote for a job before you have seen it. Some organisations want an hourly rate before anything happens at all. Resist giving this too early, but if you have to, give a range of rates and list some of the variables – level of edit that might be required, degree of complexity of the document, pressure cooker deadline, and so on.

When you receive a reasonable sample of the text, you can get started on the task of getting the job. First you need to **assess the job** for yourself – define it in terms of what you see needs to be done and why, no matter what the client might have said. Refer to Chat 13 'Project definition'. This stage includes timing yourself to see how long it takes you to edit some sample pages. From this you can work out your **hourly rate** for the level of edit you deem necessary. Add on time and charges for administrative work, consultations, possible research and so on; and consider the level of difficulty of the job – charge more for a really difficult job than for a simple, straightforward job.

It seems to me that the client is entitled to know **how you propose to go about the work** – so set out a step-by-step **timeline for aspects of the work** – charting the project.

A numbered list of steps might include:

> Step 1    Do rough hard-copy check, listing grammatical and stylistic problems and inconsistencies.
>
> Step 2    Do detailed analysis for discussion.
>
> Step 3    Hold planning consultation. (It's customary not to charge for an initial consultation.)
>
> Step 4    Edit on-screen using Track Changes.
>
> Step 5    Allow 'x' hours for additional consultations.
>
> Step 6    Make amendments as necessary and send to client.

Then I tell the client **what IS included** and **what IS NOT included** – I might include making extra copies of each section of the document for discussion with the client, and I might exclude checking a bibliography for anything other than spelling, typos and inconsistency of formatting (depending on the job, of course). You will end up with the number of hours you estimate for completion of the edit, a short list of inclusions and exclusions, and an estimate of how long overall you expect to take working on this job. Editing is an intensive activity that nobody can do for long at a stretch, so a task you estimate will take 40 hours will, of course, take more like two weeks, as you need to spread those hours over a longer time than two days.

When can you start? You need to tell them about your **availability**, and take into consideration any other jobs you are working on at present. Can you work on two or three jobs at once? Or do you need to wait until the present job is finished first?

A very important paragraph is your **disclaimer** (see Chat 9 'Disclaimers'). You are an editor and you are suggesting or recommending certain alterations that, in your view, will make the document more readable for the target audience. You need to tell the client that your alterations are recommendations only and that they are free to accept or reject any or all of them. But the client also needs to know that you will not be responsible for any repercussions should your advice not be taken, or should other alterations be made after you and the client have agreed that the job has been completed satisfactorily. Also use this paragraph to tell the client that, if the assignment alters significantly while in progress, you have the right to submit a **revised quote** to cover the additional costs you would incur.

Now you are ready to give the client your **estimate of time required** (broad or detailed) and **your rate(s)** for doing the work. Don't be backward about hours – you are entitled to work at a steady rate, not breakneck speed, and you need time for all the extras (the administrative tasks), and the client has to be prepared to pay for them. As to hourly rates, you may need to quote more than one rate for an assignment – one rate perhaps for copyediting and another for project management, research and so on. Check with others doing similar work if you don't know what rate to charge – this is a very difficult area for new editors. Don't undersell yourself, but perhaps charge a little less than the industry average if this is your first job.

Set the actual **quote** out clearly, showing your basic rate, plus GST if applicable,* and finally the total. Give a **time limit**, perhaps 14 days, for consideration of your quote.

Say how you propose to **invoice** (eg on completion or monthly). Also say how you prefer to be paid – cheque or direct deposit (see Chat 16 'Invoicing').

End with a polite, interested paragraph, mentioning the addressee's name, and offering to give further detail if required.

Send it and get on with your current work – watching your inbox won't make the job come to you any faster.

---

\* GST stands for Goods and Services Tax. GST only applies if the Australian Taxation Office requires you to register for GST (ie if you earn over a certain amount per year) and you have so registered, and the editing services are provided in Australia – jobs done for overseas clients are an 'export' to which GST does not apply.

# 16  Invoicing

Hooray! The job's done and now it's time to get paid for it – but how? If you're not used to sending invoices, and if you're like me (not good with numbers) and prefer old-fashioned methods to computerised financial management, here's a mock- up invoice that you could adapt to suit yourself.

What are the important elements?

- The name of your **editing service**, logo if any, contact details, your ABN if you have one, and one line about what your service provides – perhaps editing, writing, consulting.

- The words **Tax Invoice** if you are GST-registered,* or just *Invoice* otherwise.

- The **identification number and code** for this particular invoice. The format I use is consecutive number/year/ code for type of work. So this document would be the 157th invoice Inky has ever sent out, the year (in this example 2007) is abbreviated to 07, and the job was an edit. You can make up a list of codes to suit your work: EDIT for all editing jobs, WRTG for all writing jobs, and so on.

- Next comes the **Reference**, where you quote the document in which the agreement is – in this example, an email dated 4 January 2007. And then put the **date** of this invoice – for example, 25 June 2007.

- After that, I recommend putting in the **name of the client** (person or organisation), and this is followed by the name of the **person designated** to receive the invoice – this could be the individual you have worked directly with, a project manager, or someone in a payments office. Put the full mailing address here. If you are mailing your invoices using window envelopes, you may want to reorganise the order of the items in the invoice so that this address appears in the window. Much invoicing is done by email these days, so all that may be required is the recipient's email address plus their name, title and name of organisation.

---

\*  The Australian Taxation Office requires you to register for Goods and Services Tax (GST) if you earn over a certain amount per year. You can also register voluntarily even if you earn less than the threshold amount.

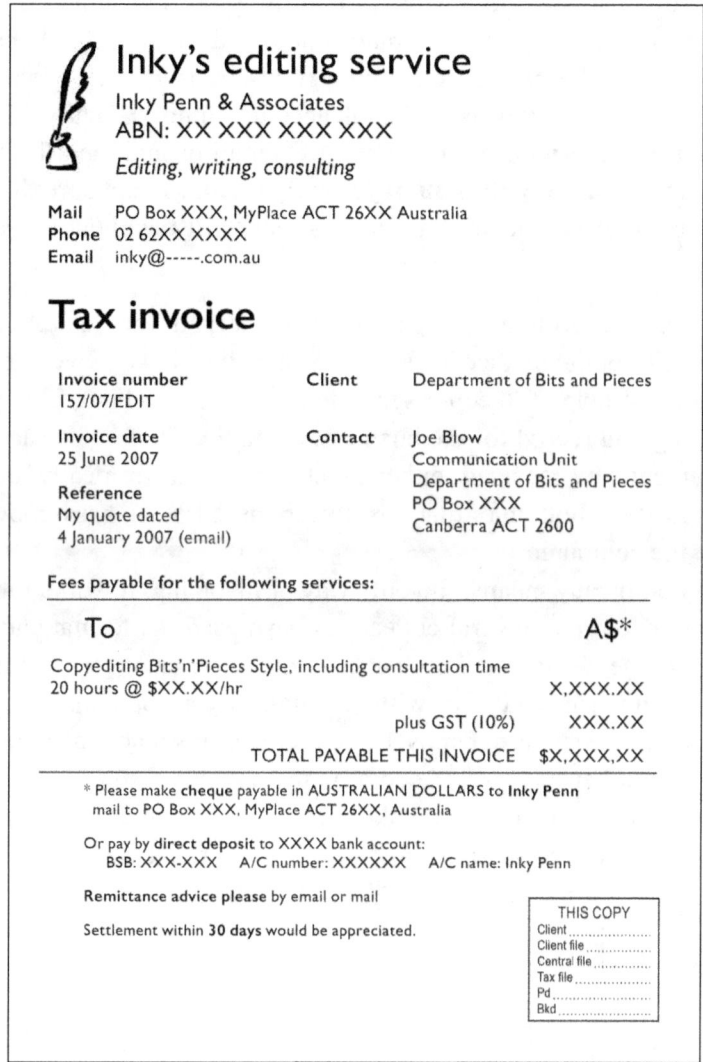

- Then comes the important bit – **a brief statement** of what work you did and your fee for the work. If the fee is based on an hourly rate, include how many hours it took, plus your hourly rate. If you are GST-registered, you need to show the amount of the GST as a separate line item – calculated by adding 10 per cent to your fee. If you are not GST-registered, or if your client is outside Australia, you do not charge GST at all: work for overseas clients is an 'export' for this purpose, and exports do not attract GST. Finally, you need to show the **total**, including the GST amount, if any. If there is no GST, you should include the following, in parentheses in the line under the total: (GST not applicable).

- You should also state **how you want to be paid**. If you accept cheques, state who the cheque should be made out to and where it should be posted. If you want to be paid by electronic funds transfer (EFT) include your bank branch number (BSB) and bank account number. Finally, I like to get a **remittance advice** from the client, by email or mail, and I always tell them that **payment within 30 days** is requested. I'm not sure that it helps much, but at least you can refer to this request if the client is really slow to pay.

The little box at the bottom is not part of the invoice, but very handy as a record of where copies of the invoice have gone. Some clients like two copies, so this can be noted. It helps to keep a separate file for each client, plus a central file as an ongoing record for the business, and a tax file for your accountant. When payments are received, either by cheque or electronically, the details can be noted at the bottom of that box. I keep these files in hard-copy form as well as on the computer.

This is not, by any means, the only way of invoicing. It works for me, and it might work for you. Several colleagues have used the format and adapted it to their own needs. It works both as a hard-copy invoice for mailing and as an electronic invoice, sent in or with an email. My accountant is happy with it (and I do like to keep him happy!), and there has been no reason to alter the format for a number of years. I keep it on my computer, so only need to alter the details of each new job, and make sure the invoice number is updated by one every time – one more tiresome job made less tiresome.

# 17   Office organisation

DIPPING INTO JANET MACKENZIE'S BOOK *The editor's companion* alerted me to one of the most challenging aspects of being an efficient editor – the state of one's workspace. Now, my workspace often leaves something to be desired: as jobs pile in on top of each other, and there are jobs in various stages of completion, my workspace starts to look more like the aftermath of a tornado.

We are not all natural-born tidy persons, but we can all do something to keep track of what we are doing, and we can all learn to develop practices that make for less clutter and more efficiency.

I work from home, so my observations here are directed to my colleagues who also work from home. If you work in an office, at least you ought to be able to keep your home relatively un-work-cluttered.

**My workspace** is the smallest of three bedrooms in my house. It's on the north side, so that natural light and solar heat pour in during winter and the eaves stop the heat from pouring in during summer. It also has a view of my garden, and I find this restful and inspirational when I'm writing and editing. It also means that I can close the door on it when work is finished for the day, and not disturb the living areas of my house.

The built-in wardrobe in the room has been converted to shelves for current work and archives, allowing me to manage hanging files in one two-drawer filing cabinet that doubles as a stand for my printer. Other stationery items and reference books are stored on shelving on two sides of the room. There's a lock-up shed that houses overflow archives until they come up for shredding.

**My computer desk** is in one corner. The main writing surface is big enough to accommodate just the job I am working on at the moment, plus a telephone. This is just as well because, with my bowerbird habits, two or three jobs would pile up on that desk at once if there was space.

**My desk and chair** are ergonomically sound. As editors, we spend a lot of time using this furniture, so it needs to be comfortable. The computer monitor needs to be at the right height and angle for you, and fitted with an antiglare screen if glare bothers you. The keyboard is best on a slide-out shelf under the main desk surface. 'Silent' keyboards are my choice – clatter drives me nuts. The chair needs to be one that does not 'grab' you under your legs and that has an adjustable back-rest.

If you have clients in your office, provide a comfortable chair. For me, that means another chair on wheels as I frequently need to have a client sitting beside me for tuition purposes.

**Lighting** is placed so that my current work is well lit. Vertical blinds help to adjust the amount of outside daylight coming into the room.

**Soundproofing** may be an issue. This is not easy to achieve if you have to use a small space in a living room, for example, but carpets or rugs on the floor, lined curtains, and a minimum of hard surfaces all help.

**Security** is very important to me, as it should be to anyone who does a lot of work in sensitive areas. All sensitive material must be kept under lock and key. Current work is locked up whenever I am not at home, and the office is also locked. Such precautions are usually necessary in order to comply with insurance requirements.

**Working hours** are not easy to stick to when you are working in part of your own home. It isn't always easy to stick to regular office hours, though it is desirable.

After all, you may have chosen to work at home because you have a baby to care for or because you want the flexibility of being able to work when the spirit moves you. For large, long-term editing jobs I do recommend sticking to a routine, but for shorter jobs and jobs that include other elements besides editing (creative writing, preparation of training programs you are going to run yourself, design work and so on), it may be important to you to work in very short bursts and to go out and meet friends for coffee to recharge the batteries. Whatever your best practice, be sure to let your clients know how they can contact you with least delay. All work and no play ... do take the weekend off if you possibly can – it's important for our health and energy levels to rest our brains completely for a couple of days in this intensive work that we do.

**Answering the phone**. No matter what sort of job I am doing at any given time, however, I do understand that most of my clients are working in full-time jobs. They understand regular working hours. So, from 9 am to 5 pm Monday to Friday, I answer the phone with my business greeting. Outside those hours, it's a much more informal greeting. This applies to both my landline and my mobile phones.

What is an ideal business greeting? Simply stating my full name seems to be sufficient.

Make sure that the message on your answering machine or on your provider's message service gives clear instructions about leaving messages or finding you on another number if the matter is urgent; and always let the caller know that you will call back promptly – and then do it!

**Health and safety** are just as important in the home office as anywhere else. Make sure that lighting is adequate so that you don't strain your eyes. Make sure that the spaghetti junction of computer leads under the desk is well controlled so that you don't trip on any of it, and that other electrical leads (to printer, heaters, fans and so on) are all properly maintained and not in a frayed or otherwise dangerous condition. Also make sure that you take proper breaks from work, and particularly from keyboard work; it is not a good idea to work for longer than about 45 minutes without a break.

**Stress** can creep into any home office situation. You are on your own a lot of the time with no colleagues to bounce problems off. Sometimes you are overwhelmed with work and you think you'll never get through it. Sometimes you are worried that you don't have enough work to pay the bills. All these situations can bring on stress. A good walk every day is a great help for clearing the mind and keeping fit. If you feel really stressed, seek medical advice and take some time off. You won't do yourself or your clients a service by struggling on when you are unwell.

\*

In short, being organised in all aspects of working at home is better than just letting it 'happen'. This means being organised as to office layout, working space, hours of work, filing and storage of files, and in matters of personal health.

Attending to these organisational details adds up to the difference between an efficient and happy freelance editor and one who is constantly on the verge of panic or serious stress-related illness.

# 18   Editor, edit thyself

OUR CLIENTS ASSUME THAT WE EDITORS UNDERSTAND what acceptable English grammar is, and can therefore check what we write before sending it to the client. Unfortunately, slapdash writing is not always mere carelessness – it is often lack of understanding. This chat is about editing one's own emails.

The example below is a composite of many such emails that I receive, or that I am asked to comment on as part of my work. As an editor-cum-trainer, a lot of my time is spent trying to avoid editing – trying instead to explain to the initiators of job applications, quotes for editing and writing, and submissions for grants how the English language works and how we can use it successfully to get jobs, editing assignments or grant money. Unless people have a good grasp of English grammar, it is difficult for them to see their own errors and thus to edit their own work.

This example serves as a jumping-off point to discuss some aspects of writing that everyone should observe, and that editors writing quotes (or expressions of interest – EOIs) should observe more meticulously than most people.

> Thank[1] for yrs[2]. I am extremely busy at present, but I can organize[3] to do it certainle[4] in about ten days.
> 
> Thankyou[5] for writting.[6, 7] Quote is $xx per hour.[8] I need to check the job first.[9] Get back to me ASAP.[10] Regards[11]

(1)   *Thank* should be *Thank you*. *Thanks* was probably intended and it could be a typo. However, it is not courteous to use shortened forms when you are not buddies with the client. I would use the full form, and there is no excuse for not checking for typos before sending.

(2)   *yrs* should be *your—*, probably *your letter* or *your invitation to quote for (title of job)*. Abbreviations such as *yrs* are often indications of lazy writing – be specific. They can also arise out of a desire to be excessively formal. Letters a century or more ago used to end *Yrs ffly* for *Yours faithfully*, and it seemed to be a mark of upper-crustiness to go overboard to use abbreviations like *ain't*. Not these days – it is just slang or uncouth.

(3)   *organize* might be acceptable in the US or the UK, but this is Australia, and the recommended spelling is *organise* (Macquarie Dictionary first-choice spelling). An exception is when you quote from an American or British source where the 'z' spelling is used. However, the whole

expression 'I can organise to do it' is poor – either you can do the job or you can't – say so outright (taking 3 and 4 together, and placing the adverb with the verb): *I would certainly be available from (specific date).*

(4) *certainle* is a peculiar kind of typo or spelling error. The correct spelling is, of course, *certainly*. The error sometimes arises when the writer is thinking the long [ee] sound and writes 'e' instead of 'y'; similarly 'possible' for 'possibly'. Or it's just sheer carelessness.

(5) *Thankyou* should be two words here: *Thank you*. It is a contraction of the full sentence *I thank you*, where *thank* is the verb. Nowadays it is joined (or hyphenated) when it used as an adjective: *a thankyou letter* or even as a noun: *The thankyou I received was a lovely bunch of roses*. We even pluralise the noun: *He said his thank-yous to his hosts before he left.*

(6) *writting* should be *writing* – this is a very common spelling error. It occurs, I believe, when the writer has a vague recollection of being taught about doubling the final consonant to add a suffix. This is true when you add *-ed* to *rebel* to make *rebelled*, for instance. However, the verb *write* does not end in a consonant when written: the 'e' at the end is silent but makes the pronunciation of the 'i' like 'pie' and distinguishes *write* from *writ*. Certainly, some words ending in 't' double it before *-ing* – *sit, sitting*; *hit, hitting*; *remit, remitting*. But the root verbs have short 'i' as in *hit* and not the long 'i' of *write*. You often see advertisements for *dinning suites*, and there was once an intriguing photograph of the striped coat of a zebra, where the caption gave details of how the *stripping* had evolved! Or, again, is it a case of careless keyboarding? We don't seem to see the same problem with *cite* and *citing* which also have the long 'i'. Oh yes, the whole expression *Thank you for writing* is redundant anyway because all the necessary thanking has been done in the first line.

(7) *Spacing after the full stop* – there should be one space after each punctuation mark. There is no space at all here when you remove my two superscript numbers. Those of us who were brought up in the typewriter era to leave two spaces after full stops and one after commas have had to struggle to conform to the computer-age requirement of one space everywhere. If you are an offender like me, always do a global 'find and replace' to correct the error before sending a piece off to a client or publisher.

(8) *Quote is $xx per hour* – not good business! It is most inadvisable to give an hourly rate without seeing the job or the plans, or (for editing) reading at least part of the manuscript first. And it may be more realistic to quote for the whole job.

(9) *I need to check the job first* – very true! This clause, in its present position, puts the cart before the horse – checking the job, reading sample pages, studying the plans and so on all come before mentioning how much it might cost. A competent editor doesn't give any costs without first reading sample pages, doing a trial edit of those pages and working out what the whole job is going to cost and what level of edit is really required – no matter what the client thinks. How often have you been asked to 'just cast your eye over this' only to find it needs ripping apart and starting over?

(10) *Get back to me ASAP* is peremptory and discourteous. A more courteous way to close the letter might be *Please let me know as soon as possible if you would like me to undertake this assignment for you*, or *I look forward to working with you* – or some similar courteous close that gives you an opportunity to show your interest in the job, if not done earlier.

(11) *Regards* appears at the end of nearly every email I receive – bor-ing! The variations are *Kind regards* and *Warm regards*. There is a gremlin somewhere that has made a lot of us opt for 'Regards' or one of its variations to close all emails. Why? It is meaningless in most cases. Use a complimentary close that means something in the context of the whole message, or use nothing at all. Often a short sentence is the most meaningful, such as *I look forward to meeting you*. The old rule for hard-copy formal letters was *Dear Sir* or *Dear Madam* and *Yours faithfully* if you didn't know the person, or *Dear (title and surname)* and *Yours sincerely* if you had at least met them. The immediacy of email has thrown those out the window, but please override the ubiquitous 'Regards'. Chatty closers like *Cheers* are for pals.

So, could we do a better job on the original message? I think so:

> Thank you for your invitation to quote for editing your memoirs. I am extremely busy at present, but this assignment interests me very much, and I would certainly be available to work on it starting after (date).
>
> I would need to see some sample pages from the book, say, one complete chapter, before I quote. My fee depends on the level of edit required, from simple proofread up to comprehensive edit, and the time required. I would prefer to quote for the whole assignment rather than give an hourly rate to edit a book of this nature. Please email a sample to me – I will then send my quote within a couple of days.
>
> I look forward to meeting you and discussing your book with you.

Better? You will have other views, and that's good. Every EOI is different and should reflect your personality. However, every EOI should be grammatically correct, according to current idiom; should have punctuation that enhances meaning and is not there for mere decoration; should use Australian spelling unless there is a good reason not to; and should be proofread for accuracy, tone and clarity of meaning.

Many email programs include 'autocorrect' and predictive text features, so that many of the above errors are now less likely. But vigilance is still important because these features can also introduce errors – you must check that what you've written is what you meant to say.

Nobody can do it for you. Think of the recipient when the email arrives on their computer monitor – would you be happy receiving the first example? We all know that doctors are supposedly bad at looking after their own health – hence 'Physician, heal thyself.' To editors who write EOIs and quotes I say 'Editor, edit thyself'.

# 19 Editing on the move

ANYONE WHO KNOWS ME KNOWS that interstate and overseas travel is part of my scene. Despite this, there has never been a missed deadline. I've written articles and done editing in aircraft, in friends' houses, on my lap in the back of a car on a long drive, in motel rooms, even in hospital waiting areas.

*Winging it* took on a whole new meaning for me at the start of a quick overseas holiday some years ago when, for me to have a break away from home at all, some editing work had to continue – no rest ... and all that.

That was when modern computer technology proved to be so wonderful. Flying in a big jet over the top of India, Myanmar and Turkey, I edited a document for a Canberra client who didn't even need to know that I was away from my home base, let alone winging it over foreign lands. While travelling, I was also able to recharge the laptop battery by plugging a dinky little device into my armrest control panel and into the computer – this was thanks to a very obliging cabin attendant.

What was the job? Well, amazingly, it was an article about early forms of transport in Australia and the role played by modern Aussie 'flyboys' in reviving some gentler forms of transport in their leisure hours.

*Winging it* means 'doing it by intuition' or, to maintain the metaphor, 'flying by the seat of your pants'. How apt!

The editing part is not guesswork – that's totally professional, though always including a modicum of personal preference and intuition, based on an analysis of the needs of the target audience. However, I have proved to myself that working away from home anywhere in the world, including in the skies, is just as easy as at stops on the road between Canberra and other places in Australia.

Editing is one profession that allows us the freedom to be anywhere and everywhere at once. We can schedule holidays (given goodwill from clients) and not miss a beat in our contracts. The ever-shrinking world is our oyster. Those few days changed my thinking about whether or not to commit to editing jobs. Provided the job is such that it can be done in small bites, there's no reason to let jobs get in the way of enjoyment of the world and what it has to offer. I 'winged it' from the UK to the US and then a long haul from the US to Fiji in the following couple of weeks. The editing work that went with me helped to fill in some of those otherwise tedious hours in the air – and has done so ever since.

A bit of planning has to go into doing things on the run. So what sort of planning is needed?

You first need to prioritise all the jobs waiting for attention. If something can wait until you get home to records and reference material, it waits. My home office is my most work-friendly environment. Having said that, what's the point of 'working from home' if you can't enjoy the freedom that it gives you? Decide what can wait and what you need to take with you.

You then need to further prioritise the tasks that can be done on the run. I do this in conjunction with a detailed itinerary, so that I know exactly what facilities will be available at each stop on my travels. Motel rooms are good because most have some kind of WiFi, and there's usually a desk or table to use as a work space.

Staying with relatives or friends is always problematic, in terms of work, because first priority has to be fitting in with whatever plans they have for fun, family get-togethers and other outings. It's therefore necessary to organise 'must do' work so that it can be done in work-friendly environments. Aircraft are OK if you choose your seating and if you can plug into the power on board – I have done a great deal of work on long flights between Singapore or Bangkok and London.

This all requires project management techniques, including charting deadlines and dates when I'll be away from my home base and then planning travel and style of accommodation to fit in with the jobs – not the other way round. After all, my commitment to my clients is paramount, and it's up to me to see that I meet that commitment by putting myself in places where it is possible for me to work to get the job done. It's not meant primarily to be a holiday.

What goes with me?

- Bare-bones hard-copy files if not stored electronically – most recent files and client contact details.
- Flashdrive (thumb drive, data stick – it has several names) on which I have loaded as much as possible of the documents required, plus any available reference material and correspondence – again, most recent material.
- Laptop computer – for air travel, its carry-case becomes my overnight bag and makes a handy footstool. Once overseas, sometimes only the flashdrive is necessary, depending on whether or not a local computer or cyber-café is available.
- Small printer if it seems I might need it and if I'm driving within Australia (it's kept stored, with a supply of paper and spare ink cartridges, in a carry bag, ready to go).

- A4 writing pad and small stationery items that could be useful.
- Chargers for mobile phone and batteries.

On even the most complex of journeys, I would take only three major items – my laptop computer with its attachments, my printer and a briefcase with the rest in it. The flashdrive is permanently slung round my neck on a lanyard for safekeeping.

Well, that's the travelling part. What about the work?

Travel has been part of my life for long enough now for me to know just what to pack for any destination. On arrival, I can set up a mini home office in minutes and be working away at an editing or writing job, either on hard copy or on-screen. Phone consultation sessions can continue, without a hiccup, while interstate or overseas – thanks to the mobile phone and 'global roaming'.

And what about telling the client?

For very short excursions, it may not even be necessary to tell clients that you will be away because today's technology makes it possible to be as close as a phone call or email anywhere.

If ongoing consultation is part of the job, it is essential to let the client know where you will be. It is unlikely that a client these days would object to your being away from your home base, provided the work keeps coming in on schedule. However, there could be legal reasons for not working on a client's material while out of the country – think about this before making plans to travel or even before taking on the job at all. Your first priority has to be the interests of the client, and playing fair with the client.

I have worked on material for Canberra clients while travelling in the UK and the US, with no ill-effects to the work or to my relationship with my clients, but only after consulting them. If I am travelling within, say, a couple of hours' drive of my home base, I frequently get on with it and only mention it later. But it is not advisable to do even that without establishing with the client before taking on the job that a certain amount of travel would be all right and would not disrupt the workflow.

The message is: don't be afraid of having a break from your home office and taking your work with you if you think you can cope just as easily on the run as at home. Plan the travel and the work carefully. Plan what to take with you. Talk to your clients about it and get their approval before taking their material away from your home base. Plan your work so that you can continue it stress-free, and enjoy seeing something of the rest of Australia or the world at the same time. It takes a bit of effort the first time you do it, but it gets easier as you become more skilled at the planning part. I recommend it as a way of having a break but not losing earning power.

# 20  Keeping in touch: emailing

EDITORS NEED TO KEEP IN TOUCH WITH THEIR CLIENTS, and there are several ways to do this: in person, by phone, in writing. Before communicating with your client, think carefully about what you want to say or write to them.

If a matter is urgent, or if explanation is required, it works better if you and your client can talk to each other. Tone of voice, gesture, facial expression, ease of interaction are all important, and these have to be replaced somehow when the only form of communication available is email.

Email is not secure. Never write anything to or about someone that you would not be comfortable saying in a personal conversation. Only send copies (cc) or blind copies (bcc) if absolutely necessary – clogging people's computers with unwanted mail is just not on. Did you ever hear the term 'the paperless office'? This is what the computer and email were supposed to bring to us – deliverance from draft after draft of reports, correspondence and other documents. Not a bit of it. We draft and redraft even more than before and sometimes even print every draft out, thus wasting more paper than ever. Try to get it right the first time by doing your drafting, reorganising, checking, self-editing on screen yourself, and only sending an email when you are satisfied that it's the best it can be. Your email to your client should be a model of the kind of acceptable English that you would like the client's book, article or thesis to be, wouldn't you agree?

One of my great annoyances is receiving a reply to an email without the original being included. When you reply to an email, do so above their original text – your recipient will be glad to have their own email there to refer to.

Another pet hate is a subject line that either changes for no good reason or that doesn't change even when the new text has nothing to do with the original subject line. Think about continuing a thread or breaking it and starting afresh.

So much for some of my pet hates. Here are some pet likes:

- emails that get to the point in the first sentence – no beating around the bush with introductions like *I am writing this email to let you know that ...*; instead, start with the next words: ... *I have suggested some alterations to Chapter 1 which you could consider*
- short, simple sentences – if a sentence rambles with conjunctions tacking on more and more clauses, look at splitting the sentence into several shorter sentences

- active voice – it makes for clarity, shorter sentences, and reader focus
- conversational language in emails to clients – you'll get a better 'tone of voice' by using *I, we* and *you* in business emails (remember, the recipient can't see your friendly smile); it's OK to use contractions in all but the most formal emails – *I've, can't, would've* etc are useful ice-breakers; go ahead and end a sentence with a preposition – *I'm not sure what paragraph 3 is about* is less stuffy than *About what is paragraph 3?*

While some informality is fine, don't try to be funny in a business email – unless you're a born comedian and humour is really going to help. Likewise, stick to non-technical language unless you are absolutely certain your client understands the jargon you are using. By the same token, be careful with the use of abbreviations and acronyms that may not be clear to the client.

Keep paragraphs short. Remember that a paragraph is a unit of thought, not of length. A paragraph should consist of a main sentence with the guiding idea of the paragraph and several supporting sentences, and that's all. There is nothing more dreary to a reader than to be faced with a screen filled with text, with no break anywhere.

Unless you are writing a rambling chatter email to a friend, describing your recent holiday, keep emails as short as possible. A single 'screenful' of information is about as much as most people can cope with at one sitting. If you need to write about two matters, try writing two separate emails.

All the conventions of correct English grammar, spelling and punctuation apply to the writing of emails. An advantage of emails is that you can, on most computers and in most software programs, check spelling and grammar as you go. But do be aware that spell checking and grammar checking tools are only guides – you still need to have a good command of spelling and grammar to make use of any suggestions that they make. And remember that spell checkers cannot always differentiate between *their, there* and *they're*, as they are all correctly spelt English words – you need to use your own judgement about some spellings and word usage.

Stick to ordinary English words, in full. Text messaging is for mobile phones – don't let the telegraphic words of that medium creep into emails.

The format of an email is partly set for you, with a place to insert the email address of the recipient, anyone to receive a copy, and a subject. Make the subject line meaningful: *Your Chapter 3* is not as descriptive as *Tautologies in Chapter 3*. Think about appropriate typeface, font size and colour. A friend regularly sends me emails that are presented on a deep violet background, with a flowery typeface, in a small size and white, and with animated decorations. I find it very difficult to focus on the message with all that going on. For most business purposes, stick to a white background, an easy-to-read typeface such as Arial, Helvetica or Calibri (all sans serif – that is, plain – easier for reading on screen), in 12 point, and probably in black (though people with vision problems may prefer a slightly larger font size and perhaps blue). If an attachment is necessary, I suggest attaching it before you write the email, to avoid forgetting it later.

To emphasise everything is to emphasise nothing. It's true. If you overdo exclamation marks, or bullets, or bold type, or underscoring, or 'high priority', you will lose the effect of their occasional use. Just because these facilities are available doesn't mean that we have to use them all the time. As with all writing, consider your reader – I'm thinking here of a client who needs clear guidance from you as their editor.

There is much more to be said about writing effective emails. There are many excellent resources on the internet. One such is *E-Write, the E-Writing Bulletin*, which discusses many aspects of writing emails and material for websites – to subscribe go to <http://www.ewriteonline.com>.

# 21 A roundup

The administrative aspects of editing are no less important than the editing itself – certainly not 'inconsequential' at all. They are sometimes awkward, difficult or a right royal pain, but necessary to the editing process. So where have we travelled on the journey through this part, where have we arrived, and where can we go from here?

## Where have we been?

We've looked at the job that's just landed on the desk as a project – a finite thing, with a beginning and an end; something that can be planned, charted, managed, and that follows much the same pattern whether a small flyer for a village bazaar or the annual report of a huge government department.

Before taking the job, it's necessary to assess it – to **define** it according to the guidelines set out in the *Australian standards for editing practice* and the *Commissioning checklist*. We need to know about the nature of the job, the target audience, the client's deadline and budget constraints. We need to take a sample of the text and work out how long the job is likely to take, the degree of complexity and the level of edit required (no matter what the client thinks that might be), and therefore how much to charge for the job.

OK, we've decided to bid for the job. Now we need to submit a formal **proposal and quote**. Let's assume you've assessed the job. Clients appreciate knowing how you plan to go about it, as well as what you will charge for what. Quoting is probably the most difficult aspect. It's a nightmare for new editors who have no idea of what to charge. Asking around seems a bit haphazard, but you do soon get a feel for what is fair for a particular job. Should there be a scale of fees that editors can refer to and follow? Given the variety of jobs, the unlimited number of so-called 'levels of edit' (really a continuum), and the huge variability of editorial proficiency in the profession, I think it is well nigh impossible to set fees beyond perhaps a suggestion of broad ranges at several major levels of edit.

Then we need to get paid for what we've done. **Invoicing** can be tricky, particularly if, like me, you're not a 'numbers person'. The basic elements of an invoice are the name of your organisation, the words Tax Invoice if you are GST-registered (just Invoice otherwise), an identifying number and code, the reference to the source and date of the initial agreement between you and the client, the nature of the work and the total amount to be paid. There are other bits and bobs you can include, and you will have individual requirements.

We then took a tiptoe through the tulips of **office organisation** – tiptoe because it's often the only way to pick one's way through the office, and mine is no exception! In an ideal world, the computer desk would have on it only the work in hand, the furniture would be such that we avoid backache and eyestrain, the spaghetti junction of electrical leads under the desk would be neatly stowed, and there would be no stress in the job because we would keep fit, well fed, and only take on as much work as we can do comfortably. But it isn't an ideal world, is it? I can dream!

We looked at a very personal area – **editing our own emails**. The emails we send to our clients should be models of good writing. They are our 'advertisements' and need to be pruned and tidied so that the client gets the best possible impression of our command of English grammar and plain English.

Appropriately for me, I included a piece about **editing on the move** – I am always on the run or moving around, either interstate or overseas, and my trusty laptop usually travels with me. It's perfectly possible to carry on editing from anywhere in the country, or anywhere in the world, provided our clients are comfortable with this. Some planning is required, but being able to do this makes life as a freelance editor much more enjoyable than it might otherwise be. I can indulge my twin passions – words and travel – and get paid at the same time.

## Where are we now?

We've got some administrative aspects under control. As editors, we're not all the best of business people, but we do need to deal with the non-editing aspects of our profession so that we get employed again.

## Where to from here?

This part is self-contained – it attempted to cover the main administrative tasks that an editor has to deal with, in some sort of logical order. It seemed appropriate to draw the main points together at the end of it. The other parts of this book contain collections of thoughts about a number of random topics, grouped as logically as possible, but not self-contained like Part 3. These other parts include information on the basics of editing, English grammar, punctuation and style, plus some thoughts on the future of words.

# itchypencil 4

## A traveller's tale

Travelling around Australia provides a wonderful opportunity to observe English 'as she is writ' for the benefit of the travelling public.

Between Canberra and Melbourne there are highway signs that tell you that the hard shoulder is 'for emergency stopping only – bicycles excepted'. Where are bicycles supposed to go in an emergency? Aha! Further along the motorway, cyclists are told they may use the soft shoulder in an emergency. Frankly, wouldn't you have thought that using the soft shoulder, which frequently means a slippery ditch, would be more likely to cause an emergency? Or can they possibly really mean that it's OK for cyclists to ride on the hard shoulder but that other vehicles can only use it for emergencies?

Roadworks abound, of course, and it's not unusual to see a notice that warns you: *No lines marked – do not overtake unless safe*. Are we to infer that if lines are marked, it's OK to overtake, whether safe or not?

And every time LANE ONE FORM looms up on the road ahead, giggles abound. Do they think we read from near to far and not from top to bottom?

Well, on one holiday, my travelling companion and I arrived at Port Melbourne to drive onto the Spirit of Tasmania. Inspection of the ticket reveals a full page of the Terms and Conditions of Carriage of Passengers printed in pale grey in minuscule print. The upshot is that nobody reads this page, which is tucked in behind the ticket and the more friendly instructions. But if you don't read it, you'll never know that, according to Clause 14(a), the shipping line is not liable for anything bad that might happen to you or your vehicle, even if they cause the damage or injury. It's all in legalese, but it's there ... or was last time I looked at such a ticket.

Safely ashore, we soon arrived at our first stopover, a very cute stone cottage in Swansea built in 1860 – the sort with crooked doors and floors, and jammed with 19th-century bits and pieces. It is a delightful hideaway, but stuck to a wall we found the following lulu of a single sentence, also concerning liability:

> The proprietor of these premises is not liable for the loss, destruction or damage of, or to, property belonging to guests on these premises unless such property has been lodged expressly for safe custody, or, has been lost, damaged or destroyed due to some negligence or deliberate or reckless act or default of the proprietor or an employee.

Fifty-eight words to say 'The proprietor is not liable if anything bad happens to your property unless you have expressly lodged it for safe custody or the problem has been caused by the proprietor or an employee.' [33 words]

There was a marvellous sign at a railway crossing near Tewkesbury, south of Burnie in Tasmania. It said LOOK FOR TRAINS – not *Look out for* … or *Watch for* … which might make sense. It was a puzzle to know what to do with any trains we might have found, and how they had become lost in the first place!

And we were amused (after we finally worked out what was intended) to read the following ditty above the toaster in the breakfast room of a B&B in Devonport:

> 5 is to dark, 1 is to light,
> Leave it on 3 and its just right. [Spelling is theirs, not mine.]

We didn't fiddle with the toaster settings.

Memories of a hill near Camden NSW known to all as Tumbledown Dick were stirred by the sight of signs that proclaimed first Break-me-neck Hill and soon afterwards Bust-me-gut Hill on the drive from Swansea to Hobart – OK for us in a car, but no doubt hard work for horse-drawn traffic.

And when we'd finally mastered the complex one-way street system of Hobart, it was time to leave this beautiful island packed with history and enormous community pride, and return to Devonport and our sailing back to the mainland. We were heartened to read, by a gravel road near Great Lake, a sign that, instead of warning us of a number of wearisome kilometres of winding road ahead, announced 'Winding road ends 3 km'. Now that's ending on a positive note!

# Part 4
## Grammar: some basics

## 22  Why grammar?

WOULD IT BE TOO SWEEPING A STATEMENT to say that without grammar, there's no style? No. Style happens only if the underlying grammar is so consistently acceptable that it almost disappears and leaves the style to shine through. If the message sent by the author doesn't reach the reader with its original meaning, with the author's 'voice' and enthusiasm, and in an easy-to-read flow of text, something has gone wrong with the way the words have been put together – not necessarily with the author's intention. *Style* can refer to an author's individual style, a house style, a specific way of writing such as plain English style, and so on.

Without considering the basics of English grammar – the morphology involved (the parts of words that form the whole words) and syntax (the ways words are assembled in sentences to make grammatical sense) – an editor cannot do justice to any author's work.

As editors, we are responsible for ensuring that the author's intention is carried out. So it's our job to see that the words the author has used are put together in a way that is meaningful to the intended audience and will get the intended meaning across with the least possible effort on the part of the reader.

You may be an experienced editor. If so, perhaps these pages will serve as a refresher or as material you can use when mentoring less experienced editors. Maybe you are a new editor – if so, perhaps these reminders of basic rules and conventions of English grammar will help you with what to watch for in your own writing and in the writing of others. If you have been editing for many years, how long is it since you attended a grammar workshop? The English language changes all the time, and these days it is changing very rapidly – and that includes what is or isn't acceptable in some areas of grammar. Perhaps these pages will serve as food for thought, as something to take on board as a new way of looking at an old grammar problem, or even just as confirmation that you were right all along!

### So, what is grammar?

Grammar means 'the features of a language (sounds, words, formation and arrangement of words, etc.) considered systematically as a whole …'

(Macquarie Dictionary). Every language has a grammar – patterns made by putting words and parts of words and other structures together to make meaning, and the rules that govern how we do it. We learn the grammar of our own language gradually as we listen to it being used around us and, later, by being taught in school. If we threw words together in any order we liked, and if we put endings on words at whim, what we say and write would look very peculiar and would not make much sense to the listener or reader. If we are speaking or writing in English, we need to understand and use the rules governing the formation of English used by most people, so that we can understand and respond to people in the same code.

## What destroys grammar?

The main culprits are:

- lack of follow-up to the basic grammar that may have been taught in primary school
- lack of any teaching of grammar in primary school (it still happens)
- the notion that grammar doesn't apply to emails
- the notion that text messaging is correct grammar (it may be, but because of space constrictions, it has to be very much abbreviated).

## How can we as editors help in these circumstances?

- We can be meticulous in our checking of grammar in everything we edit.
- We can use 'comment note' facilities in on-screen editing to explain why we are recommending certain changes, giving sound grammatical reasons but without confusing the author with jargon.
- We can read and learn more and more ourselves about grammar and pass our knowledge on to new and younger editors who don't have the breadth of experience that we might have.
- We can move with the times ourselves – English is a living language, and so constructions which may have been frowned upon a generation ago are now considered grammatically acceptable.

An important area is the editing of material written by people who have English as a second, third or fourth language. More and more, editing such material is becoming the norm for me. It may be written by people of Chinese, Japanese, African, Polish and US origin. US origin! What's the problem there? Plenty. A lot of American expressions, and even some grammatical constructions, are quite different from Australian English. Chinese native speakers have problems with articles, verb tenses, and use of prepositions. Polish people have trouble with English spelling because their own spelling is phonetic. And so it goes on.

There are also many times when I wonder whether the author (even with English as a native language) just tossed a bucketful of words and word endings in the air and let them land on the page in any order. The author clearly hasn't thought about the difficulty the reader was going to have with this mishmash of syllables. For communication to take place, there has to be a way of getting the words and meaning that are inside the author's head to the inside of the reader's head without losing anything. The *com-* of *communication* implies 'togetherness' – information flowing back and forth between people. We need a tool to achieve this, with rules that we all understand. The code we share is English grammar.

# 23  Rules, shmules!*

LET'S LOOK AT SOME OF THE RULES OF USAGE and try to identify what are genuine rules and what are not. I am not a prescriptive grammarian. A descriptive linguist like me recognises that what might have been unacceptable usage years ago is now perfectly acceptable. English is a living language, so things change all the time, often as a result of what we hear on television. We pick up and absorb American English from one show and British English from another. Perhaps the most obvious 'rule' that we have seen change recently is the *different from/to/than* one. For a full discussion of this, see Chat 27 'Relationships'.

There are some real rules – that is, those whose violation would label you as a writer of non-standard English. Here are some of the constructions that should be avoided in formal writing:

### double negatives

He *didn't never* attend university.

The crashed aircraft was proved to have had *hardly no* maintenance in the last three months.

### non-standard verb forms

He *bidded* for the house at the auction sale.

She hadn't ever *knew* anyone so kind before.

I *would of* helped if you *had of* asked me.

### double comparatives

Your second effort was better than the first, but this is *more better* still.

The music in the second half of the concert was *much more livelier* than that in the first half.

### misuse of adjectives for adverbs

The new assistant is working *real good* now.

This job is urgent, so please finish it *quick*.

---

\*   The 'rules, shmules' reduplication has crept into English from the Yiddish construction, which can indicate irony, derision or disbelief. Here it indicates skepticism (Is it still a real rule?). It can also intensify as in 'fancy-shmancy' as applied to a really smart restaurant.

**redundant subjects**
> *These plans, they* need more detailed work.
> *The weather, it*'s been very cold lately.

**pronoun case muddles**
> Tom, Jack and *myself* were selected for the team.
> *Her and me* will look at your problem for you.

**subject–verb disagreement**
> The entire shelf of books and papers *were* about to topple.
> Jim and the other boy, Peter, *was* asked to put the storybooks away.

There are others, but these are the most common traps that many people fall into. When we write, as opposed to when we have a conversation, we have to use the constructions that most people know and use – shared knowledge and shared understanding of what is acceptable. But there are many other so-called rules that are not rules at all, but some kind of folklore. Students ask me questions about them in my courses, so perhaps it is worth sharing a few of them with you.

## 'Never begin a sentence with *and* or *but*.'

Why not – occasionally? Here's a very telling piece of writing that uses both. *But*, you ask, is courtesy not an individual characteristic, infinitely variable as to its practice? *And* if that is so, how can any manual on etiquette provide guidance?

## 'Never begin a sentence with *because*.'

This 'rule' presumably came about as a way of preventing the writing of fragments, as in **Because** *I don't want to. It's raining, and I'll get wet if you make me go out*. Good writers can avoid fragments, and have no trouble using *because* at the beginning of a sentence and using appropriate punctuation: **Because** *we have access to the internet, we learn about world events more quickly than ever before*. The author of this sentence wanted to put the access to the internet up front, to emphasise it. Another way of writing the sentence is: *We learn about world events more quickly than ever before because we have access to the internet*. This version emphasises what we learn, not the access to the internet.

## 'Use *that*, not *which*, for restrictive clauses when referring to an inanimate referent.'

True, but not because the referent is inanimate. Consider these examples:

> This is a tricky situation *that* demands immediate action.
> This is a tricky situation *which* demands immediate action.

The second example is incorrect because *which* begins a non-restrictive clause. So let's compare 'restrictive' and 'non-restrictive' clauses:

- 'Restrictive' clauses are essential to the meaning of the sentence as a whole. They restrict the context of the thing to which they refer.
- 'Non-restrictive' or 'parenthetical' clauses are not essential – they give extra information. It's as if we wrote the clause in brackets or 'parentheses'.

How do we show the difference clearly? It is customary, particularly in formal writing, to prefer *that* to introduce restrictive clauses and keep *which* for introducing non-restrictive (parenthetical) clauses that just give extra information. Here's an example where *that* is used correctly:

> The course *that* covered basic English grammar was interesting.

The main clause 'The course was interesting' doesn't define what course we're talking about. We need the clause 'that covered basic English grammar' to restrict the context. This is a restrictive clause and so we don't set it apart with a pair of commas (similar to a pair of brackets).

Now, see this sentence:

> The basic English grammar course, *which* I attended yesterday, was interesting.

In this sentence, the main clause 'The basic English grammar course was interesting' stands perfectly well alone. We don't need the clause 'which I attended yesterday' to define the course. This is a non-restrictive clause. The extra information is not necessary and so we do set it apart with commas. To correct the sentence from the first set of examples, we need to insert a comma before *which*:

> This is a tricky situation, *which* demands immediate action.

This distinction between 'that' and 'which' along with the punctuation is an important difference between the two structures.

The same rule applies whether the referent is animate or inanimate, as long as it's not a person (use *who* and *whom* to refer to a person):

> The dog that I see every morning is called Rex.
> That dog, which I see every morning, is called Rex.
> My neighbour who has a dog is called Tom.
> My neighbour, who walked his dog this morning, is called Tom.

## '*Between* is only used with two, *among* with three or more.'

That certainly used to be a real rule, but it's gone out of the window. Now it's OK to write: *There was agreement **between** the leaders of Australia, the United States and the United Kingdom about recent Middle East military action.*

## '*Less* for uncountable, *fewer* for countable nouns'

My generation will probably stick to that injunction, but even the best writers are now using *less* in places where *fewer* might once have been preferred: *On no **less** than five occasions*; *There were **less** people in the stands than I would have expected.* There is a definite shift happening here from *fewer* to *less*, though *fewer* will still be restricted to countable nouns.

## 'Wishful thinking requires the subjunctive form of the verb.'

You may be glad to know that the subjunctive mood has all but disappeared into history. No longer will Tevye in *Fiddler on the Roof* have to sing 'If I *were* a rich man …': he can now sing 'If I *was* a rich man …'. But what does this removal of a whole mood do to the richness of the English language?

## 'Never split an infinitive.'

I've included this 'shmule' because it worries a lot of my editing colleagues. The 'rule' would have you write 'I expect you **to understand** already how to knit', keeping the parts of the infinitive 'to understand' together. But it is more forceful to write 'I expect you **to already understand** how to knit'. And I don't think it's possible to write 'the boxer seemed **to nearly kill** his opponent' any way other than by splitting the infinitive.

\*

Because English changes all the time, 'rules' come and go. At any given time, we are in a state of flux about one usage or another. Idiom is the word used to mean the usage characteristic of a particular form or dialect of a language – acceptability at a particular time too.

Writing is no less clear, graceful or grammatically correct if it ignores a few ancient prescriptions or proscriptions. And good writing isn't only a matter of these rather mechanical aspects that I've been concentrating on. See, a preposition at the end of a sentence, no less. Followed by a fragment (well, two fragments). I've just happily broken two 'shmules' – never end a sentence with a preposition and always write whole sentences. I could go on.

# 24 Parts of speech: some of the players

LATELY, IT SEEMS THAT MORE PEOPLE than ever before are keen to understand English grammar, either because they missed out at school or because they are learning another language and the teacher expects them to already understand the terms used to talk about the grammar of their own language – English. People say to me 'I know when it's right or wrong, but I don't know why' or 'I mix up adjectives and adverbs because I never learnt which was which, and Spellcheck is no help' or 'Why is "jury" a single unit one time and a plural idea another?' or 'I can get a message across by texting on my phone – I ought to be able to use the same way of writing in everything, but I get bawled out if I do!'

Briefly, writing by the seat of the pants, or going with gut feeling, is OK if you are quite sure that your target audience will go along with you, but it's best to back this up with a little formal understanding of how things work.

The words *adjective* and *adverb* are labels that are applied to certain words – they indicate the function of those words in a particular sentence. Many words in English can have more than one function – take 'still', for instance: in *He is sitting still*, *still* is an adverb; in *We came to a patch of still water*, *still* is an adjective. Spellcheck is no help in instances where a word is spelt correctly but is inappropriate in the context it appears in. For example, if you write *There books are on the shelf*, Spellcheck will not pick up the error because 'there' and 'their' are both perfectly good English words.

Words like *jury* can be either singular or plural, depending on what job they are doing in the sentence. *The jury delivered **its** verdict* is correct because the jury is acting as one entity on this occasion. *The jury straggled out into the street to meet **their** families after the long day in court* is also correct because, on this occasion, we think of a group of twelve separate individuals who make up the jury, each with a family – a plural idea.

*1 v these days txt msgs will b ok*. One of these days, thought transference might be possible and become OK too. For the moment, however, we have to write in the code that most people relate to, and that is standard English grammar. If we don't, we risk being misunderstood, and that is time wasting and costly in business.

What has this to do with editing? Everything! If you can't explain to an author why they should be using an adjective and not an adverb in a sentence, in my view you are not doing the full editing job. Our aim, surely, is to help the author to write well, so that next time, they will write with fewer grammatical errors. Is this doing you out of editing work? No. My experience is that editors who explain concepts to their clients are the ones who get more work – not less.

So what are these *players* in English grammar? You have probably heard of nouns, pronouns, adjectives, adverbs, verbs, prepositions and conjunctions, even if you don't know what their role is. They are known as *parts of speech* or *word classes*.

You're about to find out about a few of them.

## Nouns

Nouns name things. There are several types of noun – common, proper, collective and abstract.

- **Common nouns** name everyday things: *pen, pencil, children, party, desk, office, apple.*

- **Proper nouns** name particular things and always start with a capital letter: *Australia, Elizabeth, Mount Ainslie, Sunday, Prime Minister Andrew Fisher.*

- **Collective nouns** name groups of things: *team, audience, congregation, herd, flock, jury.*

- **Abstract nouns** name things you feel and think, but can't touch: *peace, love, hate, spirituality.*

Nouns in English have number, gender and case (see Chat 33 'Case: from Latin to modern English').

- **Number** is either singular or plural. Plural is marked by one of several plural markers: *-s, -es, -en,* as in *hat/hats, box/boxes, ox/oxen.*

- **Gender** is masculine or feminine (some non-English languages also have neuter). Gender is only sometimes marked, as in *actor* (masculine)/*actress* (feminine), but this marking is disappearing. For example, *actor* is applied to both male and female stage performers.

- **Case** is not visibly marked in nouns except in the possessive case: *Mary's* umbrella. Other cases are shown by the position of the word in the sentence – for example: Jim (subject) gave Mary (indirect object) her umbrella (direct object).

## Pronouns

Pronouns stand instead of nouns. If there were no pronouns, we would have to write the noun each time, as in this example:

> When Joe arrived at Joe's home, Joe made Joe a sandwich and read the article Joe's son had given Joe.

As we do have pronouns, we can cut out the repetition and write:

> When Joe arrived at *his* home, *he* made *himself* a sandwich and read the article *his* son had given *him*.

There are different types of pronoun – personal, reflexive, relative, interrogative, demonstrative, indefinite. The two illustrated in the sentence above are personal (he, his, him) and reflexive (himself).

Like nouns, personal pronouns also have case. *He* is subjective case, *his* is possessive case and *him* is objective case. *Himself* is reflexive – that is, it reflects on a person or thing earlier in the sentence – in this sentence 'he' in '*he* made *himself* a sandwich …'

## Adjectives

Adjectives modify (or tell you more about) nouns and sometimes pronouns. For example, in 'My *black* briefcase is missing. Yours is *brown*.', *black* modifies *briefcase* and *brown* modifies *yours*.

Adjectives can have three 'degrees of comparison'. For example: Jane is a *quick* (positive degree) worker; Pip is *quicker* (comparative degree) than Jane; Toni is the *quickest* (superlative degree) of all.

Nouns and verb participles can also act as adjectives: *cattle* (noun) truck, *rising* (present participle) sun, *driven* (past participle) snow.

## Adverbs

Adverbs modify verbs, adjectives and other adverbs, and also have three degrees of comparison. For example: He runs *quickly* (modifies the verb *runs*). She is *very* happy (modifies the adjective *happy*). This train travels *quite* slowly (modifies the adverb *slowly*). While Jane works *quickly* (positive degree), Pip works *more quickly* (comparative degree), and Toni works *most quickly* (superlative degree) of all of them.

*

There is a lot more that can be said about these parts of speech. Any good grammar book or website will tell you a lot more. The examples given here have been adapted from my book *Effective writing: plain English at work* (2nd edn).

The next chat covers verbs, prepositions, conjunctions and articles. Who needs all this terminology? We all do, as competent editors. It's part of the metalanguage – the language of language – of editing, which allows us to talk about language in its own words. And this is what's important to the 'teaching' aspect of responsible editing.

# 25  Parts of speech: more of the players

IN THE PREVIOUS CHAT, we met some of the players in English grammar – four of the 'parts of speech' or word classes: nouns, pronouns, adjectives and adverbs. Remember that words are labelled according to the function they perform in a sentence – very few words perform only one function. As a result, many words have multiple labels. Now let's meet another bunch of the troupe: verbs briefly, then prepositions, conjunctions and finally interjections.

## Verbs

The Latin word *verbum* means *word*. When our ancestors were handing out labels to some of the important kinds of words in English, they labelled as *verb* the word (or group of words) that they thought was *the* most important word in a sentence. The verb in a sentence tells us what the subject either does or is.

Verbs are so important, indeed, that we have devoted two whole chats in this part to the basics of verbs (Chat 28 'Verbs: some basics' and Chat 29 'Verbs: more basics'). And following those two is a chat about nouns pretending to be verbs (Chat 30 'Nerbs'). So we'll go on now to the next of our players: prepositions.

## Prepositions

Again, we look back to Latin to help understand these little words. *Pre* is Latin for *before*. So a preposition is positioned before a noun or pronoun or their equivalent. Prepositions show the relationship between two things: *The toys are **in the box*** (shows where the toys are in relation to the box, and *in the box* is called a prepositional phrase).

There are some words that are always followed by a certain preposition, for example: *adjacent to, independent of, culminate in*. So we might write *This building is adjacent to the bank*. In that sentence, *to the bank* is a prepositional phrase, and *adjacent to* is the accepted way of writing 'adjacent + preposition'. This currently acceptable way of writing is known as *prepositional idiom*. For more about prepositions, see Chat 27 'Relationships'.

## Conjunctions

Just like the buses, things that come together meet at a junction, and when two or more words, phrases, clauses come together they meet *with* (Latin *con*) each other at that joining place (or junction) – hence *conjunction*.

Like items or items of similar significance are joined by the *co*ordinating conjunctions such as 'and', 'but', 'or' and 'yet'. For example:

> John is tall *and* slim.
> The boys are playing cricket *but* the girls are playing hockey.

Items of different weight are joined by *sub*ordinating conjunctions, such as 'although' and 'because'. For example:

> We abandoned the cricket match *because* it rained.

## Interjections

Back to Latin: *inter-* means *between* and *-ject* comes from the verb *iacio* meaning *I throw*. So an interjection is something that is thrown in between other words but doesn't really belong there grammatically. It cannot be analysed, except to identify it as an interjection. Interjections are uttered in surprise, shock, joy and so on. Examples include:

> *Oh!* I didn't see you there.
> He is, *alas*, very ill.

\*

So much for the building blocks of sentences – the words, the parts of speech, that change their labels as soon as we know what role or function they are playing at the time. There is a lot more that could be written about them all. Most of them are covered in my book *Effective writing: plain English at work* (2nd edn). See also Chat 27 'Relationships' for examples of the several functions of the word 'down'.

Are you a better editor for knowing this bit of English grammar? Only you can tell. It certainly helps me, as an editor, to explain the alterations needed in clients' manuscripts. Clients are often seeking help with English grammar. I believe we need to help with some authority, and knowing the metalanguage of editing gives us that authority and credibility in our 'teaching' role.

# 26   The arbitrating article

ARTICLES ARE PART OF THE 'DETERMINER' FAMILY IN ENGLISH GRAMMAR. They are among the gremlins that haunt all of us, and particularly haunt people who have English as a second language, and people who, through no fault of their own, didn't get a good grounding in the basics of English grammar.

There are two kinds of articles – definite (*the*) and indefinite (*a* or *an*). We use the definite article when we are writing about a specific thing: *Please give me the book on the small table*. We use the indefinite article when we are writing about something indefinite or non-specific: *She would like a cool drink or an orange and a biscuit*. Note that *a* is used when a consonant follows and *an* when a vowel sound follows. Sometimes no article is necessary at all – when we are writing about a generality: *Books are more interesting than pamphlets*.

As an editor, can you spot errors in the expression of number? Articles don't occur in some languages, so people learning English as a second language sometimes have to learn to put them into their writing. This is an area of concern for editors too. We need to be aware, when we are editing, that 'first language interference' can occur – this is when the grammatical rules of the native language are imposed on the vocabulary of English.

Australia is a multicultural society, and many of us have the grammar of our original languages buzzing around in our heads, and we apply it to the words of our new language. The result is not always felicitous. It's a huge and complex subject, so let's look at just some major aspects of the use of articles here.

Take these three sentences for a start:

(1)   I would like *a* chocolate.

(2)   Thank you for *the* chocolate.

(3)   Chocolate is delicious.

Why do we use the indefinite article *a* in (1), the definite article *the* in (2) and no article in (3)? In (1) we use *a* because it's the first time we talk about chocolate and we're not specifying a particular chocolate. In (2) we are talking about a specific, definite chocolate, so we use *the*. In (3) we're just expressing our feelings about chocolate in general – not one single chocolate and not a particular chocolate, but all the chocolate in the world, in whatever form.

Bliss! The same thing applies in the following examples:

(4) He was later *a* minister in *the* government of ...

(5) She will be *the* Minister for Defence in *the* new government.

(6) Ministers will be sworn in tomorrow.

We might read in material prepared by writers with a background in one of the Asian languages something like 'He is member of Department of Defence' (omitting the articles *a* and *the* because these articles are not required in their native languages). Another form of interference occurs among native English speakers, where there are dialectal differences in expression. For example, it is increasingly noticeable that some American English speakers say *Give me a couple apples* whereas speakers of Australian English would say *Give me a couple of apples*.

There can be confusion about whether to use an article at all or omit it. Take this example:

(7) The events of September 2001 have given     impetus for a change in the relationship between the Commonwealth and the States.

Would you put *an*, *the* or nothing in the blank? If you put *an*, you mean just one of many impetuses. If you put *the*, you mean the only impetus you know of. If you put nothing, you mean impetus in a general, conceptual, sense. So the article can change the meaning altogether.

We also use the article the to show specificity:

(8) My brother was taken to hospital after he fell down and broke his leg. I visited him in the hospital.

In the first sentence there is no article because we mean the general concept of hospitalisation. In the second sentence we mean the specific hospital where my brother is.

Omitting the article can also bestow a certain importance on the noun:

(9) Ted Brightley, president of the society, opened the meeting.

If we put *the* before president, it somehow lessens the effect of the word – to me, at any rate. However, the definite article must be included if the name is left out:

(10) The president of the society opened the meeting.

Finally (but by no means exhaustively), there are some phrases that do or don't have articles in them depending on what's idiomatically acceptable:

(11) in the light of ...; in light of ...

(12) in lieu of ...

(13) in view of ...

(14) in place of ...; in the place of ...

Sometimes it's just the author's personal choice, but from the editor's point of view, it's often a matter of consistency.

Sometimes, of course, articles are not needed – usually when we generalise:

(15) There were boys and girls in the bus.

(16) I like cake.

The definite article is *the* and is always spelt *the*, although it can be pronounced *thee* or *thuh* depending on whether a vowel or a consonant follows: /thee/ *apples* or /thuh/ *factory*. The indefinite article is spelt *a* or *an* depending on whether a consonant or a vowel follows: *a box of oranges* or *an open book*.

We use *the* (the definite article) when we have already referred to the noun or noun phrase, or when we want to specify a particular noun or noun phrase:

(17) He bought *a* hat yesterday. Here is *the* hat he bought.

(18) Please pass me *the* book with the blue cover.

All articles are followed by nouns or noun phrases, and generally appear first in the phrase: *the* car; *the* sports car; *the* green sports car. There is one exception – when a pre-determiner of some sort is used, such as *all*, *some*, *both*. In this case, the article comes second:

(19) *All the* cars in the rally are sports cars.

(20) *Both the* boys went swimming.

The indefinite article changes form to suit the sound that follows, as noted above. So we write: **a** *book*; **a** *brown book*; **a** *very large orange and brown book*; but **an** *orange and brown book* because the **sound** that immediately follows the article is the determining factor.

Some English words look as if they start with vowels (because of their spelling), but they are pronounced as if they start with consonants, so take *a* before them. For example, in *He belongs to* ***a union*** the first sound in *union* is *y*, sounded as a consonant and followed by the vowel *u* – yunion. Some words look as if they start with a consonant, but are pronounced without sounding the initial letter. For example, in *She worked for **an hour**,* the *h* of *[h]our* is not pronounced – thus the word begins with a vowel sound.

Some words are tricky. Do you say *a historic moment* or *an historic moment*? In modern English, we pronounce the *h* as a consonant in *historic*, so it should be *a historic moment*. If you say *an hotel* (with or without pronouncing the consonant *h*), you are partially following the French *un hôtel* where the *h* is not pronounced. We have acquired a lot of words like *hotel, hospital* and *hostel* from French, but we have moved away from French grammar and we use English grammar. So we should consistently follow the English grammar pattern. We should say and write *a hotel, a hospital, a hostel* and so on.

Some abbreviations cause us to stop and think, too. Again, the choice between *a* and *an* depends on whether a vowel sound or a consonant sound follows. For example, we would say and write *She got **a** High Distinction for her essay* (where the *H* is pronounced as a consonant) but *She got **an** HD for her essay* (where the *H* is pronounced *aitch*).

Words change over time in English, and the changes can affect whether *a* or *an* is used. Take the Middle English word *napron* (part of the napery family of cloths and table linen, from the Old French *naperon*) which used to be referred to as *a napron*. Gradually people dropped the *n* at the beginning of the word, so *an* had to be used – *an apron*. Remember that, when you don *an apron* or *a napron* in barbecue weather!

# 27   Relationships

**P**REPOSITIONS ARE WORDS THAT SHOW RELATIONSHIPS BETWEEN THINGS. They are always followed by a noun or pronoun, and sometimes by two nouns or pronouns (or a mixture) joined by a conjunction. The pronouns that follow prepositions are always in the objective case (that is, *me, you, him, her, us, them*):

> The books are *on* the table.
>
> There are books *on* the table *and* the chair. [*and* is a conjunction]
>
> Come *with me* to the party. [*me* is a pronoun, objective case]
>
> Come *with Jason and me* to the party. [*Jason* is a noun, *me* is a pronoun]

The group of words headed by the preposition is called a **prepositional phrase** – *on the table, with me*. In *The books are on the table*, the preposition *on* shows the relationship between *books* and *table*.

If you are not sure whether to write *with Jason and I* or *with Jason and me*, try leaving Jason out of it – would you write *with ... I* or *with ... me*? The nouns and pronouns that follow prepositions ('are governed by' prepositions in grammar-speak) are always in the objective case. This case doesn't show in nouns like *Jason*, but does show in pronouns – the objective case of *I* is *me*. (For more about case, see Chat 33 'Case: from Latin to modern English'.)

## Which preposition to use?

There are many prepositions – usually small words, but not always: *on, in, under, through, up, with, by, above* and so on.

Some words are always followed by specific prepositions and prepositional phrases, such as:

- *adjacent **to*** (not *with*), for example:

    My house is adjacent *to* the woods.

- *responsible **to** or **for***, for example:

    I am responsible *to* my boss.

    I am responsible *for* the conference arrangements.

This is called **prepositional idiom**, meaning that it is the accepted usage at the moment, depending on meaning – that is, the currently accepted preposition to go with a noun to produce the intended meaning. Idiom is like fashion – it changes with time. What was unacceptable fifty years ago might be perfectly acceptable today, and something else will no doubt be acceptable tomorrow.

Perhaps the most obvious example of such change is in *different from/to/than*. Fifty years ago, the acceptable use of *different + preposition* was *different from*, which used to be the only acceptable way of writing this phrase – it was the sole prepositional idiom at the time. Gradually, usage made *different to* acceptable, first in speech and then in writing, even formal writing. But the jury is still out on *different than*, which seems to be acceptable in speech now, and has been acceptable as part of American English writing since at least the 1990s. However, it has not yet made it into complete acceptability for formal writing in Australian English; it will in time. The table below shows one example of multiple prepositional idioms expressing the same idea.

|  | *Speech* | *Writing* |
|---|---|---|
| This photo is different *from* that one. | ✓ | ✓ |
| This photo is different *to* that one. | ✓ | ✓ |
| This photo is different *than* that one. | ✓ | ✗ |

The purists have no doubt got hairs positively bristling on their necks by now! Why not insist on *different from*? English is a living language and usage changes continuously. My inclination is to go with the flow, so long as meaning and structural integrity are maintained. Personally, my choice is *different from*, but that is because it was what was taught at my school. However, there are plenty of ways to express meaning, and I have no objection to reading newer, more fashionable ways of saying the same thing.

Some other prepositional idioms that were the only correct forms fifty years ago, but which could now be debated, are:

      opposite to      afflicted with      similar to

and some which seem to be solidly stuck in their old form:

      emigrate from      accede to      aptitude for

Having said all that, there are always situations when you need to show different meanings by **altering the preposition** you use. For example, you:

>agree *with* a person
>agree *on* a price
>agree *between* the two of you
>agree *to* a deal
>agree *in* part (if you don't like the whole deal)

Likewise: *I am a teacher **of**, **at**, **in** or **for**,* depending on what follows.

## Position of the preposition in a sentence

We've all been told it's now OK to end a sentence with a preposition. After all, Sir Winston Churchill himself was said to have debunked the notion that you couldn't do so by saying something like *This is the sort of arrant pedantry up with which I will not put.*

But does it work every time? Is it OK to write *This is the book you wrote in* rather than *This is the book in which you wrote*? Before I answer that, let's look at what Churchill might otherwise have said: *This is the sort of English I will not put up with.* Or another example: *What shall I write about?* Should that be *About what shall I write?*

In my view, where the prepositions are clearly part of a prepositional phrase such as *in the book, at the corner*, the whole phrase is best kept together if possible. However, many prepositions are really working as particles after verbs, so I then don't have a problem with putting them at the end of a sentence as in my example *What shall I write about?*

In answer to the question above, it seems to me to be perfectly OK to write *This is the book you wrote in* just as it is OK to write *This is the book in which you wrote*. These are individual stylistic variations of the same thing – they mean the same thing and either version is perfectly clear.

The very word *preposition* is its own downfall. It means literally something that is positioned in front of something else – pre-positioned. And this is what has governed the thinking of many educators in the past – after all, if it's supposed to be in front of something, it can't be at the end of a sentence, can it? If it's at the end of a sentence, we have to call it something else, don't we? We've moved on from there! I'm happy with the term 'preposition', despite its Latin origins.

## When is a preposition not a preposition?

When it is an adverb. Just to confuse things, prepositions can also be used as adverbs – that is, they tell you more about verbs, as in these sentences:

> My friend came *in*. [adverb]
> The cat climbed *up*. [adverb]
> I can see your plan *through*. [adverb]

But:

> The cat climbed *up* the tree. [preposition]
> I can see *through* your plan. [preposition]

(Note that adverbs can also tell you more about adjectives and other adverbs. See Chat 24 'Parts of speech: some of the players'.)

The easiest way to identify prepositions is to remember that they always relate to a noun or pronoun, and are usually positioned before the noun or pronoun.

Note that there are many words that function as prepositions, nouns, verbs, adjectives and adverbs. How many ways can you use 'down', for example?

> Let's walk *down* the stairs rather than *down* the ramp. [preposition]
> My doona is filled with goose *down*. [noun]
> 'Big Arnie' would *down* me with one blow. [verb]
> The *down* train is due any minute. [adjective]
> I put the heavy parcel *down* on the floor. [adverb]

**And are there post-positions?** Yes, there are, but happily for us, not in English!

# 28 Verbs: some basics

THE VERB IS THE MOST IMPORTANT WORD IN ANY SENTENCE. Without a finite verb, a group of words is not a whole sentence – it is a fragment. *Verb* comes directly from the Latin *verbum* meaning *word* – which just goes to show how important it is.

How often have you read, at the beginning of a letter, *Referring to your letter of (date)*? It is written with a full stop at the end, as though the writer thinks it is a complete sentence. It's not. *Referring* is the present participle of *refer*, not a complete (finite) form of the verb. There is no subject either. This string of words is a fragment. To be a complete sentence it should be *I refer to your letter of (date)*. That is a complete sentence with a complete form of the verb – in this case in the present tense *refer* – and there is a subject *I*.

A sentence can consist of only a verb, though the sentence then has a hidden (understood) subject anyway, and the mood is imperative (and the sentence type probably exclamative): *Stop!*, which really means *(You) stop!* where *you* is not written, but understood to be there. You may well ask where the whole sentence is in the following exchange:

'Morning, Jim. Feeling better?' 'Yes.'

There isn't a whole sentence in sight, but we often speak in fragments. In this instance, *Morning* stands for the whole sentence *I wish you a good morning*, and *Yes* stands for the whole sentence *I am feeling better*. It is acceptable in conversation that may be part of a novel.

Here's another problem that we editors often see when we work on material written by authors who have English as a second language – muddling of verb tenses in English. For example, in *I am living in Australia since 1985* the writer is trying to say that they have been in Australia from a particular date, and at the same time to say that they are still in Australia. This is a verb tense problem. The sentence should be *I have lived in Australia since 1985*, using the present perfect tense, which consists of the present tense of 'have' and the past participle *lived* of the verb *live*. This tells the reader that it's a mixture of present and past, but that the situation is ongoing at the moment of writing.

So, what do we need to know about verbs? To express finer meaning in verb phrases, we need to understand tense, mood, voice, transitivity, the use of verb participles, agreement in number and person between the subject and verb, and some of the more complex forms of verbs, using auxiliary verbs and participles. The discussion of these aspects here will be brief – the basics only.

## Tense

Basically there are three 'simple' tenses – tense means time: present, past and future.

- Present: I *write* novels.
- Past: I *wrote* a novel once. I *bought* a book yesterday.
- Future: I *will write* a novel one day. I *will sing* with the choir tomorrow.

Have you noticed that, while we can express simple present and past tenses by using one word only, we have to use a helping word like *will* to make the future tense? Languages and cultures that do or don't have certain tenses present a fascinating aspect of linguistics – perhaps another time.

Using auxiliary (helping) verbs 'be' and 'have', we can concoct any number of more complex tenses. See Chat 29 'Verbs: more basics'.

## Mood

There are four moods that express the different attitudes of the speaker or the writer to the action or state described by the verb. Here are the terms you may be familiar with:

- Indicative (makes a statement): The grass is green. Tom kicked the ball.
- Interrogative (asks a question): Is the grass green? Did Tom kick the ball?
- Imperative (issues a command): Look at the green grass. Kick the ball, Tom!
- Subjunctive (the 'wishful thinking' mood): If I were rich, I would give money to the poor. (Here, *were* is not in the past – it's expressing a wish).

Some people include the infinitive (to be, to have) as a mood. Mood is a grey area in grammar these days, with the subjunctive mood not being used as much now as in the past.

A more modern grouping of purposes of verbs is:

- Declarative (same as Indicative)
- Interrogative
- Directive (same as Imperative)
- Exclamative.

Note that the subjunctive mood is omitted.

For more on mood see Chat 39 'What is a sentence?', and refer to Mark Tredinnick's *The little green grammar book* for more on the more recent grouping of purposes of verbs.

## Transitivity

Verbs are either transitive or intransitive. Many verbs can be either, depending on the context. *Trans* is Latin and means *across*. So a transitive verb is one where action passes across from the subject to an object – for example: *The boy kicked the ball* (action passes across from *boy* to *ball*). An intransitive verb is one that doesn't have a direct object – for example: *She appears well*. Here's an example of the same verb *fly* used transitively and intransitively: *Pilots fly aeroplanes* (transitive). *Birds fly* (intransitive).

Here's a question about transitivity: why are passive verbs always transitive? The answer will be in the next chat, Chat 30 'Verbs: more basics', which includes voice of verbs.

## 'Being' verbs

So far, we've looked at *doing* verbs. There are also *being* verbs. Find the verb and ask the question to lead you to the subject: *Tim is my brother*. Who or what *is*? Tim is. We are talking about Tim – this is the subject of the sentence. An earlier example *She appears well* includes another *being* verb – *appears*. Another such verb is *seem*, as in *This hat seems to fit you*. None of these verbs has an object – the words that complete the sentence after a *being* verb are known as the *complement*.

# 29   Verbs: more basics

SO FAR, WE HAVE LOOKED AT VERB TENSE, MOOD AND TRANSITIVITY (we'll come back to transitivity). Let's move on to one of the biggest problems of all, for both native English speakers and people who have English as a second language – voice.

## Voice

In English grammar we have two voices – **active** and **passive**. When the subject of the sentence is the doer of the action, the sentence is said to be in the active voice – that is, the subject is doing something *to* the object in the sentence. When the object is the doer of the action and the subject is the receiver of the action, the sentence is said to be in the passive voice – that is, something is being done *to* the subject *by* the object. Here's a simple example:

> The boy *kicked* the ball. [active]
> The ball *was kicked by* the boy. [passive]

When should we choose one voice over the other? Well, in English we tend to put into subject position in a sentence the thing we want to emphasise – the thing we want to talk about. In the example above, if *the boy* is what you want to emphasise, you would put *the boy* in subject position – that is, probably first – in the sentence. So we would use the active voice form of the verb. If *the ball* is more important to you, you would put it first in the sentence – in subject position. Now, the ball is not performing the action of kicking: it is being kicked – it is a passive receiver of an action. This is passive voice.

Now we come back to transitivity, as promised. A verb is either transitive or intransitive. All passive verbs are transitive. Why? Well, look at the passive example above:

> The ball was kicked by the boy.

Although *the ball* isn't performing any action, there is still action going on – action is still passing across (*trans*) from *the boy* to *the ball*. If we were to write that sentence in the active voice, it would be:

> The boy kicked the ball.

So, as the same action is happening, we say that the passive verb *was kicked* is a transitive verb. All passive verbs are said to be transitive.

What if there is no doer expressed in the sentence?

> Your proposal has been turned down.

This is called an agentless passive (no doer expressed). But we really mean that someone did the turning down – we probably mean:

> Your proposal has been turned down by the selection committee.

Agentless passives are allowable, provided the reader will certainly know who or what is performing the action, or if it is irrelevant, as in:

> Grafton was flooded.
>
> My house was burgled last night.

It is hardly necessary to say *by floodwater* or *by burglars*. Although *floodwater* has not been expressed in the sentence, the passive verb *was flooded* is still said to be transitive. The same goes for the second sentence.

Be careful with agentless passives. In business documents, particularly correspondence with people you don't know, such as job applicants, they can cause offence. Take this example:

> Your application for Position 1234 has been rejected.

The applicant's first reaction on seeing this is probably something like 'Who did this rejecting? I'm entitled to know.' You can save yourself a lot of grief by saying who the doer is (perhaps *management* or by adding an explanatory sentence or two immediately after this one, for example:

> Your application for Position 1234 has been rejected. Management appreciated your presentation, but could only choose one person out of a high-quality field for the position. Please apply for further positions with us in future.

It's probably better to write 'The Selection Committee considered your application but regrets that you were unsuccessful on this occasion' than 'Your application was considered but deemed unsuccessful on this occasion'. The first example indicates who is responsible for the decision while the second does not.

## Subject–verb agreement

**Person** in English grammar means first, second or third person. **Number** means singular or plural. Person is only obvious in pronouns:

| Person (subject) | Singular | Plural |
| --- | --- | --- |
| First person | I | we |
| Second person | you | you |
| Third person | he, she, it, (singular 'they') | they |

Examples of agreement using simple verbs:

> *I write* reports all day.
>
> *He / John writes* reports all day.
>
> *They / The managers write* reports about our reports.

See more about agreement in Chat 31 'One or more than one'.

## More complex verbs

A verb form that is more than one word long is a verb phrase (or phrasal verb). We can use auxiliary (helping) verbs to make more complex verb forms. This is a big topic, so please consult a complete grammar textbook if you want to know more.

So far, we have only looked at the simple tenses: present, past, future. If we use the verb *have* plus the past participle of the main verb, we can make the *perfect* forms of verbs (where *perfect* means *completed*). The perfect form also has three tenses: present perfect, past perfect and future perfect:

> *John has written a book.*
>> [present tense of *have* plus past participle written of write = **present perfect tense** – means it is completed (but only just; he's still crowing about it!)]
>
> *I had written three books by the time I was 30.*
>> [past tense *had* of the verb *have* plus past participle *written* of *write* = **past perfect tense** – means it was all over well in the past]
>
> *She will have written five reports by the end of this week.*
>> [future tense *will have* of *have* plus past participle *written* of *write* = **future perfect tense** – means it hasn't happened yet, but by the end of the week all that report writing will be a thing of the past]

There are continuous forms of those tenses as well. For those we enlist parts of the verbs *have* and *be* to help, and we use the present participle (ending in *-ing*) – just one example of present perfect continuous tense:

> *I **have been writing** articles for professional journals for a number of years.*
> [*have been* means that I have been doing it for some time – past – and *writing* that it is continuing = **present perfect continuous**]

## Placement of adverbs

Before leaving verbs, just a word about the placement of adverbs – try to keep adverbs close to the verbs they modify: *He **works diligently** at his job* is better than *He **works** at his job **diligently**.*

# 30 'Nerbs'

ENGLISH IS A LIVING LANGUAGE, so word classes often change. We're quite used to *hoovering* the carpet and *xeroxing* the document, where nouns have taken on verb functions. But some of these 'verbed' nouns grate.

Consulting the style guide of the American Psychological Association (APA) showed this entry which horrified me:

> The following is excerpted from the 5th edition of the *Publication Manual* ...[*]

Whoever heard of *excerpted*, particularly in a style guide? Apart from the horrible **nerb** (Nancy Allison's great word for such verbed nouns[**]), an active construction would have made better sense as a direct statement to students writing psychology theses:

> The following is an excerpt from the 5th edition of the Publication Manual ...

A search of the internet revealed more examples from business writing. Is it any clearer to write:

> Management has *boardroomed* the topic for discussion
> If the disk is full, the system may *error*
> Let's *acronym* it rather than write it out in full

than these older-style versions?

> Management has sent the topic for discussion to the boardroom
> If the disk is full, the system may make an error
> Let's use an acronym for it rather than write it out in full.

Inventing nerbs (or indeed 'vouns' – nouns made from verbs) seems to be a passion with the upwardly mobile set these days. It doesn't seem to matter that half the population has to work at understanding these new terms. They are a real challenge to the proponents of plain English because they confuse rather than clarify, despite producing slightly shorter sentences.

---

[*] APA (American Psychological Association), *APA style*, 2003, <http://www.apastyle.org/electext.html> (viewed 28 April 2004).
[**] Nancy Allison, *Nancy's wordsmithy: every noun can be ...*, 2000, <http://www.stc-boston.org/archives/articles/nouns.shtml> (viewed 29 April 2004).

Henrietta Hay in her article 'Verbing and nouning'* uses the word 'verbicide' to mean 'the wilful distortion or depreciation of the original meaning of a word' and quotes from a US comic strip *Calvin and Hobbes*, in which the two main characters have the following conversation:

Calvin: 'I like to verb words.'

Hobbes: 'What?'

Calvin: 'I take nouns and adjectives and use them as verbs. Remember when "access" was a thing? Now it's something to do. It got verbed. Verbing weirds language.'

Hobbes: 'Maybe we can eventually make language a complete impediment to understanding.'

The word *weirds* in the conversation above is an example of an adjective being 'verbed'.

A word that has jumped both word class and discipline is *architect* – it's now being used as a verb, as in *the [book] is focused on architecting and building [X] dynamic workplaces.*** The word means *designing*, a nerb from way back, but one we're comfortable with. The only people comfortable with *architecting* in this context are the people who put together websites and such. As ever, in my view, jargon should be kept for those who are familiar with it and should not be imposed on the general public.

A recent addition to the family of nerbs is *google* – not, let me hasten to assure you, with an initial capital. To use that word with an initial capital as a verb would apparently incur the wrath of the founders of that excellent search engine. We have all been guilty of suggesting to friends and students that they *google* a term – well, like *nerb*, for instance – to see what is thrown up. It's an expressive verb and there really isn't another one that does the job half as well, although we could say *Search the term on Google* (this time with a capitalised G).

So what can we conclude about the use of nerbs in public documents? They seem to be an inevitable part of the ongoing changes in English. As long as there is no other short phrase that the public is comfortable with that will do the job, use them. But they must be sensibly applicable to human situations. To me, it isn't clever for people to *interface* when they merely *meet*; why

---

\* Henrietta W Hay, 'Verbing and nouning', *Henrietta Hay* website, 14 July 2000, <http://www.henriettahay.com/language/00jul14.htm> (viewed 29 April 2004).

\*\* Peter Marquis-Kyle, 'Stop verbing those nouns', *Peter Marquis-Kyle: conversation architect* website, 30 December 2003, <http://www.marquis-kyle.com.au/mt/000426.htm> (viewed 29 April 2004).

should one be *tasked* when one is just given a job to do? And please don't let me hear again, as I was told recently, that *this room is not suitable for either officing or conferencing*. The word *greenlighted* does nothing much for me either, though we've come to accept *highlighted*.

*

Well, this little chat was *goaled* at *impacting* on you some of the effects of *verbing*. As for *nerbs* in the material you edit, please *redlight* them for urgent attention.

# 31  One or more than one

IN ENGLISH, AS IN MOST MODERN LANGUAGES, we have a singular form of a noun to express one, such as cow, and a plural form to express more than one, such as cows. The same goes for verbs. Some languages have singular (one), dual (two) and plural (more than two). Some old languages used to have even more ways of expressing number: singular, dual, paucal (a few) and plural (more than a few).

## Agreement

Verbs and their subjects must agree in **number** and **person**. 'Number' in English grammar means singular or plural (one book; several books). Plural can be expressed in a lot of different ways. Singular can be tricky sometimes too, depending on the origin of the word – what about the singular of *criteria*? It's *criterion*, Greek in origin.

A singular subject (which is always a noun, pronoun or noun phrase) must have a singular verb. A plural subject must have a plural verb.

> The *book* that I bought yesterday from the bookstore in town *is* well written.
> *He is* a teacher.
> *The blue vase* on the top shelf *was* my mother's.
> The *books* on that shelf *are* all mine.
> The main *criterion* for selection for that job *was* excellent communication skills.
> The *criteria* for the job *were* set out clearly in the advertisement.
> *My horse jumps* fences.
> *Horses jump* fences.

Note that third-person singular of most verbs in English ends in *s*, and the plural has no added *s* – *jumps* is singular; *jump* is plural. Number in verbs can be difficult, particularly for the writer who has English as a second language. The plural verb is unmarked while the singular verb takes *s* – quite the reverse of the rule for nouns. For example, *They **run** every morning* is plural to match the plural subject, while *He **runs** every morning* is singular. The number of the verb must match the number of the subject in the sentence – this is called 'subject–verb agreement'.

What would you choose here – singular or plural verb?

> A box of textbooks on various European languages *was/were* delivered yesterday.

If you said singular, you were right! It's just the box that was delivered. The fact that the box contained a lot of textbooks (plural) about various European languages (plural) doesn't make any difference. Just *a box* (singular) *was delivered*.

## Forming plural nouns in English

Number – of nouns – is usually expressed in English by the addition of a plural suffix *-s* or *-es*, as in *cow/cows*, *box/boxes*, or by some other alteration to the singular word, as in *ox* and *oxen*. There are exceptions:

- Nouns ending in *consonant + y* change the *y* to *ie* and then add *s*, as in *country/countries* (but not proper nouns such as *Mary* where a simple *s* is added: *Marys* – see more below).
- Nouns ending in *vowel + y* are pluralised by adding the simple *s*, as in *monkey/monkeys*, *key/keys*. You may see *money* pluralised as *monies*, but most dictionaries and other authorities prefer *moneys*.
- Many nouns ending in *-f* change to *-ves* for the plural, as in *loaf/loaves*, *leaf/leaves*, *thief/thieves*. Again, there are exceptions: *oaf/oafs*, *roof/roofs*, *chief/chiefs*.

This isn't the end of it, however. There are many noun plurals that follow different rules. These are mostly either very old English words or words that have been borrowed from other languages, whose plurals are so different that they just have to be learnt. They are often confusing for people with English as a second language, so we editors need to watch for errors. Here are some examples:

- Changed vowels: *foot/feet*, *mouse/mice* (but note that more than one computer mouse becomes *mouses*).
- No change at all: *deer/deer*, *sheep/sheep*, *fish/fish* (though *fishes* is also an acceptable plural when referring to fish of two or more species).
- Suffix *-(r)en*: *child/children*, *brother/brethren*, *ox/oxen*; and we can include here, or in the 'changed vowel' examples above, *man/men*, *woman/women*.

- Nouns from Latin like *memorandum* and from Greek like *criterion* have Latin/Greek or anglicised plurals: *memoranda* (L)/*memorandums* (Eng), *criteria* (Gr)/*criterions* (Eng), though *criteria* seems still to be much preferred (as in 'selection criteria' for a job).

Plurals of nouns of other origins, including French, Italian and Hebrew, often stick to their foreign-language plurals in English: *plateau*/*plateaux* (Fr), *libretto*/*libretti* (It), *seraph*/*seraphim* (Heb). However, English plurals using *-s* or *-es* are also used.

There do seem to be rather a lot of rules and variations. My advice would be to go for consistency throughout a document, bearing in mind the tone and the target audience.

There is one rule that is a must for me, however. Do not normally use an apostrophe to indicate plural. Do not write *Onion's are cheap today* or *The Beatles were popular in the 1960's*. Instead, write *Onions are cheap today* and *The Beatles were popular in the 1960s*. There is one exception – when a final *s* without an apostrophe would make a word difficult to read, as in: *Dot your i's and cross your t's* or *There are four s's in Mississippi*.

Proper nouns are also subject to a rule – people's names cannot be changed. If there is more than one person named Mary in your group, you write *There are three Marys in our group* – not *three Maries*, which means something entirely different. We also address a letter to the sisters Jane and Bev Jones as *Misses Jones*, and to the several doctors who looked after us in hospital as *Drs Benson, Cook and Garside*.

What should we do about pluralising compounds? Times they are a-changing, as the song says. We used to be told that we always pluralised the more important noun in the combination: *secretaries-general, brothers-in-law, baby sitters*. However, the trend seems to be towards pluralising at the end of the combination with a simple *s*, no matter which is the more important word. This particularly applies to compounds that are very familiar, such as *attorney-generals* instead of *attorneys-general*; and in compounds borrowed from French such as *cul-de-sacs* – we wouldn't dream of pluralising *cul*, though it is the key word in the compound.

When we add numerators to nouns in English we also pluralise the noun, as in *I bought **two books** yesterday*. A writer from an Asian-language background is more likely to write *I bought **two book** yesterday* because the rule in most Asian languages is that the numerator itself is sufficient indication of plural in such a phrase.

*itchypencil 5*

## Distracting signs

> **DRIVE N TEXT**
> **U B NEXT**

This sign appears on the roadside along a busy parkway. I couldn't stop to photograph it or I would have been booked for stopping in a 'no stopping' zone. When I first saw it, I nearly drove off the road through lack of concentration on driving. I couldn't figure the wording out.

Since then, I've realised it's addressed to all the drivers who insist on continuing to send text messages on their mobile phones while driving on that parkway at 100 kph.

It's intended as a warning to such drivers, but it's dangerous for drivers who don't text – our concentration is interrupted for the second or two it takes to absorb the unusual wording, and is therefore a recipe for an accident. I'm in favour of warning texting drivers that they will be booked if caught texting and driving at the same time, but wouldn't it be better to put the sign at the beginning of the parkway where people are less likely to already be doing 100kph?

# Part 5

## Grammar: beyond the basics

# 32  Voice: active or passive?

THE NUMBER OF TIMES PEOPLE ASK ME about the difference between active and passive constructions is countless. When writing plain English for public documents, active voice is better than passive because active is more direct, is clearer, uses fewer words than passive and so on.

But just what is *active* and what is *passive*? Is this active or passive: *The boy who kicked the football got injured in the scrum*? And this: *I was robbed*? The main clause in the first is passive and the embedded clause is active. The second sentence is passive. In both instances, the subject (*the boy*; *I*) is the receiver of the action expressed in the verb.

Basically, an active construction is one where the doer of the action is in subject position in the sentence. A passive construction is where the receiver of the action is in subject position.

In *The teacher kicked the ball*, *The teacher* is the doer of the action and is in subject position before the verb *kicked*. This is an active construction.

In *The teacher was kicked by the school bully*, *The teacher* is the receiver of the action and is in subject position before the verb *was kicked*. *The school bully* did the kicking so is the doer of the action. This is a passive construction.

In both cases *The teacher* is in subject position in the sentence. This is the position where we regularly put the topic or key noun phrase of the sentence – the bit we want the reader to grasp immediately as what the sentence is about.

In most public documents, particularly in forms or on safety labels where instructions must be clear, active is preferred. Rather than *The form must be completed and delivered by next Monday*, say *Complete and deliver the form by next Monday*.

When we're told to use more active than passive in plain English, we don't have to take that to extremes. There are many occasions when passive is better because we don't know the doer of the action, the doer is understood or irrelevant, or we just don't want to be quite so direct. Here are three examples to illustrate these instances:

> My house was broken into and my television set was stolen. [Doer: *burglar/s* but we don't know who or how many]

> Canberra was recently covered in red dust swept up from central NSW farms. [Doer: *wind*, but unnecessary to say so]

The late Bill Bloggs was loved by all those whose lives were touched by his. [Doers: *All those* and *his [life]* – the active version would not be so gentle]

Passive constructions are worst when the reader needs to know who is responsible for what but isn't told. In this example, *Your application for leave has been turned down*, the reader is entitled to ask 'by whom?' And in this letter, there are many unanswered questions about responsibility:

> Dear——, In order that your application to vary your residential lease *may be processed* [a], it is necessary that the full name of the owner *be supplied* [b]. The type of activity proposed *should* also *be described* [c] on the attached form, which *should be completed and returned* [d] to the address shown.

(a)  by whom? presumably whoever sent the letter—that is, *us*

(b)  by whom? presumably the person addressed—that is, *you*

(c)  by *you*

(d)  by *you*

Converted to active voice, who does what becomes much clearer:

> Dear——, In order that we may process your application to vary your residential lease, it is necessary that you supply your full name. You should also describe the type of activity proposed on the attached form, which you should complete and return to the address shown.

A nice balance of active and passive in a document is best.

# 33  Case: from Latin to modern English

YES, WE DO HAVE A CASE SYSTEM OF SORTS IN ENGLISH. It's important for editors to understand it so that they can, if asked, explain to authors why a certain correction is necessary. For example, we all know we need to change these sentences: *My sisters coats are in the cupboard* and *Jane is coming to the party with you and I*. Or do we? And why? (These sentences will be used as examples later in this chat.)

\*

Here's a sentence in Latin:

> Paulus amat Mariam

If a writer in the dead language of Latin around the time of Julius Caesar wanted to write *Paul loves Mary*, they could write *Paulus Mariam amat*, *Mariam amat Paulus*, *Amat Mariam Paulus* or *Paulus amat Mariam*. They all mean exactly the same because the endings on the nouns (inflections) tell us that Paul is the subject and Mary is the object, no matter what order the words appear in. *Paulus* is the nominative (subject) form of the name we understand as Paul in English. The *(u)s* ending tells us that Paul is the subject of the sentence, no matter where in the sentence it happens to be. The *(a)m* ending in *Mariam* tells us that Mary (*Maria*) is the object of the sentence, no matter where in the sentence it happens to be. So *Mariam amat Paulus* always means *Paul loves Mary*; it can never mean *Mary loves Paul*.

Conversely, if the writer wanted to write *Mary loves Paul*, they could write any of the following four: *Maria amat Paulum*, *Paulum amat Maria*, *Amat Paulum Maria* or *Maria Paulum amat*. The meaning stays the same regardless of the order of the words because the inflections on Mari-*a* (nominative = subject) and Paul-*um* (accusative = object) show the functions of the words accurately in the sentence. In other words, we can toss those words in the air and let them land anywhere – and it makes no difference to the meaning of the sentence.

## A case system

This is called a case system. It is one category in the inflection of nouns, pronouns and adjectives showing what role they're playing in the sentence. Let's stick to nouns and personal pronouns here. Latin has six cases: nominative, vocative, accusative, genitive, dative and ablative. English has these cases too, but not different endings on words to indicate those cases, as in Latin. Although nobody much actually speaks Latin these days, the system has been well preserved and is a useful basis for studying how other languages cope with the problem of indicating the function of words in sentences. If you are learning some modern languages, such as Russian, Armenian, Greek, Lithuanian and German, one of the terms you will hear used is **case**. A case system persisted in Old English, but in modern English we use, and depend on, word order, prepositions and *'s* to indicate and understand the case of nouns.

So, in English, *Paul loves Mary* means just that. It does not mean that Mary loves Paul back! In English we put the thing we want to talk about in subject position – *Paul*. The rest of that short sentence is called the predicate – *loves Mary*, and is what we want to say about the subject. *Paul* is said to be in the **nominative** (or **subjective**) case. *Mary* is in the **accusative** (or **objective**) case, by virtue of its location in the sentence. The regular form of English sentences is SVO (subject–verb–object).

In English, the **genitive (possessive)** case of nouns is indicated by the use of the apostrophe with or without a following *s*. This is inflection. Here are some examples of singular and plural possessive nouns in sentences:

> **Paul's** books are over there; **the children's** books are here.
>
> The **Joneses'** swimming pool is quite small.
>
> My **sister's** [singular *sister*] coats are in the cupboard.
>
> My **sisters'** [plural *sisters*] coats are in the cupboard.

We can, of course, show all the other cases from the old Latin system, but not by inflecting the nouns concerned:

- **Nominative** case identifies the subject (what we are talking about) in a sentence. In English, we would write *'Paul loves Mary'*.
- **Vocative** case identifies the person being addressed. In English, we would write *'Paul*, do you love Mary?', with 'Paul' being the person addressed.
- **Dative** normally indicates the indirect object in a sentence. In English we can say *Give that book to Mary* where 'to' indicates the dative; or 'Give *Mary* that book', where the 'to' is implied before 'Mary'. (We're not giving

Mary away! We're giving the book away – 'book' is therefore the direct object; 'Mary' is the recipient of the book and said to be the indirect object.)
- The **accusative** case identifies the object in a sentence. In English, we would write 'Paul loves *Mary*', where Mary is the object of the love.
- The **ablative** case is sometimes called the 'instrumental' case. To express it in English we use the prepositions *by*, *with*, *from* and so on. In 'The book was written *in Australia by Paul with Mary's help*', the prepositional phrases 'in Australia', 'by Paul', and 'with Mary's help' are all in the ablative case, expressing the instrument, manner or place of the action described by the verb 'was written'. Ablative is the case that indicates the agent (or doer) in a passive sentence: *The boy was bitten by the dog*. In Latin, the noun itself would be inflected to show the ablative case – its ending would change.

## Declension of a noun in Latin

Here is an example of what the writer in Latin needed to know. The declensions (the different forms – in this case, inflections) of the noun *lupus*, meaning *wolf*, were:

nominative: *lupus*
genitive: *lupi*
dative: *lupo*
accusative: *lupum*
ablative: *lupo*
vocative: *lupe*

## Personal pronouns

While the apostrophe is used to indicate possession in nouns (the *cat's* tail) and some pronouns (*anyone's* guess), it is not used to indicate possession in personal pronouns – precisely because there is a special form of the pronoun for possessive in the English case system: *my/mine, your/yours, his/his, her/hers, its/its, our/ours, their/theirs*.

The table on the next page shows the case inflections we have retained in our personal pronoun system:

| Person | Singular | | | Plural | | |
|---|---|---|---|---|---|---|
| | Nominative | Accusative | Genitive | Nominative | Accusative | Genitive |
| 1st (speaking) | I | me | my/mine | we | us | our/ours |
| 2nd (spoken to) | you<br>*formerly* thou | you<br>*formerly* thee | your/yours<br>*formerly* thy, thine | you | you | your/yours |
| 3rd (spoken about) | he<br>she<br>it<br>*singular* they* | him<br>her<br>it<br>*singular* them | his/his<br>her/hers<br>its/its<br>*singular* their/theirs | they | them | their/theirs |

\*   Singular *they* was introduced to the paradigm to overcome the lack of a singular gender-free personal pronoun. It is really a throwback to an older English form.

Where does that leave *it's*? This is not possessive case – just a contraction of *it is*.

Following are some examples of the personal pronouns in use.

*Nominative (subjective) case*

This case is all about the subject of the sentence:

>   **He** [subject] went to the pictures.
>
>   **I** [subject] went to the pictures.
>
>   **He and I** [compound subject] went to the pictures.
>
>>   Note: **Him and *I* went to the pictures** is incorrect because 'him' is the accusative (objective) form of the pronoun and can't be used in subject position. To test this, remove 'and I' from the sentence: *Him ... went to the pictures* – does this seem correct? Of course not.

## Accusative (objective) and dative cases

These cases are all about the object of the sentence, including indirect objects:

I invited **him** [object of verb].

I am going to the pictures with **him** [object of preposition 'with'].

> Note: Prepositions always take the accusative (objective) case form after them, but you only notice this when a pronoun follows the preposition. In a sentence such as *Come to the pictures with Paul and me*, 'me' is obviously the correct accusative form following the preposition 'with'. 'Paul' is also said to be in accusative case because of its position following 'with', but it is not inflected in any way. Another example (from paragraph 1 of this chat): *Jane is coming to the party with you and I* should be *Jane is coming to the party with you and me* (objective). If you removed *you and* from that sentence, you would never say *Jane is coming to the party with I*, would you?

In a dative construction, the prepositions *to* or *for* are usually used, if any, and they are followed by the same form of the pronoun as in the accusative case. For example:

Please give the book **to him**.

I asked him to do this job **for me**.

Send (to) **her** a copy.

> Note: This last sentence places the dative (the indirect object *her*) before the accusative (the direct object *a copy*) and *to* is then implied.

## Genitive (possessive) case

This case is all about ownership in some form or other. The genitive case is seen in English in personal pronouns only, such as the ones mentioned above: *my, mine, your, yours* and so on.

The genitive case is not always obvious, but here are some examples that may help:

> This is **my** book, not **yours**. **Your** book is on the shelf with **his** book. This one is not **his**. **Your** computer is not working so you can use **mine**. [Not an apostrophe in sight!]

> Note: Can you see that we use one form of the possessive pronoun when we use it adjectivally – that is, in front of the noun that it modifies – as in '*my* book'? We use another form when we do not specify the thing owned but when it is obvious from the context – as in '... you can use *mine*' when we know we are referring to a computer.

## A word about singular *they* (as used in these chats)

A long time ago, it was decreed that *they* could only be used as a plural pronoun, so we ended up with a frightful mess of *he/she*, the legalistic *the masculine shall be taken to include the feminine* and my personal nightmare *s/he* (a chocolate frog to whoever can pronounce it!) Along came the feminist movement and with it a recognition of the thoroughly bad manners of sexual discrimination, and so singular *they* was reintroduced into English: something very like it existed before the prescriptive grammarians did their worst – it's nothing new. Now we can say and write, even in the most formal documents, *Someone has left **their** gold fountain pen behind and **they** are welcome to claim it from my office*. In this sentence, *they* and *their* can be singular or plural, masculine or feminine – it's the non-gender-specific pronoun we lacked for centuries.

\*

Finally, as mentioned earlier, *case* is just one category in the inflection system of a language. Other categories of inflection in English are pluralisation (*box–boxes*, *woman–women*) and changes indicating gender (*actor–actress*), though the latter category has almost disappeared in the move to non-discriminatory language. Understanding case is a big step on the way to understanding other inflections in words, and a help towards spotting errors in inflections in the material we work on as editors.

# 34 'That' pesky word

A PARTICIPANT IN A TRAINING SESSION questioned the need to use 'that' in a sentence like *Management accepted that the procedure for checking the cooling system was faulty*. Her argument was that it was a short sentence and therefore perfectly clear; to include 'that' would make it unnecessarily longer.

Of course, it is fine to leave out *that* or *which* or *who* if there is no chance of ambiguity, as in the following sentences:

> He said Ann would buy the coffee.
> The person I wanted to see was away.
> Is there something I can do to help?

I'm not getting into the 'that–which' debate here – that's another story (told in Chat 23 'Rules, shmules!'). However, it's useful to look at what can happen when someone reads the first sentence without 'that':

> Management accepted the procedure for checking the cooling system was faulty.

In English we read from left to right. Well, that's stating the obvious! To be more explicit, we take in meaning from left to right in a sentence. We expect the normal order of: the subject, where the initial focus is; then a verb; then an object or other complement.

As we read this sentence, we read *Management accepted the procedure for checking the cooling system* and then come up against a brick wall. The words *was faulty* don't fit with the idea of acceptance of something. We backtrack, thus wasting precious time, and find that we really have two clauses here, and that the subject of *was faulty* is *the procedure*. So we are actually being asked to understand

> Management accepted [X] where [X] is this: the procedure for checking the cooling system was faulty.

If we pop *that* into the sentence, the problem disappears:

> Management accepted that the procedure for checking the cooling system was faulty.

That pesky little word *that* has performed a useful service in alerting the reader to the fact that there is a whole clause there that is the object of the verb *accepted*. One extra word has meant a saving in reading time of several seconds, and those seconds add up during a hectic business day.

Plain English does not always mean fewer words. Clarity of expression is paramount.

# 35 Please allow my fancying possessives before gerunds

OR WOULD YOU PREFER 'Please allow *me* fancying ...'? Debate has raged for many years over whether to use the possessive form before gerunds (verbal nouns using the present participle of the verb). There are good reasons for doing it and equally good reasons for not doing it. A lot depends on what you mean.

Take these examples:

(a) Max dislikes the **child** standing by his gate.

(b) Max dislikes the **child's** standing by his gate.

In (a), Max dislikes the child – the fact that the child is standing by his gate is incidental, merely serving to identify the particular child. In (b) Max dislikes the standing by his gate – the fact that the child is doing it is incidental.

(c) I am concerned about **your** running in the woods at night.

(d) I am concerned about **you** running in the woods at night.

In (c), it's the running that is the cause for concern. In (d) I am concerned about you – I wouldn't want you to risk danger by going out into a dark place at night.

The gerunds in the examples above are after the verb – they are in object position in the sentences. What happens in subject position?

(e) **His** singing caused the audience to applaud loudly.

(f) **He** singing caused the audience to applaud loudly.

No contest! We don't have to think whether we prefer (e) or (f) – clearly, (e) is correct. Why is that? In (e) there is one clear subject of the verb *caused*: *singing*; it is modified by the possessive personal pronoun *his* so that we know whose singing it was. In (f) there is confusion: is *he* or *singing* the subject?

Now compare these constructions:

(g) The old man was delighted at his **grandson's winning** a place at university.

(h) The old man was delighted at his **grandson**, his daughter's boy, winning a place at university.

In (h) the words *his daughter's boy* modify the noun before the gerund *winning*, so the regular form of *grandson* is used, not the possessive. This is an exception to the convention of using the possessive before a gerund.

Other exceptions are when the noun before the gerund is abstract or collective:

(i) In athletics, it's a case of **youth** getting the better of experience.

(j) The **crew** leading the passengers to the lifeboats was the captain's idea.

When the preceding noun is plural, there is some debate over whether the possessive should be used or not. What do you think?

(k) The teacher was surprised at her **students** working hard in the school garden.

(l) The teacher was surprised at her **students'** working hard in the school garden.

And could you put an apostrophe in this?

(m) I am tired of **the neighbour from hell** complaining about my cat to pay me back for my complaining about **her dog** howling all night.

It makes sense without any apostrophe, and I would hesitate to put any in.

The feeling is that noun phrases like *the neighbour from hell* and *her dog* would be made awkward with apostrophes. (Of course, *my* was put there to trap you!)

It is always possible to recast a sentence if the use of the possessive would make the sentence seem awkward, even when it seems grammatically correct. This is particularly so when indefinite pronouns such as *someone, anyone* and *somebody* precede the gerund. For example:

(n) I would be disappointed about **anyone's** thinking that of me.

could be improved by recasting as:

(o) I would be disappointed that anyone would think that of me.

To me, commonsense must prevail. As the Fowlers (HW and FG) said in 1924:

> when [a] subject is itself a number of words, the possessive sign cannot, except rarely, be used. Thus we can say *The explanation of his failing to please was so-and-so*; *his*, not *him*; ... but we cannot go so far as to write *The explanation of a-man-who-had-so-often-pleased-the-populace's failing this time to please* ... [*The King's English*, p 69]

And the high priest of public service writing, Sir Ernest Gowers (1973), wrote this about the 'fused participle':

## CHAT 35  PLEASE ALLOW MY FANCYING POSSESSIVES BEFORE GERUNDS

> All authorities agree that it is idiomatic English to write *the Bill's getting a second reading surprised everyone* ... [treating *getting* as a gerund] ... [and that it may also be correct] to treat *getting* as a participle, and write *the Bill getting a second reading surprised everyone*. [*The complete plain words*, p 149]

Gowers argues that neither *Bill* by itself, nor *getting* by itself, is the subject of the sentence but that the subject is a fusion of the two. He advocates satisfying both the purists who would stickle for the possessive and those who find the possessive odd by recasting the sentence to '*Everyone was surprised that the Bill got a second reading*'.

I personally go for the possessive with the gerund where it makes the meaning clear.

# 36   Confusions

Would you say *just between us* or would you say *just among us*? These two have come closer in meaning in recent times. Purists would have it that *among* can only be used when more than two things are involved, while *between* can only be used when precisely two are involved. ***Among*** *all the countries at the Games, Australia stood out as winning the most medals.* ***Between*** *you and me, I think she's telling fibs about her age.* It used to depend on whether we were referring to two or more than two – we kept *between* for two: th*e job was divided between you and me*, and *among* for more than two: *the job was shared among all of us*. However, it is becoming more acceptable to use *between* in both contexts and for all such situations: *Let's share the chocolates between all of us*. My preference is to stick to the traditional usage.

Other pairs of words are also confusing. I've picked out the ones that seem to give most problems (based on those that seem to come up for correcting most frequently in my editing jobs). There are plenty more.*

## affect, effect

Except in one special usage, *affect* is always a verb: *The rise in the price of petrol will **affect** the cost of holidays.* It is pronounced [affECT'] with the emphasis on the last syllable.

*Affect* as a noun is pronounced [AFF'ect] and is only used in the psychological sense of a highly sensitised state of mind, passion, emotion (from Jungian psychology). Its adjective is *affective* and the adverb *affectively*: *His decision to resign from the Board was **affectively** based, not based on reason.*

*Effect* can function as a noun or a verb [effECT']: *The effect [outcome] of his decision was to create a vacancy on the Board. The doctor's treatment effected [brought about] a cure.*

---

\*   The following examples and those in Chat 37 'More confusions' and Chat 38 'Even more confusions' were derived from a list of confusing pairs of words collected in G Snodgrass and E M Murphy, *Letter writing simplified* (revised), Pitman, Melbourne, 1986.

## imply, infer

Wishful thinking, perhaps, but I'd naively thought that at last these two were sorted out, until someone used *imply* incorrectly in a conversation. She said: 'I imply from what you say that these figures are wrong.' No, she should have *inferred* that the figures were wrong. The speaker *implies*; the listener *infers* (or 'draws an inference') from what they have heard or seen. *Are you **implying** that I am not up to undertaking the job? I **infer** from what you say that you think I'm incompetent.*

Let's finish this selection with this bugbear of many writers and editors:

## lay, lie

Confusion between these two verbs shows no sign of abating. The problem is that *lay* is both the present tense of the transitive verb *lay* meaning *place down* – *My hens lay six eggs among them every day* – and the past tense of the intransitive verb *lie* meaning *recline* – *He lay flat on the floor to rest his sore back*. The best way to see the difference in usage is to look at this chart:

| Tense | Intransitive (no object) | Transitive (plus object) |
|---|---|---|
| present | lie (recline) | lay (place something down) |
| past | lay | laid |
| perfect | have lain | have laid |

Here are sentences using each of these:

> I **lie** in the shade because I burn easily. [present]
> 
> I **lay** on my bed because I needed a rest. [past]
> 
> I **have lain** here for several hours. [present perfect – present tense of 'have' plus past participle of 'lie']
> 
> Hens **lay** eggs. We **lay** the table for dinner. [implying 'put things down on the table'] [present]
> 
> He **laid** the documents on his supervisor's desk. We **laid** the table for dinner. [past]
> 
> She **has laid** her head on the pillow already. [present perfect]
> 
> We **will have laid** the table by the time dinner is ready. [future perfect]

(There are other tenses, including past perfect and future perfect, and there are continuous forms of all of them. They are not discussed in depth here – please consult a full grammar text.)

Another confusion seems to be the reluctance of some people to use *lie* (recline) because *lie* also means *tell an untruth* – these people prefer *lay* for the present tense: *Do you mind if I lay down for a while?* (incorrect). They also tend to use *laid* for the past tense: *I laid down for a while.* (also incorrect).

**Lay** means *to put down*: ***Lay** the books on the table*. **Lie** can mean *recline* or *be untruthful*: *If you **lie** in the sun, you will get sunburnt; if you **lie** to a judge in court, you are committing perjury.* The past tenses and past participles of these verbs cause problems too. The past tense and past participle of *lay* is *laid*: *I **laid** the table for dinner*; *He **has** always **laid** his books on this desk*. The past tense of *lie* (recline) is *lay* and the past participle is *lain*: *I **lay** on my bed for half an hour*; *I **have lain** on my bed for long enough*. The past tense and past participle of *lie* (be untruthful) is *lied*: *The witness **lied** when giving his evidence; she **has lied** about her age ever since she turned 30.*

# 37  More confusions

OVER THE YEARS, MY LISTS OF COMMONLY CONFUSED WORDS HAVE DEVELOPED from editing jobs, from published books, from conversations, and in all levels of English usage, from novels to academic treatises. Here are a few, with clarifications, and how the individual words ought to be used. There are many, many more.

## adherence, adhesion

Both come from the verb *adhere*, meaning 'to stick to', but are used in rather different contexts. *Adherence* means 'clinging to' when referring to a principle, while *adhesion* means 'sticking together' physically. For example:

> If you want to be in the team, I insist on adherence to the rules of the game.
> Old sticking plaster gives poor adhesion to the skin.

## aggravate, irritate

How often do you hear *'Stop aggravating me!'*? You cannot be aggravated without first being irritated. *Irritate* is more like annoy: A mosquito bite *irritates* the skin. Scratching *aggravates* the sore – that is, makes it worse.

## alternate, alternative

The confusion between these two adjectives doesn't seem to lessen with time. In one usage they are quite different in meaning. If you see a sign on the road: 'Road closed: take *alternate* route', you need to take *the other* route – no choice. If you have *choices* about what to do with Saturday afternoon, you have several *alternative* options – the cinema, a walk, visiting friends and so on. *Alternate* can also mean first one then the other and so on: *At the banquet, the hundreds of guests were served alternate meals – lamb or beef.*

## cheap, inexpensive

Here's another pair of words that has come closer in meaning. Strictly, *cheap* means not worth much, while *inexpensive* means not costing a great deal. For example: *This dress is not very smart – it looks cheap. The other dress has some style although it's inexpensive.* The term *good value* sometimes gets mixed in with these. People often say *This restaurant is good value* when they really mean that it's inexpensive. A restaurant can be good value even when it's expensive to dine there – the cost of the food and the quantity you can eat for a certain amount of money are not the only factors in one's estimation of value.

## comprise, consist

These two are easily confused and are constantly used incorrectly because of the similar contexts in which they appear. They mean much the same thing. However, *consists* is always followed by *of* while *comprises* is not.

> The retirement village consists of forty villas.
> The retirement village comprises forty villas.
>
> The new course consists of four main sections.
> The new course comprises four main sections.

## continual, continuous

Have you noticed the road-cleaning trucks that have 'continual stopping' printed on their rears? Quite correct. They move, then stop, then move, then stop and so on – the stopping *continually* recurs. *Continuous*, however, means uninterrupted: *We had to stay indoors all day because the rain was continuous.*

## desert, dessert

There's no confusion between these when they are spoken in a sentence, but many people misspell them. My mnemonic for this is 'there's more to eat in a dessert than in a desert, so put an extra s in dessert' – *desert* is dry land while *dessert* is the sweet course of a meal.

## disinterested, uninterested

The clue to the difference in meaning between these two words lies in the prefixes *dis-* and *un-*. *Dis-* is more like *away from,* as in *distant,* while *un-* is the equivalent of *not.* So a *disinterested* passer-by may have witnessed a street accident but have no personal interest or involvement in it, or even have an opinion one way or the other about the cause of it. An *uninterested* person takes no interest at all – they couldn't care less.

## equable, equitable

I have recently seen these used interchangeably, but they are quite different. *Equable* means not easily disturbed, or, of climate, not varying much from a pleasant norm: *The coastal town enjoys an equable climate all year round.* *Equitable* means fair: *The distribution of assets was equitable for all claimants.*

## fewer, less

The distinction between these two is becoming blurred. We really should use *fewer* for number and *less* for quantity. So *fewer* should be used with a plural (countable) subject: *There are fewer members present tonight than there were at last month's meeting. Less* should be used with a singular (uncountable) subject: *There is less water in the dam this summer than there was last summer.* But nowadays, *less* is being used to cover both meanings.

## if, whether

The difference between these two has all but disappeared in colloquial speech. However, it is useful to remember the difference for use in formal writing. *If* really means on condition that: *If it rains, the tennis match will be cancelled. Whether* implies choice: *Please let me know whether I have been accepted for the course.* (Some say that *whether* should be accompanied by *or not*: *whether or not I have been accepted*. My view is that it should be used if the meaning is not entirely clear without it – otherwise it can be omitted.)

\*

All clear now? Or 'confusion worse confounded', as Milton might conclude! (*Paradise Lost*, Bk II, line 996)

# 38   Even more confusions

Here are some more words that are commonly confused — examples of some that are frequently used incorrectly, with explanations about their use in writing.

### interstate, intestate, intrastate

If my friend doesn't make a will, he will die *intestate* – that is, without having made his 'last will and testament'. If he does so while out of his home state, he will be *intestate* and *interstate* at the same time – that is, between states. *Intrastate* is different – it means within the state; so if I travel between Queanbeyan and Dubbo, both of which are in New South Wales, I am travelling *intrastate*; between Sydney in New South Wales and Melbourne in Victoria is *interstate*.

### lend, loan

My vote for the second most confused pair of words (after *lie/lay*) goes to *lend/loan*. How often do you hear 'Give me a *lend* of your pencil'. Wrong! *Lend* is a verb, so it's '*Lend* me your pencil'. Traditionally *loan* has always been a noun, so 'I got a *loan* from the bank.' However, in recent times, *loan* has become acceptable in colloquial speech as a verb. So we can say '*Lend* me your pencil' or '*Loan* me your pencil'. But it is still correct to use only *lend* as the verb in writing.

### passed, past

- *Passed* is the past tense and past participle of the verb *pass*: 'I *passed* my exams'; 'He *has passed* through Canberra many times'.
- *Past* can be several parts of speech in modern English grammar: *in the past* (noun), *the past tense* (adjective), *the bird flew past the window* (preposition), *the soldiers marched past as the general took the salute* (adverb).

## scrip, script

Someone offered to take my 'scrip' for medication to the pharmacist the other day. No, that would be 'script', short for 'prescription'. *Scrip* is the document that shows that you own shares in an organisation. *Script* is also used when you mean anything written for reading or performance, such as a play – it is short for 'manuscript'.

## shall, will

These are included here because *shall* is becoming a rarity. For purists, *shall* was the first person and *will* the second and third persons when expressing future tense: *I/we shall go, you/he/they will go.* They were reversed for emphasis: *I will go, whether you like it or not*; *You shall sweep the floor, Cinderella.* Nowadays, *will* is acceptable in all circumstances. Strangely, *shall* still exists in question forms: *Shall we dance?* See Chat 41 for more on *shall*.

## who, whom

*Whom* is declining in use in English and being replaced by *who*. The two pronouns do cause a lot of confusion. However, it pays to use them correctly because they make meaning clear. *Who* is always the subject of a clause. *Whom* is always either the object of a verb or follows a preposition. *This is the person who can help you. This is the person whom we rewarded for bravery. This is the person to whom we gave a medal for bravery.* It may help to break the sentence down to see which should be used:

> This is the person + *She* (the same person) can help you = This is the person *who* can help you.
>
> This is the person + We rewarded *him* for bravery = This is the person *whom* we rewarded for bravery.
>
> This is the person + We gave (to) *him* a medal for bravery = This is the person *to whom* we gave a medal for bravery.

Maybe that distinction will disappear eventually, and we'll all happily accept the currently unacceptable: *This is the person who we rewarded for bravery.* I will continue to observe the distinction in my speech and writing, but I'll probably be in the minority.

Already perfectly acceptable in speech is *This is the person we gave a medal for bravery to*. It dodges the need for either *who* or *whom*. I doubt whether it's yet completely acceptable in formal writing, although a preposition can certainly be used at the end of a sentence.

*

This selection may alert you in your writing and editing to some of the more common confusions in English grammar and usage – be on the lookout for many more. In speech, we get away with non-standard usage, but we cannot afford to let these gremlins get into writing, particularly more formal writing, because we risk making meaning unclear. And the aim of every writer, and certainly every editor, should surely be to make meaning completely clear for the reader.

# 39  What is a sentence?

APART FROM WHAT THE JUDGE HANDS DOWN AT A CRIMINAL TRIAL – a death sentence or a month of community service – a sentence is a string of words that makes sense on its own. Grammatically, it has a subject and a predicate – the subject is what we want to talk about, and the predicate is what we want to say about the subject.

Let's look at a few sentences:

- *Birds fly.* This is a pretty basic sentence: *birds* is the subject and *fly* is the predicate. The predicate can be as short as this or quite long, but it must contain a complete (finite) verb – either an action verb as here or a being verb as in the next example.
- *Robin is a boy.* Here the subject is *Robin* and the predicate is *is a boy*, containing the being verb *is* and some extra words saying just what Robin is – *a boy* (this is known as the complement: a being verb cannot have an object because there is no action involved – it is intransitive).
- *John kicked the ball.* The subject is *John* and *kicked the ball* is the predicate, including the action verb *kicked*.
- *John kicked the ball to the boy in the green shirt.* The subject is *John* and the rest of the sentence is the predicate, with the action verb *kicked*. The rest of the words in the predicate tell us more about what happened: *the ball* is the object of the kicking and is therefore the direct object of *kicked* (that makes *kicked* a transitive verb, where action passes across from a subject to an object by means of the verb); then there are two prepositional phrases, beginning with *to* and *in* respectively – more information about the event.
- *The dog died at the scene of the accident.* Here the subject is *The dog* and the verb is this time intransitive, *died*, because it doesn't have an object. (Some verbs can be both transitive and intransitive – in the first example, *Birds fly*, *fly* is intransitive, but in a sentence like *Pilots fly aeroplanes*, *fly* is transitive because action passes across from *pilots* to *aeroplanes*.)

All the above sentences are simple, **declarative (indicative)** sentences.*

The normal (or canonical) form of a sentence is **Subject → Predicate including finite verb**, as in the examples above. However, sentences can be written as questions, and then the order is changed and they are known as **interrogative** sentences:

> Is Robin a boy?
> Do birds fly? [the subject is still *birds*; the verb phrase is now *do fly*]
> Did John kick the ball?

Do you see how the verb has changed position? The verb, or part of it, is usually at the beginning of the sentence, ahead of the subject.

Another type of sentence is known as a **directive (imperative)**. As this suggests, it expresses an order or instruction:

> Come down to the coffee shop when you're ready.
> Finish this job before you start the new one.

Do you see what's happened to the verb? It's at the beginning of the sentence. And the subject seems to have disappeared. Actually, in each case, 'you' (the person addressed) is understood as the subject.

Finally, there's the **exclamative** sentence, or exclamation, usually uttered in fear, anger or as a warning or other extreme emotional state:

> Mummy, I had a bad dream and I'm scared!
> This is absolutely delicious ice cream!
> What a naughty puppy you are!
> Look out!

Can you find the subject in each of these exclamative sentences?

These terms (declarative, interrogative, directive and exclamative) are encompassing the old moods: indicative and imperative. Most of the writing you will do in business, and most of what you are likely to have to edit, will be declarative (the old indicative mood). If you are editing novels, however, you are more likely to come across interrogative and directive (the old imperative mood) sentences, with perhaps some exclamative sentences. There is a mood that has not been mentioned yet – subjunctive. It will need to wait for Chat 40 'Stacking sentences', because it involves complex sentences.

---

\*   For more about a fresh approach to describing sentences, read Mark Tredinnick's *The little green grammar book*, UNSW Press, Sydney, 2008. His four purposes for writing sentences are incorporated here.

## What is NOT a sentence?

A fragment is not a sentence. Here are some fragments:

- *In the morning* is a prepositional phrase that tells us more about something else, but where's the 'something else' – what happened to what 'in the morning'?

- *The blue car on the other side of the street* could be the subject of a sentence but it has no predicate so we don't know what the writer wants to say about it.

- *Running for the bus* has part of a verb (the present participle 'running') at the beginning, but not a finite verb and there's no subject so we don't know what the fragment is referring to.

- *Referring to your email* is not a sentence, though many people start their email replies with it and even put a full stop after it. However, it only has the present participle of 'refer', and there is no subject.

- *Because it rained yesterday* is not a sentence, although it has a subject *it* and a predicate *rained yesterday*. It is a subordinate clause, dependent on a complete sentence (main clause) to make a whole sentence: *Because it rained yesterday, the match was cancelled.* (Clauses and sentences other than simple sentences will be the topic of Chat 40 'Stacking sentences'.)

Ah, but what about conversations between characters in novels – do they always have to be sentences? No, they don't. When we write out people's conversations, we write them as they would be spoken, and we often speak in fragments:

> 'Are you coming to the movies?' [complete sentence]

> 'Not today.' [fragment, standing for the complete sentence 'No, I am not coming today']

> 'When, then?' [fragment, standing for the complete sentence 'When can you come, then?']

> 'Tomorrow any good?' [fragment, standing for the complete sentence 'Is tomorrow any good?']

This conversation is perfectly understandable, though not strictly good grammar.

Other situations in which you might find fragments being used perfectly acceptably are where as few words as possible are best for getting a message across quickly, such as on medicine labels, in evacuation instructions, in firearm usage instructions, on public notices where danger exists, and in advertising:

    For external use only
    Toilets upstairs
    Steep hill
    Available in blue and black
    Brand X – your passport to beauty

# 40  Stacking sentences

In the previous pages we looked at the question 'What is a sentence?' and the discussion was restricted to simple sentences. These are sentences consisting of one clause only, but a clause that makes complete sense on its own. Let me tell you about clauses and about phrases – also strings of words that make a certain amount of sense. But phrases are not complete on their own. And let's look at the difference between simple sentences and those that are not so simple: compound and complex sentences, where clauses are stacked together to make longer sentences. Here we go!

A **phrase** is a group of words that makes some sense, but cannot stand on its own because it is not a complete idea. There are noun phrases (*the tall girl*), verb phrases (*would have been seen*), prepositional phrases (*in the locker room*) and others.

A **clause** can be a sentence (*The girl hit the ball*), also known as a main or independent clause; or it can be a group of words that has a subject and a finite verb but is only part of a sentence (*when it was served to her*), also known as a subordinate or dependent clause.

Here is a **complex sentence**:

>The girl hit the ball when it was served to her.

In this sentence, *The girl hit the ball* is the main clause (also a simple sentence) and *when it was served to her* is a subordinate clause. This kind of sentence is complex because it consists of at least one main clause and at least one subordinate clause; *when* is a subordinating conjunction.

A **compound sentence** consists of two or more main clauses. In the following example there are three main clauses joined together with coordinating conjunctions *and* and *but*:

>I am good at spelling **and** you are good at grammar, **but** we both need help with report writing.

Those are three sentence structures. In addition, let me remind you about the sentence types discussed in Chat 39 'What is a sentence?': the new terms are declarative, interrogative, directive and exclamative, tending to take over from the old moods indicative, imperative and subjunctive. There was no discussion of subjunctive mood because this mood often involves complex sentences. My view of the subjunctive is that it expresses purpose, wish, condition or doubt. Here are some examples:

> I gave you a dictionary, that you might learn some new words. [purpose]
>
> God save the Queen! [a simple sentence with the implied wish: 'I wish/pray that God might keep the Queen safe']
>
> If I were you, I should pay what he asks. [condition and consequence]
>
> If I were a rich man, I would buy a big house. [a complex sentence with the subordinate *if* clause (condition) followed by the main clause (consequence); note that *were* is used to express the subjunctive, meaning 'I'm not a rich man but if only …' – so not the past tense *was*; however, having said that, the trend now is for the ordinary past tense *was* to be used in this context]
>
> If John were chairing this meeting, you wouldn't get away with such behaviour. [doubt – the subjunctive is no longer used very much in this sense, being supplanted by the indicative (declarative) *was*]

**Paragraphs** are more stacked sentences. Beware! A paragraph is a unit of thought, not of length, so don't let your writing or that of your client ramble on and on. The ideal paragraph should be organised with a topic sentence containing a guiding idea, some sentences that support the guiding idea and are linked appropriately, and a final sentence that pulls the paragraph together and points to the guiding idea in the next paragraph. Here is an example:

> You may have some **difficulty** [guiding idea] in writing a paragraph. [topic sentence] First of all, think about the idea you want to get across. Second, write a sentence that expresses that idea. Third, think about and write down the ideas that support that idea. Finally, write the paragraph, making sure that the sentences are tied together neatly with transitional devices like the ones used here – first of all, second, third and so on. [supporting sentences] Writing a paragraph will not be **difficult** [reflecting guiding idea] if you approach it systematically.

What do you suppose the next paragraph might be about? Yes, *a systematic approach to writing a paragraph* – flagged in the last part of the final sentence. For more about paragraph writing see my book *Effective writing: plain English at work*, 2nd edition, Chapter 6.

Paragraphs need to be varied in length, and there is nothing wrong with a single-sentence paragraph occasionally to make a strong point. Likewise, there is nothing wrong with a much longer paragraph if you are writing or editing a descriptive passage in a novel, for example. Always remember the target audience – business people don't have time to read rambling paragraphs, but there is nothing nicer than curling up in a big chair on a winter's day with a novel that absorbs you with descriptions of lazy summer days that unfold through long paragraphs.

\*

To finish this chat about sentences and how they can stack up, my advice would always be to think of the reader. Will short, punchy simple sentences be best to get a message across economically? Or will the reader be comfortable with complex or compound sentence structures? Finally, how long should paragraphs be? The answer to that is much the same as how long a piece of string should be, because length is not the primary consideration. If a writer can put together two consecutive, well-planned paragraphs, they can put together just about anything – it's just a matter of building on the basic foundations of appropriate sentences and appropriately stacked sentences in paragraphs that are thought through methodically.

# 41   Shall we dance?

Do you remember that song from *The King and I*? The governess, Anna, and the King of Siam got into all sorts of confused situations, some of them with words. Well, I'm looking at some more 'confusions', and one of them is **when to use *shall* and when to use *will***.

The question *Shall we dance?* is worded correctly. If we follow the rulings of the grammarians of a couple of centuries ago, *shall* expresses first person (person speaking) future tense, while *will* expresses second person (person spoken to) and third person (person spoken about) future tense. So:

> I/we shall dance tomorrow.
> You will dance.
> He/she/it/they will dance.

Reverse the pattern when it's intention you are expressing:

> I/we will dance whatever you say to the contrary.
> You shall dance.
> He/she/it/they shall dance.

This pattern was still being taught during my schooldays and persists to this day in the question form – thus, *Shall we dance?*

For most purposes, however, *will* is tending to replace *shall* when one or the other is necessary, and there are other ways to express the future:

> He's going to sing at the next concert.
> He's singing at the next concert.
> He'll sing at the next concert.

## And *then* there was *than*

You'd be surprised at the number of times it's been necessary for me to edit one or the other for being the wrong one. *Than* is grammatically either a conjunction or a preposition. *Then* is mostly an adverb of time. The two should not be confused, but they are, and it may be worth asking whether the increasing presence of different accents in Australia is a factor in the misspelling of *than* as *then*.

The correct use of *than* is illustrated below:

> You know **more than I know** about gardening. [*than* is a subordinate conjunction introducing the subordinate clause that begins *I know*]
>
> You know more **than me** about gardening. [*than* is a preposition with the pronoun *me*, objective case, properly following it]

Some grammarians allow *You know more **than I** about gardening*, on the basis that the verb *know* is understood after *I*. My view is that it is rather stiff, and *me* is quite acceptable in an informal context.

*Different than* is now acceptable in speech, but *different from* and *different to* are better established in formal writing.

*Then* is easier to deal with. Mostly it's an adverb: *We're waiting for everyone to arrive; we'll leave for our picnic then.* Sometimes it's an adjective: *The then prime minister.* And sometimes it's a noun: *Let's leave it till then.*

There's another use, which is a form of adverb described as a *conjunct*, as in this example:

> You know you want to try skiing. Then why don't you?

In that example, *then* has a sort of 'linking' role, joining the two separate sentences. Pam Peters, in *The Cambridge guide to Australian English usage* (pp 22–24), discusses various types of adverbs, including some that you may not have learned about at school – subjuncts, disjuncts and conjuncts.

While we're looking at prepositions with objective case pronouns following, let's remind ourselves of a problem area for some people – the incorrect form of the pronoun that follows the preposition:

> Please come to the movie with Jack and **I**.
>
> Please come to the movie with Jack and **myself**.

The preposition *with* needs the objective form of the personal pronoun after it. Refer also to Chat 33 'Case: from Latin to modern English'. In the first example, *I* is wrong because it's the subjective form of the pronoun – we should use *me*. In the second example, *myself* is wrong because it is a reflexive pronoun and needs *I* or *me* earlier in the sentence to reflect back on.

> Please come to the movie **with** Jack and **me**.
>
> I don't want to go to the movie **myself** unless you and Jack come **with me**.

Try leaving out *Jack and* in the first sentence: *Please come with I/me*. Which is correct? Clearly, it's *me*. Putting the words *Jack and* in makes no difference to the need to use the objective case after the preposition.

## Spelling and grammar checking tools

Why can't we just rely on these tools to fix things that we get wrong? English-language spelling tools generally only recognise English words, and sometimes, even if they're spelt correctly, will accept them as correct, no matter what the context. Although the more common errors, like the grammatical difference between *there, their* and *they're,* are picked up by most modern tools, uses of similar but incorrect words are often missed.

Microsoft Word's grammar checker tends to pick up more syntactic errors, but concentrates heavily on pulling you up for using passive voice, even when you want to use passive voice. But it won't pull you up on incorrect use of *myself,* as in the above example: *Please come to the movie with Jack and myself.*

My advice is to use such tools to check on obvious errors like spelling and typos, but don't rely on them for picking up wrong uses of words. MS Word's grammar checker is possibly a little more useful, but it won't teach you correct grammar and is sometimes actually wrong. (The result of putting this chat through the grammar checker was that it told me that a complete sentence was a fragment!)

Many of my clients have tried relying on these tools, found them wanting, and eventually come to me to have their work edited. You will undoubtedly have the same experience. There are new tools that are really useful, but even the best of these still often need you to pick and choose from the advice they offer. Nothing beats confidence in your own command of language.

# 42  May I? Might I?

WHEN SHOULD WE USE *MAY* AND WHEN SHOULD WE USE *MIGHT*? Well, opinion varies, and it's difficult to consider either of them without also considering *can* or *may* and *could* or *might*.

What do these sentences mean to you?

> I can hold the torch for you.
> I may hold the torch for you.
> I might hold the torch for you.
> I could hold the torch for you.
>
> You can go on your own.
> You may go on your own.
> You might go on your own.
> You could go on your own.

To me, they mean the following, respectively:

> I am able to hold the torch for you – my hand is capable of gripping it and holding it steady.
>
> I've been given permission to hold the torch while you do the hard work.
>
> If you need a torch held for you, I'm a possible volunteer for the job.
>
> I'm willing to save you from the effort of holding the torch if it will help you do the hard work.
>
> You are capable of going on your own.
>
> I give you permission to go on your own – you don't need an escort.
>
> There's a possibility of your going on your own, but it's not certain.
>
> What's stopping you? There's no reason you have to have company for this.

My observation is that *may* is tending to give way to *can*, so that *can* now embodies the meaning *has permission to* on top of *is able to*. Likewise, *might* is tending to give way to *could*, except where strong doubt is intended.

How about the question form?

> Can/May/Might/Could I hold the torch for you?

My preference would be for *Can* or *May*, in the sense that I'm seeking permission. *Might* seems too formal, and *Could* would only be possible, to me, if there is emphasis on *I*, in the sense that there is a choice of people to hold the torch.

In *The Cambridge guide to Australian English usage* (pp 114–15), Pam Peters suggests three main meanings for both *can* and *may* nowadays:

> be able to
> be allowed to
> be possible that

with meaning shifting depending on context. *May* doesn't seem to be used to express ability, but it can certainly express permission and possibility, depending on context:

> You **may** come with us.

*Can* is used in all three senses:

> You **can** use a razor blade [ability or permission] but please be careful.
>
> It **can** make the job easier for you. [possibility or ability, depending on circumstances]

*May* these days seems mostly to be used when there is some sense of doubt or possibility – perhaps there is some hint of 'maybe'. It also seems to be more polite than *can*. Compare these sentences:

> Yes, you **may** go now.
> Yes, you **can** go now.

Another problem area is the meaning and use of *could* or *might* in sentences such as:

> **Could** I borrow that book when you've read it?
> **Might** I borrow that book when you've read it?

Here, *might* seems to suggest a certain tentativeness.

Of course, *could* also has a role as the past tense of *can*: *She could climb mountains when she was younger.*

It's a vexed area. But English is full of such vacillations between meanings and usages. As an English-born and -bred person living in Australia, the word *tea* presents a problem to me. When someone invites me to tea, it's necessary for me to ask whether they mean a late afternoon snack (usually with the drink tea) or an evening meal. In Australia *tea* can mean either, but most commonly the evening meal. In England, *tea* is still a snack at 4 pm and the evening meal is dinner or supper.

This *may* just have stirred up a hornet's nest, but let's hope you *can* get something out of the examples – you *might* think about some words that are problems for you.

## Watch out! A roadside warning

How many hundreds of times have you seen this sign on the side of the road, quickly registered what it's about and carried on driving?

If we examine it a bit more closely, we can see that there are some glaring faults:

1. Where's the rider?
2. Where are the bicycle pedals?
3. Why should we 'watch for' riderless bicycles?

If any riderless bikes cross my path, they'll certainly get a very wide berth from me. I have no wish to have a confrontation with a riderless bike. Even if a rider were perched on a bike that had no pedals, extreme caution would be wise, particularly if they were yelling 'Look Mum, no feet!'

Finally, 'watch for' is an instruction or invitation to be on the lookout for something that we can stand still and watch for, such as whales out in the ocean, from the safety of a vantage point on land. Just watching for riderless bikes is surely not intended as an enjoyable pastime!

Can we think of a better sign? Perhaps something like this:

- Include a stick figure rider on the bike
- Include pedals on the bike
- New caption: AVOID, or GIVE WAY TO, CYCLISTS

This is just one roadside sign that could use some redesigning to make it more meaningful and more of a direct warning to other road users. There must be many more.

Note: On a visit to England, I noticed that the equivalent sign there shows the bicycle with pedals. I felt safer immediately!

# Part 6

## Punctuation: marks that matter

# 43  Pausing with purpose

PUNCTUATION IS ALL THOSE LITTLE DOTS AND SQUIGGLES that get put in and around sentences. There are quite a few of them, and sometimes people confuse them. Let's see if we can clarify the whole situation to make punctuation easier to cope with, and easier for you to explain to an author whose work you are editing.

First, punctuation is for meaning, not for decoration. It takes the place of pauses in speech, tone of voice, facial expression and even body language. It is the reader's guide to how you want them to interpret your writing. Many years ago, punctuation in some legal documents was actually forbidden – it had to be left open to the reader (probably a judge) to put their own interpretation on the words. This put a tremendous strain on writers who had to make sure that whatever words they put on paper would be interpreted exactly as they intended. Thankfully, we have punctuation to help in all documents, legal and otherwise.

Next, let's look at what can be called the hierarchy of punctuation.

## The hierarchy of punctuation

If we take the comma (,), the semicolon (;) and the full stop (.) as the three basic punctuation marks, how do they relate to each other? Let's call the comma a quarter stop, the semicolon a half stop and the full stop – well, what else?

The main use of the comma is to tell the reader where the author wants you to take a small pause, as in these sentences:

> Take your books, pens, paper and dictionary with you.
> [separating items in a series]
>
> Peter, the managing director, is sick today.
> [setting off words in apposition]
>
> Finally, let's look at this sentence.
> [after an introductory word or phrase]

There is another use of the comma – before a coordinate conjunction that joins two independent clauses, as in this sentence:

> We did not go to Europe this year, but we did go to Japan.

However, the trend now is to omit that comma when the two clauses are clearly related as they are here:

> We did not go to Europe this year but we did go to Japan.

The main use of the semicolon is to make a much stronger pause than a comma, but not as strong as a full stop, as in the following sentence:

> We did not go to Europe this year; it was more expensive than going to Japan.
> [joining two main clauses without using a conjunction when the ideas are closely related]

The main use of the full stop is to make a very definite major pause. It can only be used after a complete sentence (that is, a group of words having a subject and a complete, finite verb at least), as in these sentences:

> We did not go to Europe this year. We did go to Japan.
> [optional alternative to using a semicolon between the two sentences]

But:

> We did not go to Europe this year. Jo and Mary are just back from a holiday in South America.
> [a semicolon is not an option here because the sentences are not sufficiently closely related]
>
> It is cold in this room because the window is open.
> [marking the end of a complete statement]
>
> Would you close the window, please.
> [marking a polite request, where a question mark would be inappropriate]

The question mark (?) and the exclamation mark (!) carry just as much weight as the full stop – note they each contain a full stop.

> Why didn't you close the window when I asked?
> [marking a direct question which is a complete sentence]
>
> Run for your life! The building's on fire!
> [marking the ends of highly emotional sentences]

There are other uses for all these punctuation marks, but let's concentrate on just these.

My hierarchy of punctuation is a good guide to what you can and can't do with the main three:

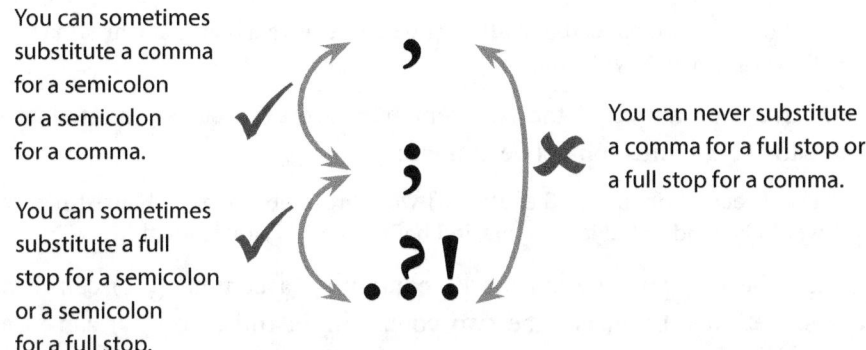

You can sometimes substitute a comma for a semicolon or a semicolon for a comma.

You can sometimes substitute a full stop for a semicolon or a semicolon for a full stop.

You can never substitute a comma for a full stop or a full stop for a comma.

As we have seen, the full stop can be used to separate two sentences (main clauses) about aspects of the same topic, or the semicolon can be used if the writer wants to keep the two closely related sentences together. The semicolon is also used to separate items in a list or a series when there is already a comma within any of the items:

> Peter, the managing director; Jane, the company secretary; and Martha, the advertising manager, will all be at the meeting next week.

The most common error occurs when we write a run-on sentence:

> The director announced that all staff would receive a bonus at Christmas, this was greeted with cheers.

This is incorrect – it is sometimes called the comma fault.

## Comma fault

This is the practice of inexperienced writers who realise that some sort of punctuation is needed and use the comma as the default punctuation mark, whether it is appropriate or not. For example:

> Thank you for your order, the goods will be dispatched tomorrow.

Here we have two complete sentences, and the comma is not a powerful enough mark to separate them – we need a full stop:

> Thank you for your order. The goods will be despatched tomorrow.

In the same way, we can't use the comma to substitute for a full stop in the example just before the heading 'Comma fault'. Each sentence is complete and the second sentence deserves its own initial capital:

> The director announced that all staff would receive a bonus at Christmas. This was greeted with cheers.

As we have seen above, if the two sentences are very closely related, it is possible to use a semicolon between them:

> The director announced that all staff would receive a bonus at Christmas; it would be paid in the last pay period before the Christmas break.

To recap, the two punctuation marks containing a comma (, ;) can swap places sometimes. Likewise, the two containing a full stop (; .) can swap places sometimes. But the comma and the full stop can never swap places. Examples:

> Please phone the President, the Secretary and the Treasurer about this matter.
>
> Please phone Joe Brown, President; Ann Green, Secretary; and Bill Moneypenny, Treasurer, about this matter.
>
> Bob is English. Peter is American.
>
> Bob is English; Peter is American.

But **never**:

> The chairman addressed the shareholders, he announced an increased dividend for the year.

The comma in the middle is wrong. Something stronger is needed to signify the end of a complete thought. In this case, it is best to use a full stop because the second sentence is not closely related to the first.

## The colon: not a semicolon

Why do people not distinguish between semicolons and colons when introducing whatever follows? My bet is that it's unfamiliarity with the keyboard – the colon can't be accessed without using the shift key, and the two are on the same key anyway. Use the colon for introducing things, as in the following examples (and right here):

> Peter announced his finding to the group: 'I can confirm that we have located the habitat of a previously lost rare species of bird this morning.'
>
> The teacher told the students to bring the following: pencils, ruler, writing paper and erasers.

The semicolon, as we have seen, is used at the end of a complete sentence where you don't want to make the break as strong as a full stop would make it:

> We did not buy a new dining suite; we had the old one reconditioned.

Another use of the colon is to show contrast between two statements, often when the second statement is not a complete sentence:

> To err is human: to forgive divine.

\*

Here we have looked at punctuation that appears *in* and *after* sentences. Other punctuation, such as quotation marks, appears *around* sentences and around words. All punctuation is there to help the reader know what the writer intended – and the editor's job is to make that intention as clear as possible.

# 44　How much punctuation is necessary?

Helping to rewrite a house style guide caused me to look at the punctuation section. This was an eye-opener – there seemed to me to be many examples of punctuation marks gone feral. It got me thinking about all punctuation marks and their necessity or otherwise.

My basic contention is that punctuation is supposed to make the text clearer, more meaningful, than it would have been otherwise. The following example (used in my book *Effective writing: plain English at work* to illustrate this point) shows what can happen to meaning when essential commas are missing:

> The work will be undertaken by Peterson Brothers Abercrombie Jones and Parker and Knight Industries.

Without commas, we have no idea whether three or four firms are involved in the work. If you can't wait to find out the possibilities, turn to the end of this chat.

Here is another example:

> When the chairman finishes the keynote address will begin.

The reader ploughs on and is brought up short at *address*, then has to backtrack and read it again, inserting a pause after *finishes*:

> When the chairman finishes, the keynote address will begin.

But do we need all of the punctuation marks that still litter our pages? Take the full stop, for instance.

## Abbreviations

In the bad old days, we put full stops after all contractions of titles and after initials, as in *Dr. A. B. Smith*. Now we're told that if the contraction consists of the first and last letters of the full title ('Doctor' here), we don't need a full stop. So now we can refer to *Dr Smith*. What about *A. B.*? The jury is out on this one. My preference is for no full stops, but also to leave a space between the letters because each one represents a whole name. *Dr AB Smith* seems crowded – let's write instead *Dr A B Smith*. To me, *Dr A. B. Smith* is a hybrid and therefore unacceptable.

What about other shortened forms? Some seem to attract a full stop in the singular but not in the plural (presumably because the letter *s* constitutes the last letter of the word) – *para.* and *paras, fig.* and *figs*, for example. There's no need to retain the full stop – to me, *para* and *fig*, in context, are meaningful and acceptable.

Then there's the *Style manual* recommendation (6th edn, p 156) that the abbreviations for Victoria and Tasmania should take full stops but that for Queensland should not – *Vic., Tas.* have full stops – *Qld* apparently does not, presumably in accordance with the 'first and last letter' principle. Why are there any full stops? Mercifully all become equal in capitals in envelope addresses: *VIC, TAS, QLD*.

The house style guide that was being updated still insisted on full stops in abbreviations like *e.g., i.e., a.m., p.m.* and *no.* for 'number'. Eh? There's something wrong in that collection. Which is the odd one out? It's *no*. This is not an abbreviation of *number* at all – it's a contraction of *numero* and so, along with the removal of the full stop after the contraction *Mr*, shouldn't have a full stop at all. The argument for retaining the full stop is that it could be confused with the negative *no*. Well! Wouldn't it be safe to assume that most authors could manage to write sentences where such confusion wouldn't arise – and if they can't, isn't that what editors are for? Granted, *e.g.* is a genuine abbreviation, but do the full stops enhance its meaning? To me personally – no. In the middle of a sentence, there's no problem with *eg* or *ie*, but given that most people don't know the difference between them, my recommendation would be not to use them at all – instead write *for example* and *that is* out in full. And there seems to me to be nothing wrong with *9 am, 5 pm* and *Candidate No 73*.

That leads to the apparent confusion about how to express the time of day – *five o'clock in the morning* is expressed variously as *5am, 5 am* and *5 a.m.* My vote goes to *5 am* because the figure *5* represents a whole word and therefore deserves a space after it, and *am* is perfectly clear without any full stops.

## Numbers and commas

Commas turn up, or don't turn up, in odd places too. In some style guides, users are told to put commas between the hundreds and thousands in all numbers: *2,500* as well as *350,000*. Some say don't bother if the number is only four figures long, so we have *2500* and *350,000* in the one document.

Others say no commas at all, but leave a space instead: *2 500* and *350 000*. Well, consistency of style is important, so I'd prefer to do the same thing throughout one document, and recommend being wary of the 'space' version because it can be confusing to the reader. Call me old-fashioned, but it seems safer to me to put the comma in both *2,500* and *350,000*.

## Quotation marks

The mix of single and double quotation marks in documents is amazing. In the dark ages of typewriters we were taught to use double quotation marks for all quotations, with single for quotations within quotations. The general rule in Australia is now the reverse of that: *'aaa "bbb" ccc'* – it avoids too much use of the shift key on computer keyboards. It seems to be taking a long time for this one to sink in, perhaps because of the quantity of American literature we read. The American rule remains the older rule: *"xxx 'yyy' zzz"*. Depending on where the document is to be published, we need to pick the appropriate rule, and not mix them in the one document.

## Em rule or en rule?

Another muddle is the en rule/em rule one. This revision of *Working words* uses the spaced en rule in text – like that. It's neat. However, some style guides suggest using an unspaced em rule in similar situations—like that, or even a spaced em rule — thus. It is not unusual for editors to see all three versions in one document, as the author clearly had no guidance from anywhere as to what to use. The spaced em rule is not my style, but the other two are fine, provided they are used consistently and provided the font being used makes one or the other more appropriate.

## Punctuation with 'however'

Editors constantly get requests for a ruling on the punctuation to use with *however, nevertheless, therefore* and similar words.

The accepted format for all such words is the same, but the word *however* causes most problems because it can be used as both a conjunction and an adverb. It can mean *nevertheless* (conjunction) or *in whatever way* (adverb).

Here are some examples of *however* as a conjunction or connective:

> I like your hat. However, I do not like your dress.
>
> I like your hat. I do not, however, like your dress.
>
> I will be at the meeting; however, I am likely to be late.
>
> I will be at the meeting; I am likely, however, to be late.

In these examples, *however* at the beginning of a clause must be preceded by either a semicolon or a full stop because it introduces a new whole sentence (main clause). It is followed by a comma. In the middle of a clause, it must have a comma on either side of it. In all these instances, *however* is not part of the clause, so must be set off by punctuation marks on either side.

When it's used to introduce a clause, *however* must not be preceded by a comma. A comma is not a sufficiently strong punctuation mark to indicate the end of a complete thought (whole sentence; main clause). The *Style manual* prefers the use of a semicolon before it. My view is that either a semicolon or a full stop is appropriate, depending on how closely related the first and second clauses are, and how much emphasis you want to show – the full stop indicates greater emphasis.

Here is an example of *however* as an adverb:

> To catch the train, I will run however fast I need to.

Here, *however* is an adverb modifying *fast*. No punctuation is required with the word at all.

## A rule for the changing English language

The English language, including its punctuation, is constantly on the move, so we're never going to see hard-and-fast (or hard and fast) rules for the use of punctuation and other devices. My only rule is to use punctuation marks to make meaning clear. If a full stop does nothing to enhance meaning, don't use it. If it does enhance meaning then use it. (Did you want to put a comma after meaning?)

Writers and editors should concentrate on conveying meaning clearly. If punctuation marks help, use them. If they don't, then don't litter the text with them.

## Speaking of which ...

Remember that sentence with no commas early in this chat? Here are three ways to punctuate it to give three different meanings to the string of words:

> The work will be undertaken by Peterson Brothers, Abercrombie Jones and Parker, and Knight Industries. [3 firms – we need the comma before the final 'and' so that the reader doesn't think one of the firms is Abercrombie Jones and the other is Parker and Knight Industries]

> The work will be undertaken by Peterson Brothers; Abercrombie, Jones and Parker; and Knight Industries. [3 firms – different from the group above – with semicolons to separate the items because one item has internal punctuation]

> The work will be undertaken by Peterson Brothers, Abercrombie, Jones and Parker, and Knight Industries. [4 firms]

I think you'll agree that punctuation makes all the difference to meaning here.

## 45  What's the point?

WELL WHAT'S THE POINT OF WHAT YOU MIGHT ASK. Just that. Where's the punctuation? If you read that first sentence aloud, it sounds all right, so apparently the argument goes: if it sounds all right without punctuation when you say it, it's all right to put it on paper without punctuation. Wrong. Let's start again:

'Well, what's the point of what?' you might ask.

Why does the punctuation make such a difference? It takes the place of tone of voice, inflection, emphasis and volume, and even has a little to do with speed. It also has to substitute for facial expression, hand gestures and other body language. It helps the reader to 'hear' the voice of the writer, so it's the writer's responsibility (ably aided and abetted by the editor) to get all the fine nuances of meaning across to the reader. This means attending to punctuation as well as to words.

Punctuation has an enormous job to do. Then why are people leaving it out, using it inappropriately, using it excessively or making one favourite punctuation mark do for every occasion?

First, they probably haven't been taught English grammar (unless they were in school before the 1970s), so they have no idea of syntax – the way words and phrases are put together, with and without punctuation, to make sense in sentences. If they had been taught grammar, they would know why a comma is necessary in *Because it rained, we abandoned the picnic.* and not in *We abandoned the picnic because it rained.* The comma is necessary in the first sentence because the subject (*we*) and verb (*abandoned*) are not in the usual position at the beginning of the sentence – the subordinate clause (*because it rained*) has been put ahead of the main clause. So a break is needed to force the reader to refocus on the main clause. There's no such problem in the second sentence, so no break is needed.

Second, nobody has taught them the difference in values between commas, semicolons and full stops (or full points, if you prefer); nor between colons and semicolons. The point has been made to me that 'readers sometimes do not "see" the semicolons or commas, and some don't know how to read through them'. (Please refer to Chat 43 'Pausing with purpose' for an easy way to remember the difference between commas, semicolons and full stops.) Depending on the font, some punctuation marks are almost invisible and might just as well not be there. A case in point is the dot-point. In the typewriter era, we used the full stop as the dot-point, and it worked perfectly well because it made a distinct impression on the paper. These days, the full stops produced by computers are so small that they are useless as dot-points, so we use bullets instead. Compare these two lists:

> The teacher told the students to bring the following:
> . pencils,
> . ruler,
> . writing paper, and
> . erasers.
>
> The teacher told the students to bring the following:
> • pencils
> • ruler
> • writing paper
> • erasers.

It's clear which is more effective. Not only that, but the bullet is so obvious that it is now considered unnecessary to put any punctuation at all at the end of any item in a bullet list of this kind except for a full stop at the end of the whole list. The bullet acts as a visual divider of the listed material. It renders unnecessary the old-fashioned 'comma + and' after the second-last, or penultimate, item. However, *and* remains necessary in a series in sentence form.

Finally, there is a tendency to use dashes—particularly em rules like these—to replace other punctuation marks—as all-purpose punctuation. They are certainly more visible than, say, a pair of commas as I've just used. This is a legitimate use, but use dashes sparingly – particularly to indicate a break in thought or an afterthought, as in this example, using a spaced en rule:

> There is nothing more I can do for you – it's up to you.

In romantic fiction and love letters, dashes have their place to indicate breathlessness or haphazard thinking:

> She ran after him – her feet hurt – she kept going – she reached him – they embraced.

But we're not breathless romantics, haphazard thinkers, or editors of love letters, are we? Get the point?

# 46   The powerful 'postrophe

GRAMMAR'S IN STYLE AGAIN, IT SEEMS. Would that mean the same thing as *Grammars in style*? There are some who would like to get rid of the apostrophe altogether, but our language and the meaning we attach to what we say and write would suffer. It's quite a powerful little squiggle. *Grammars in style* tells us that *style* has a variety of *grammars* and perhaps that each one imparts some different meaning to the style in which we are writing. However, *Grammar's in style* is intended to mean that grammar is stylish, fashionable, the 'in' concept in writing. Let's hope that's the meaning you got. It's short for *Grammar is in style* – it's a **contraction**.

It's believable too – grammar is talked about more now than for many years because a lot of people in Australia, particularly many of those who attended state schools after the mid 1960s, are realising that they missed out on learning English grammar at school. If they learnt another language at school, they probably learnt the grammar of that language. If they were very lucky, they realised then that their own language must also have a grammar. And if they were extremely lucky indeed, they managed to learn some English grammar, either by consulting their parents or by studying it on their own. Those schoolchildren are now in middle management and even more senior administrative positions, having to write reports and all manner of documents at work, and perhaps wanting to learn another language where the teacher expects a working knowledge of aspects of English grammar. They are seeking training in basic English grammar; they are talking about it; they have made the word 'grammar' fashionable – yes, *grammar's in style* and Australian schools are beginning to teach it again. And this brings us back to whether or not an apostrophe is necessary.

Let's look at another example: *Your brothers briefcase is black* is easy enough to understand when we say it aloud. Clearly you have a brother, and he has a black briefcase. So, isn't it perfectly correct as it is in writing? No. First, the *s* at the end of *brothers* looks remarkably like a plural and this is confusing to the reader – the reader expects the sentence to be about more than one brother. Second, in writing we need to indicate ownership in nouns by using the apostrophe, plus or minus a following *s*. The singular should be *Your brother's briefcase is black*, while the plural should be *Your brothers' briefcases are black* (if you have more than one brother, and your brothers have at least a briefcase each).

## Apostrophes for omission

The apostrophe is used to show that something has been omitted.

### Contractions

In informal writing *should not* can become *shouldn't*, and *it is* can become *it's*. *It's* is a contraction of *it is*. When we mean the abbreviated form of *it is*, we write *it's*: *It's a fine day.*

Sometimes placement of the apostrophe is a problem. It is correct to put an apostrophe where letters are left out of a word, but it needs to be exactly in the right place. So, the shortened form of *should not* is *shouldn't*, not *should'nt* because it's the word *not* that has had the letter *o* left out.

The apostrophe is often overused in writing. In formal writing, such as business letters (including emails), reports, business manuals and so on, it is best to avoid contractions such as *can't*, *don't* and *I've*. They may have a place in more informal writing, such as in these informal chats with you, or in the speech of fictional characters in a novel, for example: *I didn't get to the shops, so I haven't bought any bread.* So a correct sentence would be:

> *It's* [contraction of *it is*] a good day to give the house *its* [possessive case of *it*] annual spring clean.

A clumsy contraction that it's best not to use, unless absolutely necessary in conversation in a novel, is *wouldn't've* (meaning *would not have*). It is never a good idea to have more than one apostrophe in a word – multiple contractions such as *wouldn't've* are frowned upon.

### Dropped letters

Apostrophes sometimes drop right out of words. Would you *'phone for a 'cab to get you to the 'plane in time, or take the 'bus*? Neither, I suspect. All these curtailed words have become commonplace – we mostly don't use the words *telephone, taxicab, aeroplane* and *omnibus*; instead we use *phone, cab* (or *taxi*), *plane* and *bus*.

Other instances of omission of letters include:

> Jack **O'Brien** [where *O'* means *descendant of* or *of the family* Brien]
>
> We leave at 12 **o'clock** sharp [where *o'* is short for *of the*]

## Apostrophes for possession

Whole books have been written about the use of the apostrophe to indicate possession. This can be confusing. My rule is just a few lines long – it's set out below. The rule applies to all nouns and to pronouns like *somebody, anybody, anyone*, which act like nouns. For now, here are some correct examples:

>This is the **boy's** cap.
>
>These are the **boys'** caps.
>
>The **men's** shoe department is on this floor.
>
>In the **1960s** [no apostrophe], the miniskirt was fashionable.

### *Is the possessive apostrophe dead or dying?*

Let's hope not. Which is the clearest of these three?

>This is her brothers house.
>
>This is her brother's house.
>
>This is her brothers' house.

The first example doesn't tell you how many of her brothers own the house. The second and third examples are more explicit – they tell you that the house is owned by one or more than one brother respectively.

And let's not forget possessive pronouns. *This book is his but that one is her's …* Is that correct? No, the case system of personal pronouns (see Chat 33 'Case: from Latin to modern English') is such that apostrophes are not needed for possessive case; the possessive case of *her* when the thing possessed does not follow is *hers*. And what about *Its a good day to give the house it's annual spring clean …* Correct? No, *its* should be *it's* (contraction of *it is*), and *it's* should be *its* – possessive case, therefore no apostrophe (see above).

### *Possession pure and simple*

When you want to express possession (ownership) you have two options as a rule – one is to use the *of* structure: *this is the home of my father*. The other is to use the apostrophe: *this is my father's home*. If we choose the latter structure, how do we know where to put the apostrophe?

## How does it work?

Suppose you want to indicate that a boy owns a hat. You could write *the hat of the boy* and dodge using the apostrophe altogether, but it wouldn't be a natural expression. We would much prefer to put the owner of the hat first, followed by the hat – it makes for a much more natural expression and is shorter. So how do we decide where to put the apostrophe?

Remember that language was designed to be spoken in the first place, so whatever we write ought to sound right as well as give the reader the correct message. It's time for my three-step rule.

### Step 1

Write down the owner – in this example: *the boy*.

### Step 2

Put an apostrophe after the owner: *the boy'*.

### Step 3

Say that aloud with the thing owned – *hat*. Does *the boy' hat* sound right? No. We naturally want to put an *s* (representing a /zed/, buzzing sound) after *boy'*, thus: *boy's*. So that's exactly what we write – we put an *s* after the apostrophe if it sounds right: *the boy's hat*.

In the earlier example, the same procedure applies to *the home of my father* which becomes *my father* + apostrophe + *s* (for the sound) = *my father's home*.

What about plural owners? If all the boys in the group have hats, we follow exactly the same three steps:

- Step 1:  **the boys**
- Step 2:  **the boys'**
- Step 3:  Say that aloud with *hats* after it: *the boys' hats*. Does that sound right? Remember, we put an *s* after the apostrophe only if we need to in order to make it sound right when spoken aloud. It sounds fine without an extra *s*, doesn't it? So … **the boys' hats**

What happens when the possessing noun ends with an *s* or an *s* sound, as in the names *Dickens* or *James*? We treat them exactly the same way as other nouns:

The novel by Charles Dickens becomes *Charles Dickens's novel*.

The chair that James sits on becomes *James's chair*.

There may be some confusion here because many years ago it was the norm to write *Dickens' novels* and *James' chair*, leaving the reader to assume the extra *s* sound (when spoken) at the end. These days, consistency of treatment is more important.

## Other variations

So, are there any occasions when we don't put an *s* after the apostrophe in possessive case? Yes – for instance: The princess is wearing a tiara; it is *the princess's tiara*. But all the princesses in the room are wearing tiaras – look at the sparkle of *the princesses' tiaras*. Try putting an extra *s* after *princesses'* – a bit of a mouthful, you'll agree. So don't do it – the context has to tell us whether we are referring to one or many princesses.

There is one important exception to the 'consistency' rule – Biblical names ending in *s* are traditionally treated differently: we write *Jesus' teachings*, not *Jesus's teachings*.

There is, of course, a difference between *it's* and *its*. *It* is a personal pronoun, so is part of the personal pronoun case system, and when we mean the possessive form, we use *its* (no apostrophe): *The cat had a mouse in its mouth*. Remember that personal pronouns come to us in various forms depending on their case (see above and Chat 33 'Case: from Latin to modern English') – there are no apostrophes in personal pronouns. The only pronouns that have apostrophes are those that act like nouns, such as *someone*: *Someone's coat is on the chair*.

## Compound expressions

Where do you put the apostrophe to indicate possession in compound expressions? For example:

> the policy of the Department of the Attorney-General
>
> the umbrella of my brother-in-law

You put them at the end of the compound:

> the Attorney-General's Department's policy
>
> my brother-in-law's umbrella is black
>
> my three sisters-in-law's dresses were specially made for them
> [but: my three sisters' dresses were different colours]

We saw earlier that, where there is a plural owner (as in *brothers'*), the apostrophe goes after the *s*. Where there is joint possession – there is one thing belonging to or associated with two or more people or things – one apostrophe and *s* are placed after the second of the two owners or associates:

> Mary and Joan**'s** room is the second on the left.
> [Mary and Joan share the one room]

Where the possession is not joint – there is more than one of the thing, each belonging to or associated with different people or things – each owner or associate takes an apostrophe:

> Peter**'s** and Paul**'s** rooms are on opposite sides of the corridor.
> [Peter and Paul have a room each]

### *Irregular plurals plus possession*

Some plurals cause confusion when possession is expressed – is it *the ladies' and gentlemens' washrooms* or *the lady's* (or even *ladie's*) *and gentlemen's washrooms* or *the ladies and gentlemens washrooms* … or what? In fact, it's none of those. It's *the ladies' and gentlemen's washrooms*.

The problem about the separate washrooms for ladies and gentlemen is that *gentlemen* is an irregular plural. The plural of *gentleman* is not *gentlemans* – it's *gentlemen*. But if we just follow the three-step rule, we can't go wrong:

> Step 1: gentlemen (whose washroom it is – separate from the ladies' washroom)
>
> Step 2: gentlemen'
>
> Step 3: gentlemen's → ladies' and **gentlemen's** washrooms

### *Possessive or adjectival: is it really ownership?*

Does it matter whether we write *Fort Street Boys' High School* or *Fort Street Boys High School*? Probably not. The first example is what the school was called many years ago, and the apostrophe implies that the boys had some ownership in the school. The second example is the current spelling, where the word *Boys* (no apostrophe) has taken on the sense of an adjective rather than a possessing noun, distinguishing this school from a similar school for girls, perhaps. So the apostrophe has been dropped. But we can't drop the apostrophe in *He went to the men's locker room* because the plural word *men* doesn't end in an *s*. We can probably get away with *The ladies gym is on the first floor*.

## CHAT 46   THE POWERFUL 'POSTROPHE

I once belonged to a club in Sydney which was originally known as *The Girls' Secondary Schools' Club*, as though there was some sort of ownership by the girls of both the secondary schools and the club as a whole; and ownership of the club by the secondary schools that were attended by girls. Complicated, eh? Well, the club finally realised that the apostrophes could go because there was no real ownership – just an adjectival sense distinguishing the schools from those attended by boys, and the club as a place where girls who had attended secondary schools could have lunch, freshen up in the middle of a hectic day of shopping in Sydney, and so on. It became *The Girls Secondary Schools Club*. You may know of similar examples.

\*

Enough confusion over apostrophes? Well, I'll be back ... ah, does *I'll* stand for *I will* or *I shall*, or doesn't it need an apostrophe at all? Omit the apostrophe at your peril and risk confusing your readers. Well, *'til next time*, in Chat 47 'Apostrophe do's and don'ts', happy apostrophising!

# 47   Apostrophe do's and don'ts

The apostrophe is certainly one of the gremlins that beset writers and editors. There is, for example, a very common confusion about the use of the apostrophe to indicate simple plural. Generally, the apostrophe is quite unnecessary.

Driving around eastern Australia, I've been keeping my eyes open for signs – street signs, signs pointing to places to visit, signs telling me where to buy this or that. One day the following came to my attention:

- a list of specials at the greengrocery, the blackboard specials outside announcing NEW POTATOE'S, SPANISH ONION'S and BRUSSEL'S SPROUT'S for sale
- a sign over a shop that sells and rents videos: VALLEY VIDEO'S
- a poster advertising a local entertainment: ITS MAGIC!
- and on a television program, a transcript of a spoken comment which included the words *on Alan Jone's program* – the broadcaster referred to is Alan Jones and not Alan Jone.

## Blackboard special's

Yes, you're right, that apostrophe shouldn't be there, but that *apostrophe + s* is often seen in advertising, whether on blackboards outside shops or in advertisements. Many people who did not learn English grammar at school are confused about whether and where to use apostrophes, so they use them whenever they put *s* at the end of a word. But the apostrophe is used to show possession or omission.

So the first example above is a simple plural and when plural is intended, no apostrophe is necessary (except in very rare instances) – *NEW POTATOES, SPANISH ONIONS* and *BRUSSELS SPROUTS*. The writer is under the impression that the apostrophe has to be used to indicate plural, but this is not true in most cases. The first item in the example offends doubly because the plural marker is actually *-es* and not just *-s*. The third item in this example, *Brussel's sprout's*, is also wrong on two counts – first, the apostrophes are not needed because there is no possession intended and, if there were, it would have to be *Brussels'* or *Brussels's* because the name of the city is *Brussels*, not *Brussel*; and second, it is not necessary to put an apostrophe in sprouts to make it plural. Little wonder that this kind of usage is known as the greengrocer's apostrophe and is certainly not advocated. However, my support does go to the preservation of the apostrophe – in its proper place.

The second example is also a simple plural and should be written without an apostrophe: *VALLEY VIDEOS*.

The third example shows the confusion that can occur between *its* meaning *belonging to it*, and *it's* – a contraction meaning *it is* (apostrophe used to indicate omission). The correct spelling here would be *IT'S MAGIC!* Another example: *It's ours! I know it because of its colours; there's theirs over there.*

In the fourth example, the correct spelling is *Alan Jones's program*, and the pronunciation should reflect this with *Jones's* being pronounced [djownzez]. To say *Alan [djownz] program* is to have listeners believe that his surname is *Jone*. To write it as *Jones'* is to show confusion about where to put the apostrophe.

My three-step rule for using the apostrophe to indicate possession in nouns is very simple and is set out in Chat 46 'The powerful 'postrophe'.

## Other plurals and the apostrophe

What about the plural of Jones? Their family name is *Jones*, not *Jone*; so we need to be careful about the placement of the apostrophe in various inflections of the name. Suppose the whole Jones family, collectively known as the Joneses, owns a houseboat. Here's how to write it using the apostrophe, using my three-step rule:

- Step 1: Write down the possessing noun – *the Joneses*
- Step 2: Add an apostrophe – *the Joneses'*
- Step 3: Add an *s* only if the whole expression sounds better with it – does *the Joneses's houseboat* sound better? No – it sounds like [djownzezez]. So don't add the *s*. It is *the Joneses' houseboat* (definitely not *Jone's* or *Jones'* or *Jones'es* or *Joneses's*).

### Minding your p's and q's and similar problems

The poor little apostrophe comes in for a lot of comment, but what about the question of whether to use apostrophes in plurals of single letters and numbers, such as *Mind your p's and q's* and *Your 3's look like 8's*? The apostrophe is used in these sentences because the combinations *ps* and *qs* would be confusing to read otherwise, and the numbers – *3s* and *8s* – may look strange without them as well. Years are different – *in the 1960s* or even *in the '60s* are substantial enough to not need the apostrophes, though in *the '60s* does need an apostrophe at the beginning to indicate the omission of some figures. (But see *In the eighties …* under the heading 'Do's and don'ts?', below, for the *Style manual* view.)

By the same token, *Dot your is and cross your ts* is difficult to read. The *Style manual* (6th edn, p 88) weighs in on this one, suggesting that italics could be used for the *i* and the *t*: 'Dot your *i*s and cross your *t*s', but admits that the apostrophe version is still clearer: *Dot your i's and cross your t's.*

Here is another saying: *If if's and an's were pots and pans …*[*] Italic or nothing at all could be used here: '*ifs* and *ans*', 'ifs and ans'. They are marginally clearer than single-letter words pluralised like this, but the apostrophe version is still clearer.

## Tim had enough of her 'maybe's'

This sentence was tossed around some time ago on the forum of the website WordWizard <http://www.wordwizard.com>, where a contributor wrote:

> In the category of 'Words Used as Words', it [the *Chicago manual of style* (14th edn) (CMS)] suggests that you omit apostrophes if you italicise the words but use an apostrophe if you put the word in quotes.
>
> For example, "Tim had enough of her 'maybe's'."
>
> That seems a little confusing, so I'm going to omit the quotation marks I added to indicate what came directly out of CMS.
>
> Tim had enough of her "maybe's".

Maybe, maybe not. Should it be necessary for me to write such a sentence, I'd probably just write: *Tim had enough of her maybe's* – no quotation marks around the word. Or I might omit the apostrophe altogether: *Tim had enough of her maybes.*

Lynne Truss, in *Eats, shoots & leaves*, cites various uses for what she calls the 'tractable apostrophe', including the following (p 45):

> It indicates the plurals of letters:
>> How many f's in Fulham? (Larky answer, beloved of football fans: there's only one f in Fulham) …
>
> It also indicates plurals of words: What are the do's and don't's?

---

\*   The rest is often left unsaid. It is: '… there'd be no work for tinkers'.

## Do's and don't's?

Please join me in taking issue with Ms Truss on this. To me, the sentence is much better as: *What are the do's and don'ts?* An extra apostrophe, as in *don't's*, is unnecessary.

What about *In the eighties, the 80's, the 80s or the '80s?* The *Style manual* (6th edn, p 170) doesn't care for any of them; it prefers *in the 1980s*, in full, no apostrophe. My top preference is the same, but *in the eighties* or *in the '80s* are tolerable, provided they are not used in formal writing.

If there is more than one TAFE college in a town, we write *There are three TAFEs in this town*, not *TAFE's*. And you don't need apostrophes in sentences such as *He was an actor in the 1930s* or *I bought three DVDs yesterday* – they would do nothing to enhance meaning.

Here are two other sources of confusion involving apostrophes that you wouldn't normally encounter in writing, but which are very common in speech.

(a) He's coming to the movies with us and then we're going to he's place for supper.

The second *he's* (***he's** place*) should be **his** – he owns the place. *His* is the possessive form of *he*, and is pronounced with a short *i* – not an *ee* sound.

(b) Is you're confusion showing?

You want to edit that question? So do I. But there are many people who wouldn't spot the error in it, so these two examples should serve to alert you to keep your eyes peeled in your own writing and when editing others' material.

In (b) that should be *your*, not *you're*. There are two rules at work here. The first is the use of the apostrophe to indicate omission. When we leave letters out of words, we replace them with an apostrophe. So *you are* becomes *you're* in casual speech – but that's not what's intended here. The second rule concerns case in personal pronouns. *Your* is the possessive form of the pronoun *you*. Personal pronouns in English have what's called case – subjective, objective and possessive case. This follows the old Latin case system, though is not as extensive as in Latin. (See Chat 33 'Case: from Latin to modern English'.)

The converse occurs as well, of course. It's much more common to come across *Your an idiot!* in writing, at least in informal writing. Needless to say that should be *You're an idiot!* So, why is this included here? Because it needs emphasising – it's a very common mistake.

## The disappearing apostrophe?

Street signs in Australia no longer have apostrophes. One school of thought believes that the apostrophe will eventually disappear from English. Perhaps not just yet. It has its uses.

Long live the apostrophe – in the right place!

# 48  The humble hyphen

WE ALL KNOW THAT HYPHENS ARE USED TO JOIN WORDS TOGETHER, to avoid ambiguity of meaning, and to split long words at line ends. There are endless 'rules' about the use of hyphens, and just as many exceptions to those rules. As recently as twenty years ago, the rules were quite strict – nowadays there is more freedom of choice. Not being a prescriptive grammarian makes me tend to use as few hyphens as possible. Sir Ernest Gowers wrote:

> The author of the style-book of the Oxford University Press of New York (quoted in Perrin's *Writer's Guide*) says "If you take hyphens seriously you will surely go mad". I have no intention of taking hyphens seriously. [*Complete plain words*, p 183]

Compound words and phrases evolve over time in English. An example is *headmaster*, which was originally two words, *head master*, then hyphenated as *head-master*. Finally the hyphen was dropped and the word was set solid (to use a typographical term), as indeed happened with *stylebook* – *style-book* in Sir Ernest Gowers's quotation above and before that *style book* (two words). Similarly, while many words consisting of a prefix and another word contain a hyphen – *re-enter*, *pre-eminent*, for example – more commonly used compounds have dropped the hyphen: *cooperate*, *coordinate*, both perfectly clear, despite having two of the same vowel next to each other, each pronounced individually, the first a long vowel and the second a short vowel. The hyphen is useful, but shouldn't be overused.

When a compound phrase is used adjectivally in front of the modified noun, the convention is to hyphenate, as in *an up-to-date edition*, but when it is used adverbially it is set out as separate words, as in *this edition seems to be up to date*.

If confusion could arise without hyphens, put them in. For example, you *recover* from an illness, but you *re-cover* your favourite chair. You advertise a *little-used car* rather than a *little used car* if you mean that it hasn't been used much. And you ask your students to bring *four foot-rules* and not *four-foot rules* or even the perfectly correct *four foot rules* if you want to be clear that they are to provide four rulers each a foot long.

Lists of hyphenation do's and don'ts appear in the *Style manual* (6th edn, pp 88–94), and there are a few useful conventions in my book *Effective writing: plain English at work* (2nd edn, [3.12], [7.7]). But some constructions defy attempts to hyphenate meaningfully. Take this one, sent to me in 2003 by Ara Nalbandian when he was editor of *The Canberra editor*:

> The ADF has always organised some functions into networks. For example, the offensive fire support system is a very good example of how sensors gain information on targets that can be attacked by joint fire support assets.

What are the real meanings of *offensive fire support system* and *joint fire support assets*? Do you use hyphens anywhere to clarify them? Does *offensive-fire* or *fire-support* help? Not really. The whole paragraph needs to be recast for clarity.

As Gowers recommends, we should watch out for ambiguity that can occur when a hyphen is omitted in a construction such as: *When Government financed projects in the development areas have been grouped ...* (*Complete plain words*, p 184). Here, the reader is sent off on a false trail and has to re-read to make sense of the words. A hyphen between *government* and *financed* would have clarified the main subject and verb. (See also Chat 55 'Ambiguity, vagueness and other traps'.)

The em and en rules are also often referred to as *em-rules* and *en-rules* – unnecessary as *em* and *en* are perfectly good whole words in printing terminology. (The same goes for the *el* – a very small printer's measure, about the size of ... guess what: a hyphen!) I'm glad to see *website* as one word being advised by most dictionaries nowadays.

A lot of line-end hyphenation on a page is not as attractive as carefully cast sentences that make sense within the marginal boundaries and have a good visual effect even with a ragged right margin.

The hyphen used to be all we had on typewriters to indicate word joins and dashes in text. Now, with computers, we have *em* and *en* rules or dashes, and we should use them. The main use of the *en* rule is to show a range, as in *pages 1–16*, and the main use of the *em* rule is as a dash like this—to indicate an afterthought, perhaps. In this revision I am using – yes, a spaced *en* rule as a dash. You'll read more about these dashes in Chat 49 'Dash it!'

Whatever you use a hyphen for, use it sparingly and to enhance meaning.

# 49   Dash it!

If there's one punctuation mark that people ask me about more than most other marks, it's the dash – what it is, when to use it, what kind of dash to use, how to produce it on the computer.

When all we had was a typewriter, we used the hyphen to serve as the dash as well. As a hyphen it looked like this:

> This is a fast-moving train. [no space on either side of a single hyphen]

As a dash it could be shown as space–hyphen–space or hyphen–hyphen with no space on either side (see also Chat 48 'The humble hyphen'):

> There was nothing else for it - we had to run for cover.
>
> There was nothing else for it--we had to run for cover.

But now we have computers with em rules and en rules. If we use the hyphen as a dash, the autocorrect facility in some programs such as Microsoft Word will often convert these to em rules and en rules anyway:

> There was nothing else for it – we had to run for cover. [spaced hyphen becomes en rule]
>
> There was nothing else for it—we had to run for cover. [unspaced double hyphen becomes em rule]

The **em rule** (—) is often called 'the dash'. It is called 'em' because it was the width of the capital letter 'M' in print typesetting. The **en rule** (–) is just called 'the en rule'. It is half the width of the em rule and the width of the lower-case letter 'n' in whichever typeface is being used. For example, an em rule in Georgia 16 point looks like this: —, and an en rule looks like this: –; while in Arial 16 point they look like this: — and –.

The em rule is formed in MS Word on a PC by holding down the Ctrl and Alt keys plus the minus key on the numeric keypad. The en rule is formed by holding down the Ctrl key with the same minus key. The other option is to go to Insert, select Symbol, then go to the Special tab and select *Em dash* or *En dash*. This option is available to Apple Mac users as well. If Mac users wish to use the keyboard, however, the em rule is formed by holding down the Option and Shift keys plus the hyphen key on the left of the + key. The en rule is formed by holding down the Option key and then pressing the hyphen key.

The whole family of dashes is:

| hyphen | - |
| en rule | – |
| em rule | — |
| double em rule | —— |

Let's concentrate on the em and en rules here (and a reminder: no hyphen is needed in 'em rule' or 'en rule' because *em* and *en* are whole words). There are other dashes or dash-like characters – the underscore, the tilde, the swung dash, the wave dash, and so on – which have their uses in certain contexts and in certain languages.

## When to use the em rule (usually unspaced)

The em rule is used to:

- express abrupt parentheses:
    We went far away—far away from the cares and demands of city life—to write up our research.

- amplify or explain:
    What could the message mean—that the bus had broken down?

- show abrupt change:
    I talked to them for an hour about the psychological effects of classical music versus pop music on behaviour in institutions—but I see I'm boring you.

## When to use the en rule

The unspaced en rule is used in the following instances:

- ranges of figures and other spans:
    pages 345–7
    2001–02 financial year
    27–29 June
    69–71 Mort Street
    June–July planting guide
    Canberra–Goulburn–Sydney bus timetable

- association between separate entities:
    Commonwealth–State arrangements
    hand–eye coordination

- linking parallels in series:
    Australia–Scotland test match
    Australian–American research

The spaced en rule is used:

- when there is at least one compound term in the expression:
    the New South Wales – Victoria border
    the financial year 1 July 2010 – 30 June 2011

- in the same way as the em rule – parenthesis, explanation or abrupt change – if that is the house style:
    Your old fax machine is beyond repair – trash it.

This is my preference too for all instances of the dash – and also, I'm pleased to say, for this revised edition of *Working words*, the publisher's. In your writing and editing, follow your style guide.

## When to use the double em rule

The double em rule is used in bibliographies and references when two or more publications are by the same author – the author's name can be replaced by the double em rule after the first entry. For example:

   Murphy, Elizabeth M. *The job-hunter's guide*, Pitman, Melbourne, 1988
   —— *Effective writing: plain English at work*, 2nd edn, Lacuna, Sydney, 2014

It can also show sudden breaks or that something is deliberately being omitted:

   I'm sure he said, 'Let go, or I'll——'.
   It is alleged that the boy, J——, who cannot be named, was injured in the schoolyard fight.

*

There are many more variations on the use of hyphens, em rules and en rules in writing. As editors, we need to watch for consistency of usage and meaningfulness. Fashions change in the use of these punctuation marks, as they do in all aspects of writing. As we use and get used to new and different technologies, new practices will become the 'in' thing.

Having dashed that off, I'd better dash to——, well, perhaps to start the next part of this book!

# itchypencil 7

## 'Norf'k' – and the geese and cows

A recent trip to Norfolk Island started with a language challenge. At the tiny airport, a man called out: 'Whutta-waye?', addressed to someone standing near me. My linguist's ear picked up the sounds, and as soon as possible, a visit to a shop was organised to buy a book on the Norfolk language – pronounced [Norf'k laengwidj]. Imagine my delight at discovering the shopkeeper was a Pitcairner [Pitkerner] who spoke the local language. She described it as a pidgin, being a mix of Yorkshire Dales English and Tahitian. It has been described also as a creole and just patois, but 'creole' seems to be the most apt description. The language is certainly a pidgin that has become the native language of the entire Pitcairn community on Norfolk, and is not restricted to the uneducated. It is a living language, with all the nuances of any other language.

The language mix originates from the English of the *Bounty* mutineers and the Tahitian women they married in Tahiti. Their descendants went to Pitcairn Island and experienced great privations on that very small rocky blip in the ocean. In 1856 the whole population of Pitcairn Island moved to Norfolk Island with the blessing of the British government, who by then had closed down the second of two penal settlements there. The Pitcairners (194 of them) formed the third settlement of the island, and are thriving there today. Today's Norfolk has developed to include modern terms. Many English words, with typical Norfolk pronunciation, are in the mix.

Spelling of Norfolk is wildly variable. The language was never written down, so there is a great deal of individuality in pronunciation and spelling, when attempts are made to write it. A number of locals, including Beryl Nobbs Palmer and Alice Inez Buffett, both true islanders, have written dictionaries and texts on the language.

By the time I'd rested for a day or so and soaked up a bit of nice warm sunshine, a tour of the island and some of its tourist spots seemed like a good idea. And there it was again – the bus driver on the first tour greeted us all with *'Whutta-way yorlye?'*, thankfully followed by the English 'How are you all?' It was now easy to work out that what the man had called out at the airport was 'How are you?' addressed to a single person. At the end of the tour, dotted with bits of Norfolk from the driver, he then asked *'Whuthing yorlye gwen doo morla?'* Well, by now, we were getting used to it, and told him what our plans were for the next day!

There are some odd omissions in Norfolk – there is no word for *children*. So they have to be described as little people: *lekl salan*. And there are many words that betray their Tahitian origin, such as *hilli* which means lazy or anything to do with lethargy – the sort of laziness that stems from sitting in the hot sun for a while. A conversation can go something like: *'Come to me yu es sullun se gut a hilli side you bin sit out in ar hot sun!'* (Seems to me you are in a relaxed, lazy mood after sitting in the hot sun.) *'I guddet strawng!'* (I have a very bad attack of that lazy feeling!) A local eatery, Hilli, encourages you to 'come and laze' with them – it was a relaxing experience.

What about the geese and cows? Well, during one of the penal settlements of Norfolk Island, the governor imported geese to help keep vermin and pests down. They were so successful that they were allowed to stay and have continued to breed. They hang around the old Kingston penal settlement area in a great gaggle, and you have to give way to them. It's a beautiful area, with wonderfully restored buildings and lighters from the penal days. Same privilege applies to the cows: local farmers are allowed to graze their cows on the nature strips and any open grass, and drivers must give way to them. Our bus driver described them as 'our best council workers' – no need for mowing with the cows around.

This is a bit rambly, but that's what Norfolk Island does to you. It's a beautiful island of steep grassy hills, flat coastal areas, and those distinctive triangular pines. Well, I'd better *'jug-a-lorng'*.

# Part 7

## What is style?

# 50 A reflection on 'style' from 1804

WHAT IS 'STYLE' IN WRITING? The other day a book fell off my bookshelf into my lap. It seemed to be saying 'Read me!' It is a battered and well-used book with pages falling out of it or hanging in there by a thread. The pages are yellow with age. It fell open at a section on 'style', so – thanks, book, you've got your way.

The author of the book, which is mostly about English grammar, added an appendix on style, and I'm going to share some of it with you. Don't go looking for the book – it's out of print. It's *English grammar* by Lindley Murray, published by John and Charles Mozley, Derby in … ? Well, that's a good question. When it was published, the date of publication wasn't always included in the book. It contains an 'Introduction' dated 1795, followed by an 'Advertisement' promoting the book as a second edition – this is dated 1804. So it's more than 200 years old. It has a companion: *Murray's exercises*. Both were acquired at a favourite place of mine, Berkelouw Book Barn, Berrima, NSW.

These books have been waved about in training sessions and passed around for students to read to support my view that there's nothing new under the sun – plain English style was definitely the go in 1804. Murray talked about 'perspicuity and accuracy' as qualities of style in writing which 'require the following properties: *purity, propriety* and *precision*'. What did he mean by these?

- By *purity*, he meant using the words that belong to the English language and not using words from other languages. There has always been a tendency for some writers to show off by using Latin and French words – for example, *per annum* and *tête-à-tête*. English is a rich language, and we can just as easily write *a year* and *private conversation*.

- By *propriety*, he meant using just the right word for the occasion and the meaning, avoiding slang, technical jargon when it may not be understood, and ambiguity. His examples are still relevant today: avoid slang such as *topsy turvy, hurly burly, currying favour*; jargon such as *We tacked to the larboard and stood off to sea* (to a non-sailor); ambiguity such as *She gave her mother her coat*.

- By *precision*, he meant expressing an idea, and no more or less than that idea, in a sentence. Examples of imprecision abound – ranging from sheer loquaciousness to utter obscurity. As editors, we've all seen it in commercialese, legalese, academese and bureaucratese. Some sentences ramble, with embedded clauses, or tacked-on ideas; others are allowed to wander off on paths totally different from where they started. Such sentences are confusing, requiring several readings (are we actually meant to understand?) or they are blunt to the point of being unintelligible.

Murray urges writers to construct sentences that are neither very long nor very short. He considers a number of things that he regards as 'most essential to an accurate and a perfect sentence', including *clearness*, *unity* and *strength*.

- *Clearness* is helped by keeping parts of sentences together that belong together, such as parts of verbs, and adverbs close to the verbs they modify; and by avoiding the ambiguity caused when a phrase could relate equally to what came before it and what came after it.
- *Unity* means sticking to one main point in a sentence and not wandering off with changes of person or tense. An example from Murray is: *After we came to anchor, they put me on shore, where I was welcomed by all my friends, who received me with the greatest kindness.* Murray points to the shift from *we* to *they* to *I*, and the mix of ideas. He suggests: *Having come to an [sic] anchor, I was put on shore, where I was welcomed by all my friends, and received with the greatest kindness.*
- *Strength* means giving every word in a sentence its due weight and force, so that the sense is brought out to best advantage. A strong sentence is pruned of all redundancies, uses the little words such as *but*, *and*, *or*, *which*, *whose*, *where*, *then*, *therefore* and *because* judiciously – Murray calls them the 'joints or hinges upon which all sentences turn'. He regards a strong sentence as one that has harmony of words – words that are easy on the ear when spoken and that make the sentence flow smoothly.

There is more, but Murray concludes with the following:

> The fundamental rule for writing with accuracy, and into which all others might be resolved, undoubtedly is to communicate, in correct language, and in the clearest and most natural order, the ideas which we mean to transfuse into the minds of others.

Ring any bells? That's plain English style, isn't it? It's a style that, as editors, we would all hope to achieve for our authors, so that whatever they write comes across to their readers clearly and accurately.

Murray goes one step further. He writes:

> Did we always think clearly, and were we, at the same time, fully masters of the language in which we write, there would be occasion for few rules. Our sentences would then, of course, acquire all those properties of clearness, unity, strength, and accuracy, which have been recommended. For we may rest assured, that whenever we express ourselves ill, besides the mismanagement of language, there is, for the most part, some mistake in our manner of conceiving the subject. Embarrassed, obscure, and feeble sentences are generally, if not always, the result of embarrassed, obscure, and feeble thought.

We often can't do much about the thinking behind the work we are given to edit, but we can think it through ourselves and try to give the text the meaning we believe the author intended. So editing, for me, starts with clear thinking and then proceeds to the mechanics of our craft.

## 51   Plain English is the style

**P**LAIN ENGLISH IS THE NAME given to a particular style of writing that has been adopted as the ideal style for business and government writing. It is clear, unambiguous, brief without being blunt, easy to grasp at first reading, and it is based on sound English grammar principles – more on these later.

Part of my life consists of conducting courses in effective writing, writing in plain English and plain English at work. When people ask for training in 'plain English', they frequently want to learn about those aspects of English grammar that were not taught at school, or were not reinforced later even if they were taught in primary school. They realise that a good grasp of the mechanics of English is at the root of learning to write plain English. This, in itself, is something of a turnaround in general understanding of what plain English is all about. In the late 1980s, facilitators like me would have been told that the participants didn't want to know about English grammatical structures – that they just wanted to learn how to write plain English, as though the two did not go with each other. The current attitude is healthy – it doesn't separate grammar from plain English.

In order to write plain English, one has to realise that it is not a simple form of English, it is not babytalk and it is not a different form of English from the form that we use every day in conversation. We all learnt our native language as children, at mother's knee and then at school – this became the code for communication that we share in the community where we live. For those of us brought up in an English-speaking environment, it was the English language. For others, English is a second or third language, and non-native speakers of English may have to jump a few more hurdles before they feel able to regard English as their everyday conversational language. We have to assume here that you, the reader, understand that.

The knowledge that we share is knowing that there are naming words (nouns) and action words (verbs), as well as a variety of other kinds of words, and that they are strung together in a very particular order to make sentences that we recognise as acceptable English syntax. We don't necessarily need to know the labels we put on these words and structures, but we do need to know how to use them. Having got the mechanics right, we can then play with the superstructure to make it 'plain', as preferred in business writing, rather than flowery, poetic, academic, or any other style, depending on the reason for writing at all.

There are just a few aspects of these mechanics that we need to pay attention to, in order to make writing plain for business readers. In essence, the principles of sound English grammar are these:

- recognising that English is a subject–verb–object language and that word order is important for meaning – we don't have a full case system where the ending of a word indicates its role in a sentence (like Latin, and some modern languages such as Russian), so we need to put what we're talking about in subject position in a sentence and what we're saying about the subject in the predicate (verb certainly, plus object if any)

- knowing how to express tense (variations on simple past, present and future), mood (traditionally indicative, imperative and subjunctive) and voice (active and passive) – see below under the heading 'Voice: active or passive'

- structuring paragraphs so that they are easy for the reader to follow the progression of thought from beginning to end

- using words so that they express what you want them to express – writing in the 'code' that most people understand as standard English

- avoiding some of the more common writing errors such as shifts in time and person; lack of parallel structure in series and dot-point (or bullet) lists – see below under the heading 'Parallel structure in lists'; lack of agreement between subject and verb, or between pronouns and what precedes them; failing to punctuate for meaning.

Plain English is a layer of style over the top of sound English grammar. It is the style preferred for business writing because business people are very busy and do not have time to work out your overly complex syntax or confusing style. (Included is government writing because the people who read government publications or correspondence are frequently in a hurry and need to get the message quickly and clearly.)

What has this got to do with editors? Editors need to understand the principles of writing in plain English so that they can correct writing that is not clear, and so that they can explain their alterations to the author. Yes, it is my belief that part of our job as editors is to help authors to write more clearly next time – we can't do that if we don't know a bit about the terminology to use when talking about it.

The main points to watch for when editing for plain English are:

- sentence length and readability
- parallel structure in lists
- voice: active or passive
- use of verbal nouns
- choice of words for the target audience and the topic
- use of jargon.

## Sentence length and readability

We need to control and vary sentence length because business people don't have time to luxuriate in longwinded Dickensian prose. Nor do we want to bore readers with strings of super-short sentences that sound as if they'd been fired rapidly from a peashooter.

Several short sentences are often easier to read and understand than one very long sentence.

Sentences become long by having more and more whole ideas added on, and on and on, or by having several side issues embedded in the main sentence. We need to ensure that we don't write sentences that drone on with added-in and added-on subordinate clauses and descriptive phrases. Here are some tips on sentence length:

- Try to start new sentences wherever new ideas appear.

- Try listing similar items in bullet-point form if a long sentence cannot be broken up. We need to write our lists using parallel structure where the message shines through because the structure is totally predictable.

- Go for variety in sentence length – writing too many very short sentences is nearly as bad (for the reader) as writing too many very long sentences.

If an author combines unrelated ideas into one sentence, the reader becomes confused. Take a sentence like this:

> James is a top student of psychology although he also has interests in linguistics and anthropology and he has recently written a journal article on aspects of psychology and ageing.

There are two main ideas here: the *psychology* idea and the *other interests* idea. Combining them has made the sentence difficult to read. It would be better to separate the ideas into two sentences:

> James is a top student of psychology and has recently written a journal article on aspects of psychology and ageing. He also has interests in linguistics and anthropology.

As I stated above, sentences generally become too long by (1) adding on more and more ideas and (2) qualifying with more and more subordinate clauses. Below is a sentence that was published in a newspaper advertisement as an explanation of the term *Account Statement* (also used in my book *Effective writing: plain English at work* (2nd edn, [10.2]). There is no doubt that this sentence does need some work:

> 'Account Statement' means a printed statement setting out the essential details of those transactions effected on a member's Account during the period to which the statement is expressed to refer and of which transactions the Society is aware, together with such adjustments (if any) as the Society believes are necessary to properly reflect transactions effected during a period prior to that to which the statement is expressed to refer and which were omitted or improperly recorded on the statement for that prior period and such further entries as the Society may pursuant to these Rules be authorised to make.

Try to find the main ideas in the sentence and eliminate as many add-ons and qualifiers as possible. How many sentences would you recommend? By the way, the sentence is otherwise grammatically correct – but it's also totally unreadable. Why? Because it's one long sentence that consists of 99 words – too many for one sentence, it uses too many passive verbs, there are many qualifications of the initial statement, and it uses unfamiliar words. None of this is very helpful as an 'explanation' to bank customers.

Here are a couple of easier ones (from [10.3] of *Effective writing*):

> **(1) Add-on type of long sentence:**
> Courses for next semester will include one-day seminars on stress management, plain English awareness and personal development and will be held in the small meeting room, and there will also be two-day workshop courses on effective writing, effective listening and reading, and report writing. (44 words)

**Possible solution:**

Courses for next semester will be held in the small meeting room. They will include one-day seminars on stress management, plain English awareness and personal development. There will also be two-day workshop courses on effective writing, effective listening and reading, and report writing. (12+14+17 words)

**(2) Qualifier type of long sentence:**

For files, general papers, maps and plans which are more likely to have to be housed in the supporting data section, I think that it would be useful to include a half a page of notes on each in the library where we customarily keep one copy of everything of value, as well as a reasonable amount of details for microfilm, which has specific storage requirements for masters in particular. (70 words)

**Possible solution:**

Files, general papers, maps and plans are more likely to have to be housed in the supporting data section. I think that it would be useful to include a half a page of notes on each in the library. We customarily keep one copy of everything of value in the library. We should also include a reasonable amount of details for microfilm. This has specific storage requirements for masters in particular. (19+20+12+11+9 words)

## Parallel structure in lists

Parallel structure in lists means that the same structure is used in each list item or point, so that the reader doesn't come upon any nasty surprises in structure that can throw them off course and force them to read the sentence again. Sticking to the same structure for items in any kind of list or series in a sentence makes it easier to read.

Parallel structure is where each item begins with the same kind of word. In the following example, each item begins with the present participle of a verb:

> The training will include:
> - **reviewing** the basic structures of English sentences
> - **writing** cohesive linked paragraphs
> - **learning** to apply the principles of plain English.

The author's aim, with the editor's help, is to get a message across. If the reader has to continually jump from one structure to another, the message will get lost. Starting with chapter headings, for example: *Preview, Task analysis, Theory and research, Guidelines for action, Evaluation, Exercises*; these are all nouns or noun phrases, so are parallel. And the same goes for simple word associations – words go with words, numbers with numbers: *a two-headed, six-footed monster*, not a *2-headed, six-footed monster*; and associated parts of speech should match: *Japanese–Australian relations*, not *Japanese–Australia relations*.

What's wrong with *My uncle enjoys tennis, swimming and to water-ski*? The noun *tennis* and the gerund (verbal noun) *swimming* are parallel, but *to water-ski* is the infinitive form of a verb, so is out of sync with the other two. Change it to *My uncle enjoys tennis, swimming and water-skiing* – problem solved!

Parallel structure is really important in lists where you have an introductory sentence or phrase with several bullet-point items following. The reader expects each of the items to be a conclusion of the introductory words.

Look at this example:

> To clean the feed rollers:
> - Take out the development unit and place it on a clean sheet of paper
> - removing the feed rollers next;
> - and the rollers should be cleaned with a damp cloth

The first bullet point is a complete sentence with the verbs *Take out* and *place* both in the imperative mood and active voice. The second bullet point does not contain a finite verb – *removing* is the present participle of a verb. The third bullet point goes into passive voice – *should be cleaned*. Punctuation is variable too. How can we fix this?

Make all the bullet points follow the same structure/pattern. There are several solutions, but here is one that uses the imperative mood and active voice in each item:

> To clean the feed rollers:
> - take out the development unit and place it on a clean sheet of paper
> - remove the feed rollers next
> - clean the rollers with a damp cloth.

## Voice: active or passive

We need to use rather more active voice than passive because active is direct, clear and unambiguous, and shows who is responsible for what. Passive voice has its place, but we need to beware of ducking responsibility when the reader has a right to know who is responsible for certain actions.

- Active voice is when the doer of the action (or agent) is in subject position in the sentence, and where the receiver of the action (or patient) is in object position in the sentence. For example:

    The boy [doer] kicked the ball [receiver].

- Passive voice is the exact opposite: the receiver of the action is in subject position and the doer of the action is in object position. For example:

    The ball [receiver] was kicked by the boy [doer].

- Active voice is preferred in business writing because it is shorter than passive and it is clear who is responsible for what.

- Passive voice can result in an 'agentless passive' where we don't know who is responsible for the action. Sometimes this can be a problem: *Your application has been rejected.* 'By whom?' the reader is entitled to ask, particularly if it's something that affects them personally. Sometimes it doesn't matter: *The low-lying parts of the town were flooded twice last year.* Obviously, water was the doer of the action but we don't need to say so.

- As with sentence length, variety is good – mix active and passive, but aim for more active than passive in business writing.

## Use of verbal nouns

Verbal nouns are those nouns that are derived from verbs: *direction* from *direct*, *management* from *manage*, *discussion* from *discuss*, and so on. (They are also known as 'nominalisations'.)

As a general rule, verbs are more dynamic than the nouns derived from them, so it is better, in business writing, to use the verbs. For example, *The workers will discuss the project with whoever is responsible for coordinating it* is clearer, shorter and more 'alive' than *The workers will hold discussions about the project with whoever has the responsibility for its coordination.*

## Choice of words for the target audience and the topic

We need to use everyday words – words that we are comfortable using in conversation. It should not be necessary for the reader to consult a dictionary every minute or so to understand what we are writing about. Many people feel that using everyday words is somehow showing themselves up as ill-educated. Not a bit of it! Using everyday words shows consideration for the reader.

Why write *utilisation* when we could write *use*, or *domiciliary* when *home* or *home-based* is easier and means the same thing? We're not in the business of educating the reader in vocabulary extension – we're aiming to get a message across with as little effort for the reader as possible, not to provide an opportunity for a Sunday afternoon 'curl up with a good book'.

Here are some good principles:

- Use words you would use if you were speaking to the reader – conversational words.
- Use plain words and phrases, not pompous ones. For example, *total* is better than *aggregation*, *try* is better than *endeavour*, *help* or *make easy* is better than *facilitate*, *workable* is better than *viable*.
- Avoid redundancies. For example, *We will cooperate* is better than *We will cooperate together* – 'together' is implied in 'cooperate' anyway.
- Avoid fillers (a kind of written throat-clearing). For example, in this first sentence of a business letter *I am writing to inform you that it would seem that there is a possibility that some staff have anticipated ...* could be cut to *Some staff may have anticipated ...*
- Avoid wordy phrases. For example, *if* is better than *in the event that* or *under circumstances in which*.
- Avoid overdoing nouns in strings as adjectives. For example, *Inadequate staff performance review opportunities have led to ...* is a mess that would be better written as *Inadequate opportunities to review performance of staff have led to ...*
- Avoid overworking clichés and foreign words. Keep your writing fresh and in English. An example is *RSVP* – it has even been used as a verb: *Are you RSVPing this invitation?* Many people have no idea of the meaning of RSVP – from the French *répondez s'il vous plaît*, meaning *reply if you please* – so replace it with *Please reply*. Likewise, most people don't know the full form of Latin abbreviations like *e.g.*, *i.e.* and so on, so it's better not to use them. Instead, use the full English words – *e.g.* means *for example* and *i.e.* means *that is*.

## Use of jargon

If you are editing technical writing intended for technical people to read, the jargon of that industry is perfectly acceptable. This only works within a very proscribed circle of readers. The golden rule about using jargon is: when in doubt, don't. However, there are times when a technical term is the best term available – in that case, it needs to be explained, and there are several ways of doing this:

- Explain it in a glossary.
- Explain it on the spot.
- Use a scenario to show how a difficult concept works in practice.

\*

There is a lot more to plain English and to editing for plain English, but I hope the points set out here will alert you to some of the main problem areas to look out for in the next business or government document you edit.

There is nothing new about plain English. Let me quote from a very old grammar textbook, *English grammar*, by Lindley Murray, which was the focus of Chat 50 'A reflection on style from 1804'. Here's what Murray had to say about long and short sentences:

> A train of sentences, constructed in the same manner, and with the same number of members, should never be allowed to succeed one another. A long succession of either long or short sentences should also be avoided; for the ear tires of either of them when too long continued. Whereas, by a proper mixture of long and short periods, and of periods variously constructed, not only the ear is gratified; but animation and force are given to our style.

Not much has changed in two hundred years!

# 52 Strong, plain sentences

Is 'strong' and 'plain' redundancy? Or are they different concepts? As pointed out in Chat 51 'Plain English is the style' and Chat 53 'How *not* to write', we need to pay attention to some aspects of style in order to make writing plain for business readers. Those aspects include controlling sentence length, using more active voice than passive, using parallel structure in bullet-point lists and using everyday words. Plain English.

Plain English, to me, is based on sound grammar. Sound grammar tells me to make subject and verb agree in number, to avoid redundancy, to avoid starting a sentence with an empty *it*, to avoid ambiguity, to use standard spelling, punctuation and sentence structures – for a start. Sound grammar alone isn't enough. To be clear to the busy reader, we need to observe at least the four points listed in the opening paragraph.

Let's take this to a slightly different level. Current literature makes much of 'strong' versus 'weak' language – not only in business writing, but in everyday conversation as well. 'Strong' sentences are both grammatically sound and written in plain English. On top of that, some points come in for special mention.

## Revise weak *be* verbs

A *be* verb can be strong, as in *John is better at maths than I am*.

The weak *be* verb is in sentences like *The contribution of this group is to the overall wellbeing of the whole company* and in passive constructions like *The clock was broken by the girl*.

These sentences can be made strong by eliminating the *be* verb altogether. In the first example, look for a noun, usually ending in *-ion*, that has been derived from a verb, and then use that strong verb: *This group contributes to the overall wellbeing of the whole company*. In the second example, turn the passive voice into active: *The girl broke the clock*.

## Avoid starting sentences with *It is* and *There is*

There is nothing wrong with *There is* when used appropriately, as in this sentence. However, the phrases *It is* and *There is* can lead to wordiness and are sometimes empty of meaning.

**Weak**: It is essential that you complete the report today.
**Improved**: You must complete the report today.

**Weak**: There are at least two solutions set out in the textbook.
**Improved**: The textbook gives at least two solutions.

## Avoid agentless passives

Rewriting agentless passives in the direct, strong active voice improves many a sentence:

**Weak**: Assignments are graded according to the criteria set out in the course guide.
**Improved**: Tutors grade assignments according to the criteria set out in the course guide. [Now we know who will do the grading.]

Instructions, too, are more likely to be followed if they are short, snappy and in active voice:

**Weak**: This medication should be taken before meals.
**Improved**: Take this medication before meals.

## Unpack long sentences

Sentences that ramble have no place in business writing. Rambling occurs in two main ways – by adding on and by embedding. Here is an example of a sentence – yes, it is one sentence – containing both add-ons and qualifications:

> Would any person who on Friday 24 January 20__ witnessed the accident between a yellow and blue motor vehicle and a box trailer approximately 15 km north of Canberra on the Federal Highway at approximately 3.00 to 3.15 pm or the driver of the truck with the Apex Building Company sign at the front who was in the vicinity of the accident on that day or any other driver who may be able to help identify the driver of the said truck or the fact that the truck was in the vicinity at that time please contact Messrs Justice, Scales & Company, Solicitors of Canberra on [phone number].

That sentence is too confusing for anyone to respond to the solicitors' plea for help. My solution is to look for the main points and make every main point a new sentence. The trick is to spot the joining devices:

> On Friday 24 January 20__, an accident occurred between a yellow and blue car and a box trailer. It occurred about 15 km north of Canberra on the Federal Highway at about 3.00 to 3.15 pm. Did you see this accident?
>
> Or were you driving an Apex Building Company truck on that date? Such a truck was seen near the accident.

Or can you help identify the driver of the Apex truck? Did you see the Apex truck near the accident?

If you can help, please contact Messrs Justice, Scales & Company, Solicitors, of Canberra on [phone number].

Many factors contribute to the strength or weakness of a sentence, and sometimes several problems appear in the one sentence. The following sentence was sent to me as an example by Ara Nalbandian in 2004, when he was editor of *The Canberra editor*:

Bennett, by refusing to believe that the coastal route was a main approach, neglected the defence of the area.

Here the subject *Bennett* is separated from the verb *neglected* by a long string of words. It would certainly be more telling to unite subject and verb, and one solution is:

By refusing to believe that the coastal route was a main approach, Bennett neglected the defence of the area.

Another solution that might appeal, depending on the context of the sentence, is to break the sentence into two sentences, in order to return the subject *Bennett* to the beginning:

Bennett refused to believe that the coastal route was a main approach. He therefore neglected the defence of the area.

## A weakening pronoun

An interesting comment on weak versus strong language is that people who use the pronoun *I* too much in speech tend to weaken themselves. Take a statement like *I have a real problem with Mandy; she never finishes anything on time*. Who exactly has the problem? It looks as if the speaker has the problem, whereas in fact Mandy has the problem. Why not say so? *Mandy has a real problem; she never finishes anything on time*. And another one: *I'm not surprised there are lots of flies in the room. I noticed the door was left open for a long time*. Somehow, this use of *I* shifts the blame for something onto the person who made the statement – it's weak; it's not assertive. What's wrong with being strong? *Of course there are lots of flies in the room. The door was left open for a long time*. Blame is shifted off the speaker.

So, what's the difference between 'plain' and 'strong'? Not a lot. To me, it's a different slant on the same thing.

# 53   How *not* to write

GRAMMAR BOOKS – OLD AND NEW – FASCINATE ME. The oldest in my collection is *English grammar* by Lindley Murray (generally known as *Murray's grammar*) first published in 1795 – my edition is dated 1804. More of this later.

One of my acquisitions is a lively little grammar book, *How not to write: simple guidelines for the grammatically perplexed* by Terence Denman, published in 2005. It doesn't cover every aspect of English grammar, but it does give grammar tips in ten of the most commonly perplexing areas for workplace writers: sentence length, passive and active voice, imperative mood for instructions, verbs rather than abstractions, verbs from adjectives, simple tenses with fewer auxiliary verbs, case and personal pronouns, the possessive, the apostrophe for other uses, and the comma.

In each chapter, the author includes practical exercises and demolishes some writing myths, including the one that says you can't have a comma before *and* – as has been inserted at the end of the last paragraph. And there are others: that you can't start a sentence with *but*, *and* or *because* (I just did); that *get* isn't a proper word (arguing with my mother about this got me nowhere at the time); that *that* and *which* are always interchangeable; and more.

The author believes that 'good business writing should aim for the four Cs': it should be correct, clear, concise and conversational. By 'conversational' he does not mean exactly 'write as you speak', but he says:

> too much office writing gets into a tangle by moving too far away from the everyday words that we use when we're talking to someone. It's a good idea to listen to anything you have written. Then ask yourself whether you would have used the same words if you had been explaining it face to face or on the phone.

Sound advice, as is almost all of the advice in this book. We agree in our dislike of the abbreviations *e.g.* and *i.e.* and the Latinate *prior to*, and with his championing of the singular use of *they*.

This is a useful grammar aid for people at work. It's written in an informal style, with short, clear examples, and has some useful information on basic grammar terminology, lists of everyday words you can use to replace their pompous alternatives, and ten tips on writing in plain English.

And what about *Murray's grammar*? Well, there's nothing new under the sun – Murray was advocating 'clearness' and 'unity' two hundred years ago: 'Whatever leaves the mind in any sort of suspense as to the meaning, ought to be avoided' and 'long, involved and intricate sentences are great blemishes'.

It's always good to welcome a new grammar book, and Terence Denman's *How not to write* continues the tradition of sensible guides to good, clear, cohesive workplace writing without getting into too much technical detail. It's a good read, and worthy of a place on your shelf.

# 54  Avoid style crampers

**D**ON'T LET GRAMMAR GREMLINS CRAMP YOUR WRITING STYLE, slow you down as you edit, or drive you to dictionaries or serious grammar textbooks too often. Some of these gremlins crop up in material submitted for editing by people with English as a second or third language. Some occur in everyone's writing, from time to time. This chat provides some brief points (most of which we chat about in detail elsewhere) to keep in mind when editing.

## Articles

We use *a*, *an* or *the* in noun phrases – *a* or *an* as the indefinite article: *a* book, *an* open book (*a* before a consonant, *an* before a vowel or vowel sound); *the* as the definite article: *he grabbed **the** last piece of cake*. When we generalise, we often don't use an article at all: *Books are stored on shelves in libraries*. More detail about articles is in Chat 26 'The arbitrating article'.

## Plurals

The most common plural endings on nouns are *-s*, *-es*, and *-en* – book*s*, box*es*, child*ren*. However, there are many unusual plurals like *mice, geese, sheep, data, criteria*. And there are some downright weird plurals – for example, the plural of *mouse* (the one you push around your desk to operate your computer) is not *mice*: it's *mouses*. See also Chat 31 'One or more than one'.

## Plurals plus numerators

In many languages, a numerator is sufficient to indicate plural as well, but not in English. An Asian person might write *I bought **two book** at the shop*, whereas the correct English way would be *I bought **two books** at the shop*. See also Chat 62 'Editing ESL writing'.

## Prepositions

These little words show relationships between words. There are many kinds, such as prepositions of place, time and so on: *the ball is **under** the table*; *I will complete it **before** dinner*. Prepositional idiom also dictates which preposition should be used to indicate the particular relationship with the same word in various contexts: *I am responsible **to** my boss* but *I am responsible **for** the annual report*. Read Chat 27 'Relationships' for more about prepositions.

## Verb tense for meaning

Tense means time, so if you are talking about something that started a while ago but is still going on, you would use a continuous tense: *I **have been living** in Canberra for twenty years*. Tense is one of the hardest concepts for many people to understand, and it is explained in Chat 28 'Verbs: some basics'.

## Proximity of adverbs and verbs

Place adverbs as close as you can to the verbs they modify. *He **worked diligently** at the task of tidying his study* is better than *He **worked** at the task of tidying his study **diligently***. See Chat 29 'Verbs: more basics'.

## Proximity of subjects and verbs

Keep the subject of the sentence and its verb as close together as possible, instead of embedding material in between. ***My brother is** over there in the brown suit* is better than ***That man** over there in the brown suit **is** my brother*.

## Subject–verb agreement

Make sure that a singular verb is used with a singular subject, and plural with plural:

> A huge **quantity** of old computers **was** dumped this morning. [*quantity* is singular]

> **Two litres** of milk **are** needed for this recipe. [*litres* is plural]

> Toast and marmalade **is** a popular breakfast. [*toast and marmalade* is one dish, so is regarded as singular]

## Apostrophes for possession and omission – not plural

Whole books have been written about the use of the apostrophe. This can be confusing. My rule is just a few lines long, and is set out in Chat 46 'The powerful 'postrophe' and Chat 47 'Apostrophe do's and don'ts'.

Here are some correct examples:

This is the **boy's** cap. These are the **boys'** caps.

The **men's** shoe department is on this floor.

Please arrive at six **o'clock**.

In the **1960s**, Twiggy gained great fame as a model.

## Possessive pronouns

The remnants of a case system in English occur in the personal pronouns – *I, me, my, mine*, for example. Because a special form of the pronoun is used to show possession, there is no need for an apostrophe at all: *my, mine*; *your, yours*; *his, her, hers*; *its*; *their, theirs*. So what's *it's*? This is a contraction meaning 'it is'. Case is the topic of Chat 33 entitled 'Case: from Latin to modern English'.

\*

To sum up, don't let these gremlins cramp your style – make them work for you. Working words are words that are put together in such a way that the reader understands exactly what they meant to you when you wrote them.

# 55 Ambiguity, vagueness and other traps

JUST AS THE LACK OF A HYPHEN CAN CREATE AMBIGUITY, so can the lack of other punctuation marks, as can lexical and structural problems in writing. Remember these examples from earlier chats? In the clause *When Government financed projects in the development areas have been grouped* ... we are sent off on a false trail by the lack of a hyphen between *government* and *financed* (Gowers, *The complete plain words*, p 184). Similarly, in this sentence *As soon as the principal finishes the keynote address will be given by Professor Jones*, we are sent off on a false trail – this time by the lack of a comma after *finishes*.

## Ambiguity

Many people think that ambiguity means having two possible meanings. The prefix *ambi-* in *ambiguity* literally means 'two', in the same way that *ambidextrous* means able to use both hands equally well. In recent times, *ambiguity* has come to mean having more than one meaning rather than just having two meanings. The prefix *ambi-* can now mean *both, around* or *on both sides*, and so *ambiguous* can mean simply open to various interpretations – at least two.

There are three main types of ambiguity to watch for when editing or writing (not to be confused with vagueness).

The first type of ambiguity is **lexical**, where a word can have more than one meaning in the context, as in the notice *Bear left at the zoo gate* – are we instructed to turn left when we reach the zoo gate, or did someone leave a bear at the zoo gate? Other examples are *She can't bear children*, or *I took your picture*, or *The case is closed*. In *Ann drove the office car as well as Peter*, does that mean *Ann drove the office car as efficiently as Peter drove it* or that *Ann and Peter both drove the office car?*

Another type of ambiguity is **surface structural**. This is where the ambiguity arises from syntax that depends on emphasis for meaning – a change in spoken emphasis changes the meaning of a sentence but the desired emphasis is not obvious in writing. This occurs because in writing we lack the ability to transfer spoken emphasis to paper. We end up with ambiguous sentences like *I asked how old Barney was*. This could mean either that I asked after 'old Barney's' health (emphasis on *how*) or that I wanted to know Barney's age (emphasis on *old*). Another example is *We inspected the new managers' offices*. Depending on the emphasis, this means either *We inspected the new offices that have been prepared for the managers* (emphasis on *offices*) or *We inspected the offices that have been prepared for the new managers* (emphasis on *managers*).

And a third type is **deep structural** – also syntactic, but meaning depends on the reader's knowledge of what was in the writer's mind. You really have to get inside the head of the author to be able to interpret the sentence correctly. Phrases like *china egg container* are structurally ambiguous, as are sentences like *The police shot the rioters with guns*. In these examples, there is no lexical ambiguity and emphasis is not a factor. Think about the following three sentences and look for two interpretations for each – solutions later on:

> Visiting relatives can be a nuisance.
>
> The duck is ready to eat.
>
> When fire broke out at the hostel, the residents sought safety in their pyjamas.

## Poor reference, ambiguity and misuse of words

Ambiguity can also occur when pronouns like *which* and *it* are incorrectly used:

> The groundsman asked the players to help him patrol the oval and surrounds during the planned demonstration which would show that they cared about their sportsground.

What does the *which* clause refer to – the patrolling or the demonstration?

> When the result was announced so promptly, it surprised us all.

What does *it* refer to – the result or the promptness of the announcement?
Loosely related, misuse of certain words can cause confusion for readers:

> I heard where you are thinking of entering the Masters Games as a swimmer.

*Where* implies place, and place is not intended here. The writer should use *that* instead, making a noun clause *that you are thinking of* ... and this is the object of the verb *heard*.

Now, to put you out of your ambiguity stress, here are the possible meanings of those earlier examples:

## CHAT 55  AMBIGUITY, VAGUENESS AND OTHER TRAPS

> It can be a nuisance to have to visit relatives.
>
> Relatives who visit you may not be welcome at the time.
>
> The duck is cooked and we can sit down to a meal of roast duck.
>
> The duck is hungry and will eat the food we offer it.
>
> The residents were already in their pyjamas and rushed outdoors to safety.
>
> The residents put their pyjamas on in the belief that wearing pyjamas would make them safer.

All of these 'traps' are set out in detail in my book *Effective writing: plain English at work* (2nd edn, [8.4]).

The writer's intention must be perfectly clear. Any ambiguity must be eliminated, and this is part of the editor's job.

**Pronouns** can cause problems. In the sentence *She gave her mother her hat*, we don't know whose hat was given to mother. And whether to use *that* or *which* is a decision that has to be made with a view to making one meaning clear. Compare the following:

> The police investigations that could cause embarrassment will not be publicised.
>
> The police investigations which could cause embarrassment will not be publicised.
>
> The police investigations, which could cause embarrassment, will not be publicised.

The first sentence makes it clear that the investigations not to be publicised are those that could cause embarrassment. The third sentence makes it clear that none of the investigations will be publicised. But the second sentence is ambiguous.Can you see why? Were all the investigations to be withheld or only those that could cause embarrassment?

Ambiguity of a sort also occurs when we write sentences with **dangling modifiers** – modifiers that have no word to which they are clearly related. These can cause mirth, but should be weeded out of the documents we edit:

> Waving frantically, the taxi sped right past the old lady.
>
> While turning the page, my coffee spilt on my book.

Oh, for an editor! There are many times when I read my newspaper, or the instructions on a form, or a textbook, or even a pamphlet from my bank or insurance company, and wish someone had bothered to edit these documents. Mind you, if they had, there wouldn't have been as many giggles emanating from my office as there have been.

Here's one example that came to light in a weekly email I used to receive from the Plain English Campaign (UK), who gave me permission to quote this from the Letters to the Editor page of *The Times*, London:

> Having recently considered applying for a new credit card, I felt I should do the right thing and reacquaint myself with the Terms and Conditions under the Credit Act 1974. Where better to start than with the General Notes?
>
> '18.1 Even if you have no right to cancel this Agreement under the Consumer Credit Act 1974, you will have the same right to cancel this Agreement, and the same responsibilities if you cancel this agreement, as if you have a right to cancel this Agreement under the Act.'

The comment from the writer of the letter is 'Is it just me?' and well might he ask!

Another example: in my capacity as a Justice of the Peace, I was once asked to witness a statutory declaration by a young couple from one of the embassies in Canberra. They arrived with the document already signed. They had to sign it again because the instruction in the document is *Sign here before a Justice of the Peace*. Well, that's what they thought they had done – signed it *before* turning up at my house to have it witnessed. But *before* also means *in the presence of*, doesn't it? – nasty trap for people with English as a second language.

The moral of these two examples? Write or edit down to shorter, understandable sentences that use unambiguous words.

Looking for **vagueness** is also part of the editor's job. If we place an ad in the paper that states *Nurse required for local hospital*, we shouldn't be surprised if we get a mixture of midwifery nurses, theatre nurses, intensive-care nurses and so on applying. The ad is vague. Which of the following phrases is least vague?

> The chairman's adviser
> The chairman's most trusted adviser
> The chairman's most trusted adviser on Middle East negotiations
> The chairman's most trusted adviser on foreign policy

Yes, the extra words make the third phrase more precise.

When someone says to me 'I am in two minds about that', my response (at least under my breath) is 'Please make up both your minds which mind to use, and make a decision.' Ambiguity and vagueness only delay decision-making in the workplace.

# 56   Sentence structure snares

As editors, we often have to explain grammatical structures to our clients, particularly to first-time authors. Having a 'gut feeling' that something is right or wrong isn't enough – we need to be able to see the trap that the author has fallen into and rescue the situation and then do our best to see that the author learns not to repeat the mistake. Here are some of the traps that even experienced authors fall into. You may well argue that some of them are not 'traps' at all, but deliberate ploys for making a point in the text. That makes them all the more difficult to alter, and makes it all the more urgent that we editors know what underpins the usage, so that we can 'correct' or 'leave well alone', depending on the context.

## Fragments

A fragment is a part of a sentence, or a deliberately unfinished sentence. Grammatically, anything that is not a complete sentence (with a subject and predicate, containing a finite verb) is a fragment. They're fine in speech. We use them all the time in conversation:

> 'Hullo, John, how are you today?' [sentence]
>
> 'Fine, thanks.' [fragment]
>
> 'I've catered for eleven for lunch. I hope that's all right.' [2 sentences]
>
> 'Ten. No Jim. Meeting in Sydney.' [3 fragments]

The fragments here are perfectly understandable because they are either answers to questions or they are comments triggered by someone's earlier comment. There is no need to write full sentences when direct speech is being recorded, provided the context makes the words clear. However, how about this very common letter-starter?

> Referring to your letter of 10 September. Please send ...

The first part is a fragment because it does not have either a subject or a finite (complete) verb. *Referring* is the present participle of a verb. And who or what is doing the referring? Here's a solution:

> I refer to your letter of 10 September. Please send ...

Here the subject is *I* and the finite verb is *refer* – we have a complete sentence.

The editor needs to establish whether fragments are OK in the context – perhaps as part of a conversation in a novel or in punchy advertising writing – or should not be allowed because of the more formal nature of correspondence, reports, academic theses, or other documents where the target audience would expect the conventions of English grammar to be observed.

## Questions in surveys and forms

Surveys and forms often contain traps that make it impossible to fill them in meaningfully, usually because the writer hasn't given enough thought to the grammar. The temptation to use a fragment to save space shouldn't render the question meaningless.

Here are a few examples from actual forms. Think about what's wrong with them and how they could be better expressed before looking at the suggested alternative at the end of each item.

### Confusion

1. (from a preschool enrolment form)

    Hand? _____

The parent completing the form has to guess that the preschool wants to know whether little Tommy is left-handed or right-handed at the moment (handedness changes frequently in small children before it settles down). Now, I know a parent who decided that the question was confusing for most parents. She wrote in the blank: 'Two'! It wouldn't have taken much effort for the school to ask something more explicit:

> Which hand does your child currently favour for holding things like a spoon (left or right)? _____

### Negativity

2. (from a survey conducted by a firm which installs gas heating)

    Is your home unheated? Yes ____ No ____

People tend to think positively rather than negatively. It is better to couch questions in positive terms rather than ask respondents to write what amounts to a double negative – that is, 'No (it is not unheated)' when it is already heated. It would be better for the form writer to write:

> Is your home heated? Yes ____ No ____

## Unanswerable

3. (from a questionnaire handed out to patrons leaving a local cinema)

    How many times do you go to the movies in a year?

    Often __ Sometimes __ Rarely __ Never __

If patrons are coming out of the cinema, the *never* option can't possibly apply to them. The form writer should consider the target consumer and, in this context, omit the *never* option:

    How frequently do you go to the movies in a year?

    Often __ Sometimes __ Rarely __

## Double-barrelled

4. (from a government form)

    Are you unmarried and in receipt of a pension? Answer YES or NO __

This question forces the respondent to answer *yes* or *no* to each part of the question – the question can't be answered by everyone with one *yes* or *no* at the end. It needs splitting into two questions (or two parts of one broader question):

    Are you married or unmarried? Answer YES or NO __

    If you are unmarried, are you receiving a pension? Answer YES or NO __

Examples 2, 3 and 4 above are all structural snares that writers often fall into and that editors sometimes don't pick up because the words look normal at first glance.

*

There's more to grammar than meets the eye, isn't there? As editors we need to be watchful for traps that our authors may have fallen into, and not let errors resulting from their falling into those traps slip by into print. It is very easy to think something is right because we see it a certain way a number of times, but just one of these structural traps can put a reader right off a whole article or a whole book.

# 57   1 or 2 words about numbers

THE NEWSLETTER *AUSTRALIAN STYLE* (June 2005) headlined an article called 'Figuring out numbers' by Dr Robert Eagleson, a long-time advocate of plain English and friendly colleague to me for many years. I have some reservations about this article.

The article recommends dropping *all* numbers presented as words and replacing them with figures – just like that. You know, there are 2 ways of writing numbers – 1 is in words and 1 is in figures. Did you like that sentence?

The article asks: 'What principle makes 4 July acceptable, but not 4 sheep?' Well, to me, it's the principle of not comparing oranges and bananas. 4 July, even at the beginning of a sentence like this, is perfectly acceptable to me because dates would be cumbersome if their numerical elements were written as words. But 4 sheep would only be acceptable to me in something like a list of livestock for sale:

>   4 sheep
>   10 goats
>   2 cows

In running text *four sheep* is perfectly clear.

I'll go along with the use of figures at the beginning of sentences, provided they are substantial. Years, sums of money, percentages are all generally OK:

>   1939 saw the start of the conflict.
>   $15,000 was raised for charity.
>   75% of the students passed with Credit or better.

The conventions for using words or figures for numbers are certainly fuzzy. What's magical about 1–9 or 1–99 as cut-off points for using words or figures to express numbers? It's more important to consider the reader and use either words or figures as seems appropriate for easy reading, particularly in workplace documents. It would bother me to see figures becoming so widely used in other writing – novels, essays, poetry and so on – that we abandon words altogether.

Unfortunately, without anyone even having to advocate it, figures will probably take over to a large extent in due course. In many business documents, it is probably easier to absorb the numbers in a sentence like *15 students divided into 3 groups of 5 to discuss the case study* more quickly than if the numbers had been written as words.

There are other instances of figures creeping into common usage, not to mean numbers but as substitutes for other words. I once received a note in my mailbox advertising Australia Post's service *mail2day* (they would email you and tell you if there's anything to collect, thus saving journeys and precious petrol).

The SMS phenomenon has grabbed many of us by now, but do we have to let the use of figures as shorthand for words of all sorts spill over into the text of emails, reports, instructions and other workplace documents? This is not what Eagleson is advocating, of course: his plea is merely that we use figures where numbers occur in text. As such, it deserves serious debate among editors. But one thing leads to another.

SMS is with us, and it has to be asked whether the use of figures will come to this in ordinary email writing:

> I have 1 passenger so far 2 Melbourne 12 Oct 4 the conference …
>
> CUL8R

# 58  Say what you mean – *in actual fact*

A PROSPECTIVE CLIENT ONCE ASKED ME to quote a *ballpark figure* for an editing job. Well, *basically, at the end of the day*, my policy is to *avoid like the plague* doing this because the figure quoted becomes the *bottom line*. Now, I don't mind giving a rough quote *per se*, but *personally* my thinking is that it would be better to *get down to tin tacks* and work out a proper quote once I've *scoped* the task. *To be honest with you, with all due respect*, perhaps it's a *tad* thoughtless to ask for a rough quote and then want something more definitive later.

*It's not rocket science* to recognise that all the phrases in italics are expressions that are in current use. As long ago as 2004 the Plain English Campaign ran a survey among its newsletter readers to find out their most detested tiresome expressions. The full list was in *Plain English Campaign's weekly update: 19 March 2004*. It is no longer readily available, but write to <info@plainenglish.co.uk> if you want to know more. The following expressions are just some of these that I particularly dislike, with my comments alongside:

- *24/7* – shorthand for *24 hours a day, 7 days a week*
- *at the coal face* – probably because I'm not at it anymore as a teacher
- *at this point in time* – because it's pure Sir Humphrey (from *Yes, Minister*)
- *he/she* – or worse, *s/he* – if something like this is needed, why not spell out *he or she*?
- *heads up* (verb) – why not just *heads* as in *heads the organisation*?
- *I hear what you say* – usually means *I hear but I don't listen, and I probably won't take any notice anyway*
- *implementation architecture* – when all that's meant is *ways of doing things*
- *in a holding pattern* – for anything other than aircraft, this just means *we're at a standstill*
- *level playing field* – when we mean that everyone is *on the same terms*, and …
- *move the goal posts* – this seems to make things unfair again when we had a perfectly good level playing field

- *on a daily basis* – what's wrong with *daily*?
- *please do not hesitate to contact us* – why not just *please contact us*?
- *push the envelope* – seems to have developed as a replacement for *think outside the square* or *extend the boundaries*
- *quality time* – is something we have with a member of the family when we're on a guilt trip
- *window* – something we have when we can see a blank space in our diary.

Are there are any peculiarly Australian terms that are creeping into our writing (particularly business writing) that annoy you? If there are, why not write them down and send them to me. You can contact me via my website <http://www.emwords.info>. There are plenty of expressions that are used in speech – *chewy on yer boot, kangaroos in the top paddock* and so on – but there don't seem to be any that we use in business writing, unless we still use *shoot through* – short for *shoot through like a Bondi tram*.

Over to *your good self*.

# 59  Colloquialisms – colourful but *clunky*

COP THIS, MATES! *Let's have a chinwag and I'll give you the good oil.* Maybe a diversion from serious stuff into the realm of Aussie slang would be a bit of fun.

I have relied almost entirely on one reference book – *A dictionary of Australian colloquialisms* by G A Wilkes, published by Fontana in Melbourne rather a long time ago – in 1978. It's a fun read to this day, though there are newer editions and plenty of other books about slang. I've also consulted a few websites.

So what is slang? The Macquarie Dictionary's first definition is:

> language differing from standard or written speech in vocabulary and construction, involving extensive metaphor, ellipsis, humorous usage, etc., less conservative and more informal than standard speech, and sometimes regarded as being in some way inferior.

A second definition is 'vulgar or abusive language' from which we get the term *slanging match* – 'a quarrelsome exchange, especially of abuse'.

Wilkes's book is about 'colloquialism'. So what's the relationship between that and slang? Back to the dictionary, which gives as its first definition of *colloquial*:

> appropriate to or characteristic of conversational speech or writing in which the speaker or writer is under no particular constraint to choose standard, formal, conservative, deferential, polite, or grammatically unchallengeable words, but feels free to choose words as appropriate from the informal, slang, vulgar or taboo elements of the lexicon'.

Its second definition is 'conversational'.

So much for the serious side of this! I'm choosing from Wilkes's book some colloquialisms that, to me, fit in the 'slang' category.

## Cop this!

Remember Roy Rene ('Mo') in radio and early TV sketches? No, of course you don't. But he often came to blows with another member of the cast (Harry Griffiths) and said 'Cop this, young 'Arry' before giving Harry a clip under the ear. The expression has become part of Australian colloquial language and has changed its meaning a bit. We use *Cop this!* when we want to draw someone's attention to something unusual. A 1970 citation (Wilkes, p 91) quotes journalist Max Harris: 'Have you ever copped the way those girls serve the community at the Sydney Telephone Exchange? Flat out like lizards drinking, all day long'.

## Flat out like lizards drinking

This is an extension of *flat out*, or *flat out* is a contraction of the full expression, meaning *without a moment to spare*. The earliest citation by Wilkes (p 207) is a 1944 quote from a book by Jean Devanny *By tropic, sea and jungle*: 'The mother [kangaroo-rat] went one way and the young one another ... It ran straight, as flat out as a lizard drinking'.

## Shoot through

This means 'to absent oneself, usually in a hurry, and often for improper reasons'. It is a shortened form of the full version 'shoot through like a Bondi tram', the reference being to a tram from Sydney city to Bondi Beach that used to travel rather fast down a hill to its destination. Trams are long gone from Sydney, but the expression has remained.

A 1962 citation in Wilkes's book (p 44) is from John Morrison's *Twenty-three*: 'He shot through like a Bondi tram the minute the telegram arrived'. A variation on this is *went through* as in Kylie Tennant's *The honey flow* (1956): 'We collected Mike from where he and Hertz was mixing it, and we went through like a Bondi tram.'

However, the expression *went through* can mean something different, depending on where in Australia you live. In my experience, if a Melburnian says that a business has *gone through* or that it *went through*, it usually means that it *went broke*. A further variation with the same meaning is *went south*.

## Kick the tin, the bucket and others

*Kick* is a verb that gets used in a variety of colloquial expressions: *kick on* (to carry on despite adverse circumstances), *kick in* (of a motor, to start), *kick the tin* (to make a contribution when someone rattles the collection tin), and, of course, *kick the bucket* (to die). The precise origin of this eludes me, but one suggestion (courtesy of ABC Classic FM Breakfast 'Word of the day' from 18 February 2004) is that a suicide, or a person being strung up to a tree, dies when the upended bucket they're standing on is kicked away so that the suddenly tightened rope makes the neck snap. Ugh!

## Poke in the eye with a burnt stick

Well, all things are relative, and if something is *better than a poke in the eye with a burnt stick*, it's probably only marginally acceptable. In my family, we meant the same thing when we said *better than a slap in the face with a wet fish*.

## Chinwag

This appears in a number of lists of Australian slang on the web, but no origin is given, as it stands to reason; the Macquarie Dictionary says it means 'a chat; a conversation' (noun) or 'to talk at length; chatter' (verb) – so it's obviously from the action of your chin wagging up and down as you speak. And if you get the *good oil* from me, I'm giving you *the drum* or, according to the Macquarie Dictionary, 'information or advice usually confidential or profitable'.

\*

Well, mates, *the good oil* is that *Chrissie's* just around the corner and you'd be a *fruit loop* not to get your *chook* prepared in advance – *ridgy-didge*. Make sure you've got your *cossie* ready for the surfing season and have a *bonza hol*.

## itchypencil 8

## Only in Melbourne!

Merging computer files and merging correspondence with address lists are commonplace in offices, and I don't think anyone or anything is in danger as a result. Have you ever seen a couple of trams 'merging'? The word takes on a whole new meaning in Melbourne.

While I was driving in Melbourne one day, my car was stopped at traffic lights at a huge intersection where trams cut across the road from several directions. Trams from at least two directions actually turn into the same road. While we waited, there was time to take a photo of the sign through the front window of my car.

GIVE WAY TO MERGING TRAMS, it says! Absolutely, say I. Have you ever seen one tram 'merging' with another – it would have been an amazing sight. It was almost a pity to have to leave the scene when the light turned green for me, but perhaps such a 'merging' would not have been a pretty sight. The experience could leave the trams concerned feeling rather sore! No wonder the spot is also marked as a TRAM ACCIDENT BLACKSPOT AREA.

# Part 8

## The future of working words

# 60  Inclusiveness: who is 's/he'?

DO YOU REMEMBER THE OLD LEGAL DOCUMENTS (leases, agreements and the like) that started by stating something like 'Throughout this document, *he* embraces *she*' or 'In this book, *he* is taken to include *she*' or more pompously 'The masculine gender shall be taken to subsume the feminine gender'? OK, being embraced is fine, but in the right place and at the right time – not in print.

Inclusive, including non-sexist, language has become something of a talking point again at present – it surfaces every now and then – so let's share some of the thoughts of others on this topic as well as my own.

A textbook for secretarial students published in 1971 included three chapters contributed by me. One chapter contained the following: 'The degree to which the secretary will deputise whilst *her* employer is away depends on …' In 1986 my job was to edit a new version of the book, and this passage became 'The degree to which the secretary will deputise while *the* employer is away depends on …' Around this time, too, the publisher asked me to make sure that *he* and *she* were used in alternate chapters of this book to refer to the same office worker – in hindsight a weird attempt at even-handedness and singular construction, when avoidance, pluralising or 'singular *they*' would have got over the problem.

An interesting attempt to stick to singular constructions and third-person singular personal pronouns appears in both editions of Janet Mackenzie's book *The editor's companion* in which she writes:

> I have exploited the precision of the singular by following an arbitrary convention, referring to the author and the designer as *she* and to the reader and the publisher as *he*. Does it bother you?  [2nd edn, p 43]

The absurdities of exclusive language are legion. Two examples I used to give in my 'Sex and language' lecture to students of Sociolinguistics at the Australian National University in the mid 1980s are the oft-quoted example 'Man, being a mammal, breastfeeds *his* young', and one that confronted me when I sat an examination in 1984: 'Do not turn the page until the supervisor starts the examination. The student should put *his* name in the top right hand corner of every page'. (A wit actually asked the supervisor to spell his name for us!)

To be fair, there are some cogent arguments against inclusive language. One of the most telling I've seen was from Dr David Frost, then Professor

of English Literature at the University of Newcastle, who had been given the task (in about 1993) of preparing a draft 'non-sexist' version of the Anglican Church's prayer book for Australian use. His comment to the Liturgical Commission of the day was that 'the imposition of "inclusive language" in the prayer book would add up to bad English, (and not just bad theology).'\*
Two of Frost's examples stand out:

> Psalm 22, verse 6:
> Older version 'But I am a worm, and *no man* ...'
> New version: 'But I am a worm, and *not human* ...'
> Frost argues that the original meaning is distorted in the new version.
>
> Opening words of the Service for the Burial of the Dead:
> Older version: 'Man that is born of a woman hath but a short time to live ...'
> New version (a): 'Humanity has but a short hour to live ...'
> New version (b): 'Mortals, born of a woman, have but a short hour to live ...'
> Frost argues against (a) because it 'suggests [that] the race may be terminated next week'. He equally dislikes (b) for its obvious emphasis on mortality (rapid at that!) which is not the prime significance of the original Hebrew.

As Janet Mackenzie says: 'The over-zealous elimination of bias can falsify history' (2nd edn, p 43).

With those warnings about the risk of inaccuracy and banality in inclusive language, I still have to come down on the side of inclusiveness as a general rule. We don't have to go overboard, and we should remember that *man* is often intended to refer to the whole human race and may be difficult to replace in some contexts. (As I used to tell my Sociolinguistics students, speakers of Old English (before 1000 CE) used *man* exclusively in the generic sense – they had other specific words for male and female persons: *wer* for the male and *wif* for the female. We see the earlier forms today in *werewolf* (man + wolf) and *midwife, fishwife* or *housewife*. Gradually *wife* became restricted to married women and the form *man* took over the semantic role of *wer* while still retaining its alternative generic function.)

The website of Charles Darwin University used to have a page in 2005 that set out for its students the following guidelines, which start out straightforwardly enough:

---

\* David Frost, 'Why "inclusive" language adds up to bad English', *AD2000* vol 6 no 6 (July 1993)<http://www.ad2000.com.au/why_inclusive_language_adds_up_to_bad_english_july_1993.html> (viewed 22 March 2005).

Ensure that your use of personal pronouns is inclusive:
- leave out the pronoun or rewrite the sentence to avoid the pronoun
- repeat the relevant noun
- rewrite the sentence in a plural form

and then this:
- use 'she or he' or 'he or she'
  – some writers use 's/he' but most avoid it because it looks a little ugly within the text.

It certainly does! My first encounter with *s/he* was years ago in a report on language variation in Sydney. It appalled me then and still does. You can't even pronounce it! *He or she* for occasional use is acceptable, but pluralising or using singular *they* may be better.

Singular *they* is almost a non-issue now. It's here to stay. It's simply a return to usage that was perfectly legitimate before the prescriptive grammarians got stuck into it in the late 18th century. In 1975, linguist Ann Bodine asserted that 'prescriptive grammarians have, at least since the end of the 18th century, claimed either that English has **no** sex-indefinite pronoun, or that *he* in fact **is** the English sex-indefinite pronoun'.[*] Elizabeth Flann, Beryl Hill and Lan Wang write in *The Australian editing handbook* (3rd edn, pp 87–88): 'The generic *he* is no longer acceptable to a great many readers, writers and book buyers, and *they* appears to be emerging as the most acceptable alternative. … Editors … need to keep up to date with what is happening in the language.'

My push for 'singular *they*', over some years from about 1986 onward, was finally gratified when, in 1995, the Australian Government Attorney-General's Department supported its use in public documents prepared by them.[**]

Flann, Hill and Wang also warn us to watch out for examples of exclusiveness on the basis of race, ethnicity, gender and so on and quote the following sentence from a medical textbook: ' "Doctors often have difficulty in communicating with their female patients because they have not experienced what it is like to be a woman"—[this] assumes that all doctors are men' (p 76).

There are some legal requirements to consider. These are set out in the *Style manual* (p 55): 'Linguistic discrimination can take various forms that

---

[*] Ann Bodine, 'Androcentrism in prescriptive grammar: singular "they", sex-indefinite "he", and "he or she"' in *Language in Society*, vol 4 (1975), pp 129–46.

[**] Attorney-General's Department – Corporations Law Simplification Program, *A singular use of THEY*, Simplification Task Force, Attorney-General's Department (Australia), 1995.

may marginalise or exclude particular segments of the population – whether unwittingly or not'. There is no place in public documents for stereotyping, uninformed comment, prejudice or insensitivity.

To return to what triggered this rush of blood – a rash of references to sexist and non-sexist terms in 'WordFun' (a favourite, but sadly now defunct, email wordplay list to which I used to subscribe in Yahoo Groups). Comments in *WordFun Digest Number 649* included:

- Synthetic, artificial or manufactured are better than man-made.
- A chair is not a good replacement for chairman or chairwoman.
- A chair is something made of wood or metal or cloth. It usually has fewer ideas than a decent chair(wo)man.
- A chair is an inanimate object and many women prefer to be called Chairman or Madam Chairman.
- On the BBC recently, I heard the term 'personfully' used in preference presumably to the sexist 'manfully'.

Going overboard is all too easy. Do we really have to put up with *personhole* for manhole? As the WordFun contributors note, it would be but a step to *personkind* for mankind, *woperson* for woman and *personage* for manage.

Finally, before I scuttle out and find somewhere to hide while you gather your inclusive thoughts together, if you were in Canberra in the mid 1980s, you will remember local ABC newsreader Kevin Chapman. One night, at the height of the frenzy for inclusive language at all costs, Kevin began the 7 pm news with 'Good evening, here is the news read by Kevin Person-person.'

# 61    International English

Time was when you used your *judgment* about which spelling of a word to use when writing or when editing material. The custom was, when editing in Australia, to use the spellings we had known from school – largely British English spelling. Spellings such as *color* were frowned on and we all wrote *colour*. Then we started to think more amiably about American English spellings and they have crept into our writing. We also questioned whether we should follow the Oxford Dictionary's first choice and write *recognize*, or *recognise* – the first choice of the Macquarie Dictionary. We have allowed either, provided there was consistency throughout the document. As the world shrank, the situation gradually became more confused, and it was difficult to keep tabs on which spelling ought to be used.

My own preference is to follow the Macquarie Dictionary, which gives *-ise* as the preferred spelling in Australia, while it still offers *-ize* as an alternative spelling. The preference in the Oxford Dictionary is *-ize* with *-ise* as an alternative. American spelling (as in *humor, neighbor*) is bound to become more common in Australia as travel, television and the internet continue to make the world smaller. If the target audience is outside Australia, we must edit so as to make the finished document acceptable worldwide. My own spelling has shifted to 'minimalist' for many words – hence *judgment* in the first sentence.

In July 2003, at a conference held in Milan, Ron Blicq, Project Coordinator and Senior Editor, INTECOM International Technical Documentation Study Group, spoke about the issue of international spelling – not spelling based on what country the editor lives in, but spelling based on the cultural norms of the expected readership of the document. The Study Group's objective was 'to identify which spelling and usage we should recommend for documentation that would be written in English' but would 'receive worldwide distribution'. The upshot is the *INTECOM Guidelines for writing technical documents for an international audience* that provides spelling and usage guidance for English-language documentation intended to be read in three different situations:

- primarily in countries where British-based spelling, terminology and usage are the norm

- primarily in countries where US-based spelling, terminology and usage are prevalent

- by people in a broader range of countries, with some accustomed to British and some to US usage.

The introduction to the guidelines contains the following:

> What will quickly become apparent is that the Project Group has mostly suggested using US spelling and usage for English-language documentation that will have worldwide use. Our rationale is simply that people who are accustomed to US spelling practices find British spelling to be strange or quaint, or may even think the writer cannot spell correctly. On the other hand, most people who use British spelling and usage have also been exposed to US spelling and usage, so that even though they don't use it themselves (as, for example, in Great Britain), they recognize [sic] it and more readily adapt to it.

This rationale seems arrogant and makes me wonder why we should kowtow to this insular point of view. Words that are spelt differently in British and US settings are set out in the guide like this:

*harbor* (US); *harbour* (Br); Intl: *harbor*

If a word can be spelt two different ways, but the Study Group recommends just one spelling for all documentation, no matter what the audience, it just gives the recommended spelling:

*antagonize*

The guidelines include advice, where applicable, on recommended plurals where there is a choice, for example:

*memorandum* pl: *memorandums* (rec) or *memoranda*

It puzzles me that no choice is offered in this entry:

*addendum* pl: *addenda*

Why not offer *addendums* as well and then make a recommendation? Some entries are surprising. Some examples:

- of *autumn* and *fall*, the recommended international usage is *autumn*
- of *e.g.* and *eg*, the recommendation is *eg*
- of *e-mail and email*, the recommendation is *email* (I applaud the last two)
- *analyze* and *baptize* are recommended but *advertize* is not.

Some are worth a query, such as:

*burned* (US); *burnt* (Br); Intl: *burned*

The context and syntax make the difference here. You will notice that the past tense of *spell* has been given as *spelt* throughout this book. My inclination was to use *spelled* because my school taught that there was a difference between the past tense (*spelled*) and the past participle (*spelt*). I have happily bowed to the preference of the editor of the first edition of this book. After all, a horse can be 'spelled', can't it?

And there are some strange omissions. For example, why are *hood/bonnet* and *fender/bumper* in the guidelines, but no mention of *trunk/boot*? (Guess which of these pairs is preferred for international audiences.*)

At the end of the main section of the guidelines (only 24 pages at that time), there is a section of nine short articles which explain or expand on the guidelines and attempt to give the rationale underpinning the decisions of the Study Group. Some of these are interesting. For example, why must we use *m* as the abbreviation of *metre* and *L* as the abbreviation of *litre*? Because *M* is the abbreviation for *mega*, and to use lower-case *l* for *litre* risks confusion with the number *1*.

The recommendation for punctuating a list of bullet points takes a step backwards in time – in Australia we have largely abandoned the commas recommended here at the ends of lines and the 'comma + and' at the end of the second last line (*Style manual*, 6th edn, p 143).

This brings me to my final point: while the guidelines document might be a useful reference tool, it is highly prescriptive (despite the word 'guidelines'); it seeks to force writers and editors into a mould (or should that be *mold*) of bland international English – let's call it McDonald's English. English is a living language and should be allowed to live and grow. There are some Australian usages (for example *utility* or *ute* for the US *pickup* – a light truck with a tray) that Australian writers prefer to use in their novels and other writing. Don't these deserve a place in English written for international audiences? I don't believe that American readers are so un-worldlywise that they can't see *recognise* and know it's the same as *recognize*.

The guidelines are now available at <https://www.tekom.de/upload/alg/INTECOM_Guidelines.pdf>.

---

\*  No prizes for guessing *hood* and *fender* – the US words. And, while it isn't listed, my money would be on *trunk* rather than *boot* for US/international usage.

# 62   Editing ESL writing

WOULD A FEW POINTS IN THESE PAGES ON EDITING the work of writers whose first language is not English be useful? The term 'ESL' (meaning English as a second language) in the heading has always concerned me – it is there because it is generally accepted and understood, but my preference would be 'ENL' (English as a new language) because English could be the second, third, fourth or fifth language a person has acquired.

My admiration is enormous for people from other cultures who not only master spoken English but manage to write business letters, scientific reports, doctoral dissertations, or anything else in remarkably good English.

My editing work includes a lot of English written by people whose first language is Japanese, Chinese, Russian, Polish, German, French, Vietnamese – you name it. When people from another language base write English, grammar of their first language can 'interfere' with their writing in the new language. It's called 'first language interference' (abbreviated to '$L_1$ interference'). The writer uses English words and phrases plus whatever English grammar they have absorbed, but there are still gaps in understanding the grammar of the new language, so we get a bunch of English words structured in the style of the first language.

The problems that crop up most frequently with writers from Asian cultures are these:

- lack of or misuse of articles
- wrong tenses of verbs and wrong choice of verb in the first place
- misuse of prepositions
- misplacement of adverbs
- lack of plural marker on nouns.

There are other problems, such as phonetic spelling (usually by writers from Russia or Poland) and sentences structured in the German way with the main verb at the end. But I'll stick to the Asian writing hiccups here, with an example or two of each and a suggestion about helping the writer to see the error, fix it and learn from the experience. (The examples are all real – they have been altered slightly to ensure anonymity.)

## Lack of or misuse of articles

(a) The female road accident rate was lower than **[the]** male rate and most of **[the]** accidents happen to the people aged under 40 years.

It's necessary to explain that nouns and noun phrases in English have an article (*a/an* or *the*) in front of them when we are being specific and not generalising. It would be possible to argue for no article before *accidents* but only if we remove *of*, and then we would perhaps write *people* and not *the people*, thus making a more general statement than the present sentence.

## Wrong tenses of verbs

(b) The percentage of older women **rented** private home **has been increased**, while the percentage of older women **lived** in public housing **has been decreased**.

There are several problems here: *rented* should be either *renting* or *who rented* and *lived* should be either *living* or *who lived*. *Rented* and *lived* can't be used as simple past-tense verbs because their subjects are not *women*. The two verb phrases *has been increased* and *has been decreased* are wrong because, without revealing the whole context, the intention was to show an increase and a decrease in the proportions that just happened – not that was made to happen. We'll return to *home* without an *s* later.

(c) I **have wrote** the email about your suggestions …

(d) … six visitors who **flied** all the way from London.

These are two examples of confusion about the way past tenses and past participles are formed in English. The first, *have wrote*, is clearly the result of making use of the past tense to serve as the past participle – and there are plenty of English verbs that behave this way. The second, *flied*, is probably the result of applying logic – if you can have *try/tried* why not *fly/flied*? Irregular formations like *flew* and *written* (which defy logic) are particularly tricky for writers with a non-English background.

## Wrong choice of verb

(e) What **departs** Mr X and his colleagues from the other members is …

The writer is clearly thinking about *sets Mr X apart* or *Mr X departs in principle from his colleagues*, but the verb required here is *differentiates* or *distinguishes*. The writer needs help in understanding the links between words and the various meanings that they can have, depending on context.

## Misuse of prepositions

(f) ... give the poor opportunities **of** getting out of poverty.

English idiom is very hard to keep up with. There! Fifty years ago, it might have been frowned upon to end a sentence with a preposition. Another change: now we can write *different from* and *different to* with impunity, though *different than* is still only beginning to be recognised as acceptable in formal writing. Usage in writing always follows usage in speech – it's only a matter of time before *different than* will be perfectly acceptable in writing as well as in speech. Same here: idiom has it that we write 'opportunities *for* getting out' or 'opportunities *to* get out' but not 'opportunities *of* getting out', though we can write 'chances *of* getting out'.

## Misplacement of adverbs

(g) ... the people conform to their religious laws **strictly**.

Here *strictly* is misplaced; it belongs with the verb *conform* because it tells more about the verb – placing it further from the verb only weakens its effect. Better is: *conform strictly to* ... In some cases, shifting adverbs can alter the meaning – try shifting *only* to every possible position in a sentence like *She only bought bread at the shop yesterday* and see how many different meanings you give to the sentence.

*Only* she bought bread at the shop yesterday. [She was the sole person who did.]

She *only* bought bread at the shop yesterday. [She didn't buy anything else OR She was the sole person who did.]

She bought *only* bread at the shop yesterday. [She didn't buy anything else at the shop.]

She bought bread *only* at the shop yesterday. [She didn't buy from anywhere else.]

She bought bread at *only* the shop yesterday. [Unlikely construction but could mean: She didn't buy from anywhere else.]

She bought bread at the *only* shop yesterday. [There is just the one shop.]

She bought bread at the shop *only* yesterday. [The bread is still quite fresh.]

She bought bread at the shop yesterday *only*. [She didn't buy bread any other day.]

## Lack of plural marker on nouns

(h) ... some people cannot afford to live in those **area** where they can easily access facilities,

(i) ... rented private **home** ... lived in public **housing**. [from example (b) above]

In example (h) it should be *areas* (in English we pluralise the noun as well as using a plural determiner – here *those*). In example (i) the writer has apparently inferred from the correct *housing* that *home* is also the right construction, but it should be *homes* because these are seen as individual residential units, and so plural. One of the most common errors made by Asian writers of English is to omit the plural marker because there is no need for it in their first language. Native English-speakers go to a shop and buy *one book* or *two books*, whereas an Asian person might buy *one book* or *two book*, the numerator being quite enough to show plurality – how sensible.

\*

What can we, as editors, do to help writers from other cultures learn English structural conventions?

We certainly need to be on the lookout for all these types of errors, but more than this, we need to do what we can to help such writers to develop their English writing skills by explaining the corrections we make and expanding on them as necessary and if we have time. For example, an error may be *he bought green jacket at store*; we may correct this to *he bought a green jacket at the store*. The writer won't learn from this correction unless there is an explanation: 'We use the indefinite article "a" before a noun or noun phrase (adjective + noun here) where the jacket was one of many green jackets on sale, so non-specific, and the definite article "the" before "store" to show that we mean a particular store'. If you have time to enlarge on that to explain when you would use *an* instead of *a*, so much the better. One detailed explanation of a particular type of error correction in a document is enough – the writer will appreciate the help and may avoid the same mistake next time. I have referred to the editor's 'teaching' role earlier (see Chat 2 'Who exactly are you, editor?' Here is one case where it can help a lot to take off your editing hat and put on your teaching hat (if you are suitably qualified) to help the writer new to English to find their way through the complexities of our written language. Real language acquisition is a long-term process.

# 63   Whither grammar and plain English?

Someone asked me recently what I thought about the future of plain English. As this is an important question, I would like to spend some time chatting about the future of grammar and the future of plain English. This is sheer crystal ball gazing, and may not coincide with your opinion of where we're heading.

English is a living language because we are all different, we have different needs, we use our language for different purposes, and we are of different generations. Some of us are very comfortable with new technology. Some aren't. I suggest that, if we are to continue to communicate meaningfully with each other, we need to recognise the changing nature of language, and the changing nature of technology – at the same time.

This quote from Geoffrey Chaucer is relevant, believe it or not:

> Ye know ek that in forme of speche is chaunge
> Withinne a thousand yeer, and wordes tho
> That hadden pris, now wonder nyce and straunge
> Us thinketh hem, and yet thei spake hem so ...[*]

What Chaucer's saying, in essence, is that language changes and words that used to be valued highly for a particular meaning can appear strange at a later time.

How true! One example would be *awesome* – it used to mean 'inspiring awe' and gradually came to include the idea of 'fear' or 'dread'. Later still it came to mean 'extremely impressive' or 'of high quality'. And in most recent times, it seems to have lost some of that feeling of awe. When I tell someone I can do an edit for them in a few days, the response is often 'Awesome!' meaning nothing more than 'That's good.' Another example would be *absolutely* which has changed its meaning from 'completely' or 'perfectly' (as in 'fitting perfectly') to an expression of total agreement: 'Absolutely!'

I take particular note of what Geoffrey Chaucer writes – after all, he is my Great[many times] Uncle Geoffrey. Absolutely!

---

[*]   Geoffrey Chaucer, 'Troilus and Criseyde, Book II', from *The works of Geoffrey Chaucer*, 2nd edn, ed F N Robinson, Houghton Mifflin, Boston 1957 (first published c. 1385).

I've been around long enough to have done my writing by hand, then on manual, electric and electronic typewriters, word processors and now computers. I've been pushed into using mobile phones and text messaging. I've gladly accepted new technology such as my GPS to get me from place to place and flashdrives to cart my work with me wherever I travel. The 'instant' messaging world has to be managed carefully, but I'm all for the easy, swift contact afforded by video-conferencing facilities that I can use for worldwide training and discussion purposes. I've dodged being labelled a dinosaur by growing with modern technology and the language changes that have come along with it.

So what's all this got to do with the future of grammar and plain English? Heaps. English is a living, changing language, just as technology is constantly changing. The English language changes all the time, with new words added, old words dropped, words changing meaning, words imported from new industries and from a huge range of other languages. On top of that, the so-called 'rules' of grammar change as people speak English differently from the way their parents and grandparents spoke it. In my schooldays, we had to address our teachers as Miss So-and-so or Mister Something, but fashions change and teachers now like to be addressed by their given names. The same goes for writing – usage reflects the manners and conventions of the day.

The jargon of the information technology (IT) industry is becoming part of everyday speech and writing. Who would have thought, a few short years ago, that 'text' could be a verb as well as a noun?

The term *plain English* might seem to many to date from some time in the 1980s. Not a bit of it! Here's another quote from Lindley Murray's *English grammar* of more than two hundred years ago:

> The first requisite of a perfect sentence is Clearness. Whatever leaves the mind in any sort of suspense as to the meaning, ought to be avoided. Obscurity arises from two causes: either from a wrong choice of words, or a wrong arrangement of them.

Nothing new under the sun, is there? Murray is describing exactly what we call 'plain English' today.

Without going into detail, plain English is simply:
- controlling sentence length
- choosing everyday words over pompous words
- preferring active verbs over passive verbs as far as practicable
- using dynamic verbs rather than 'dead' verbal nouns
- being positive, avoiding foreign or jargon terms, being game to use personal pronouns and not get bogged down in third-person writing.

It's not just the words either. However well constructed a piece of writing is, it will fall flat on its face if it *looks* unreadable, so we need:

- plenty of white space
- variety of paragraph lengths
- type that's easy to read
- as few frills as possible, particularly in business writing.

The content needs to be relevant to the topic and the audience, the language needs to be meaningful to the age group we're writing for, and pages that are nothing but 'a sea of black ink' are to be avoided.

Whither grammar and plain English?

Sound grammar is the basis of all good writing and always will be. The basic patterns of English grammar will probably not change much in the future – they may get bent a little to accommodate 'mobile speak', but they will always have to be patterns that every speaker of English recognises and can respond to. Plain English is based on sound grammar and is getting plainer all the time. It is tending towards telegraphic English in some instances, and here we need to exercise care. Whatever is written to remain on any sort of record needs to be understandable both today and in the future. Even the quote from Chaucer above is reasonably understandable by today's speakers of English, and follows pretty much the same grammatical patterns that we observe today. As writers and editors we need to consider the person who will read what we write and the reason for writing. We always will. English grammar, pretty much as we know it, is with us for the long haul, and plain English will be around for as long as business people need to read clear reports without having to re-read obscure passages – they don't have time for re-reading.

*

As a famous Australian broadcaster on the BBC (Wilfred Thomas) used to say, at the end of every broadcast: 'Thank you for having me at your place'. I echo that sentiment.

# References

*Australian standards for editing practice*, 2nd edn, Institute of Professional Editors (IPEd), 2013, available at <http://iped-editors.org/about_editing/editing_standards.aspx>.

*Commissioning checklist*, Canberra Society of Editors, 1994, available at <http://www.editorscanberra.org/?s=commissioning+checklist>.

Denman, Terence, *How not to write: simple guidelines for the grammatically perplexed*, Piatkus Books, London, 2005.

Flann, Elizabeth, Hill, Beryl and Wang, Lan, *The Australian editing handbook*, 3rd edn, Wiley, Milton, Qld, 2014.

Fowler, H W and F G, *The King's English*, Oxford University Press, Oxford, 1924.

Gowers, Sir Ernest, *The complete plain words* (rev Sir Bruce Fraser), HMSO, London, 1973.

Mackenzie, Janet, *The editor's companion*, 2nd edn, Cambridge University Press, Melbourne, 2011.

*Macquarie dictionary online*, 2019, Macquarie Dictionary Publishers, an imprint of Pan Macmillan Australia Pty Ltd, <http://www.macquariedictionary.com.au>.

Murphy, Elizabeth M, with Hilary Cadman, *Effective writing: plain English at work*, 2nd edn, Lacuna, Sydney, 2014.

Murray, Lindley, *English grammar, adapted to the different classes of learners. With an appendix, containing, [sic] rules and observations for assisting the more advanced students to write with perspicuity and accuracy*, John and Charles Mozley, Derby, and Paternoster Row, London, c. 1804 (1st edn 1795).

Sabto, Michele, *The on-screen editing handbook*, Tertiary Press, Melbourne, 2003.

*Style manual: for authors, editors and printers*, 6th edn, rev Snooks & Co, Commonwealth of Australia, John Wiley & Sons, Australia, 2002.

Wilkes, G A, *A dictionary of Australian colloquialisms*, Fontana, Melbourne, 1978.

## Further reading

*APA Style*, APA (American Psychological Association), <http://www.apastyle.org> (viewed January 2019).

Attorney-General's Department – Corporations Law Simplification Program, *A singular use of THEY*, Simplification Task Force, Attorney-General's Department, Canberra, 1995.

Bodine, Ann, 'Androcentrism in prescriptive grammar: singular "they", sex-indefinite "he", and "he or she"', *Language in society*, vol 4 (1975), pp 129–146.

Bond, Helena 'Quoting: a vexing professional issue', *Offpress*, Society of Editors (Qld), October 2001.

Eagleson, Robert, 'Figuring out numbers', *Australian Style*, June 2005.

Gee, Robyn and Watson, Carol, *Better English*, Usborne Publishing, London, 1983.

Guide to grammar and writing, Capital Community College, Hartford, Connecticut, <http://www.ccc.commnet.edu/grammar> (viewed January 2019).

Hewings, M, *Advanced grammar in use*, Cambridge University Press, Cambridge, 1999.

*INTECOM Guidelines for writing technical documentation for an international audience* , INTECOM International Language Project Group, <http://www.tekom.de/upload/alg/INTECOM_Guidelines.pdf> (viewed January 2019).

Johnson, E, 'The ideal grammar and style checker', *TEXT Technology*, vol 2 no 4 (July 1992), pp 3–4.

Murphy, Raymond, *English grammar in use*, 4th edn, Cambridge University Press, Cambridge, 2012.

Peters, Pam, *The Cambridge guide to Australian English usage*, Cambridge University Press, Melbourne, 2007.

Putnis, Peter and Petelin, Roslyn, *Professional communication principles and applications*, Prentice Hall, Sydney, 1996.

Ross-Larsen, Bruce, *Edit yourself: a manual for everyone who works with words*, W W Norton & Co, New York, 1996.

Seely, John, *Oxford A–Z of grammar and punctuation*, 2nd edn, Oxford University Press, Oxford, 2009.

Snodgrass, G and Murphy, E M, *Letter writing simplified* (revised), Pitman, Melbourne, 1986.

Tredinnick, Mark, *The little green grammar book*, University of NSW Press, Sydney, 2008.

Truss, Lynne, *Eats, shoots & leaves: the zero tolerance approach to punctuation*, Profile Books, London, 2003.

'Writing and editing tips', *Communication Skills*, Air War College, <http://www.au.af.mil/au/awc/awcgate/army/writing_tips.htm> (viewed January 2019).

# Index

In this index, italicised entries indicate particular words discussed in the text (eg definitions and explanations of words that are often misused).

**A**
*a/an*, 101–4, 214, 243, 245
abbreviations, 168–9;
    *see also* shortened forms
ablative (instrumental) case, 128–9
*absolutely*, 246
academic editing, 38–40, 41–2
accepting or rejecting jobs, 43
accreditation of editors, 9, 22–3
accusative (objective) case, 105, 127–30, 155
acknowledgements, 39
active voice, 112–13, 125–6, 201, 205–6, 209–10
*adherence/adhesion*, 141
adjectives
    misused for adverbs, 90
    part of speech, as, 97
adverbs, 90, 155
    part of speech, as, 97
    placement, 115, 244
    prepositions as, 108
*affect/effect*, 138
agentless passives, 113, 206, 210
*aggravate/irritate*, 141
*alternate/alternative*, 141
am (time), 169
ambiguity, 28, 46, 217–20
    deep structural, 218
    lexical, 217
    road signs, in, 82, 83, 160, 231
    surface structural, 217–18
American English, 70, 102, 106, 239–41
*among/between*, 93, 138
*and*, 91
apostrophes
    disappearance of, 186
    indicating omission, 176, 185, 215–16
    indicating plural, 182–5
    indicating possession, 128, 135–7, 175–81, 215–16
    when not to use, 121, 129

articles (grammar), 101–4, 214, 243, 245
Asian-language background, 102, 121, 242–5
Australian standards for editing practice, 11, 21, 22–3, 27, 42, 55, 249
authors, *see* clients, relationship with
auxiliary verbs, 110, 114–15
*awesome*, 246

**B**
backing up files, 12–13
*because*, 91
*being* verbs, 111, 209
*between/among*, 93, 138
Bible text
    Biblical names, possessive of, 179
    inclusive language, 236
British English, 70–1, 239–41
budgeting, 52
bullet points, *see* lists
business cards, 12
business writing, *see* plain English
*but*, 91

**C**
*can/could*, 157–8
Canberra Society of Editors, viii–x, 11, 21, 34, 49
    Commissioning checklist, 11, 21, 55, 80, 249
    The Canberra editor, ix, 19, 22, 34, 188, 211
case (grammar), 96, 97, 105, 127–32
    Latin, 127–9
Chaucer, Geoffrey, 246
*cheap/inexpensive*, 141–2
clarity of meaning, *see* plain English
clauses, 151
cliché, 56, 207
clients, relationship with, 6, 8, 17, 24–7
collective nouns, 1, 95, 96

colloquialisms, 31, 143, 144, 226–7, 228–30
colons, 166–7, 173
commas,
　comma fault, 165–6
　difference between comma and semicolon, 163–7
　number separator, as, 169–70
Commissioning checklist, 11, 21, 55, 249
communication *see* effective writing
communications technology
　email, 12, 15, 33, 76, 77–8
　internet, 13, 21, 53, 79, 239
　mobile phones, 11, 68, 76, 78, 122, 247, 248
　SMS, 78, 88, 95, 122, 225, 247
　video-conferencing, 247
complex sentences, 151–2
compound nouns, 121, 179–80, 187
compound phrases, 187
compound sentences, 151–2
*comprise/consist*, 142
computers, 12–13, 15, 21, 77, 189
　cloud, 13
　flashdrives, 13, 75, 76, 247
　hardware, 13, 15, 60, 67, 69, 74, 75–6, 81, 170, 247;
　software, 13, 33, 40, 78;
　　*see also* Microsoft Word
confidentiality, 42–3
conflicts of interest, 42, 43
conjunctions, 91, 96, 100, 170–1
*consist/comprise*, 142
*continual/continuous*, 142
contractions, 168–9, 176, 185
contracts, 61
copyediting, 11
copyright, 33–4
*could/can*, 157–8
courtesy, 31, 34
creoles, 192–3
crib sheets, 31–2

**D**
dangling modifiers, 219
dashes, 170, 174, 188, 189–91
dates, 224

dative case, 127–31
deadlines, 43, 52
declarative (indicative) mood, 110–11, 147–8, 152
declensions, 129
deep structural ambiguity, 218
definite article, 101–3, 214, 245
Denman, Terence, 212–3, 249
*desert/dessert*, 142
determiners, 101–4, 214, 243, 245
detestable expressions, 226–7
*different from/to/than*, 105–6, 244
directive (imperative) mood, 110–11, 148
disclaimers, 35–7, 63, 82
discriminatory language, 235–8
*disinterested/uninterested*, 142
dot points, *see* lists
double comparatives, 90
double negatives, 90
*down*, 108

**E**
editing practice, *see also* editors
　'seven deadly sins' of, 20–23
　skills and expertise, 11, 43, 44
editing societies, 8, 10, 22, 23, 27, 39, 42, 56; s*ee also* Canberra Society of Editors; Institute of Professional Editors (IPEd)
Editors Queensland, 60
editing tools, 12–13, 14–17, 156, 189; *see also* computers; Microsoft Word
editors
　accreditation, 8–9, 22–3
　definition, 8
　ethics, 41–5
　mentors, as, 10–11, 38–9
　professional development, 22
　professionalism, 9, 41–5
　responsibilities, 9–11
　role, 5–7
　skills, 11, 43, 44
　teachers, as, 9–11, 100, 215
　travel and working, 74–6, 81
*effect/affect*, 138

effective writing, 10, 14, 200;
    *see also* plain English
  emails, in, 77–9
  feeble thought = feeble writing, 199
  ideas, expressing, 38
  purity, propriety, precision, 197–9
Effective writing: plain English at
    work, 2nd edn, 98, 100, 152,
    168, 187, 191, 203, 219, 249
*eg*, 169, 207
em rule, 170, 174, 188, 189–91
email, *see also* communications
    technology
  invoicing and, 64–6
  quoting in, 61, 64, 71
  disclaimer in, 357
  writing, 20, 26, 70–3, 77–9, 81, 88,
    149, 176, 225
emphasis in writing, 70
en rule, 170, 188, 189–91
English
  as second language, 24–5, 39, 88,
    101, 109, 242–5
  changes in meaning over time, 246
  first language interference with, 25,
    101–2, 242–5
  future of, 235–48
  international, 239–41
*equable/equitable*, 143
ergonomics, 67
ethics in editing, 41–5
evaluation of projects, 55–6
exclamation marks, 79, 164
exclamative sentences, 148
expression, *see* effective writing;
    grammar; plain English
expressions of interest, 20, 61, 73

**F**
*fewer/less*, 93, 143
filing, 12, 14–15
first language interference, 25, 101–2,
    242–5
Flann, Hill and Wang, 21, 237, 249
fonts, 13, 78, 79, 170, 173
forms
  home office, 12
  need for clarity on, 223

Fowler, 1, 21, 136, 249
fragments (of sentences), 149–50,
    221–2
freelancing, 80–1
full stops, 163–7, 168, 169
future of English
  grammar and plain English, 246–8
  inclusive language, 235–8

**G**
Gantt charts, 53–4
generations, differences among, 11
genitive (possessive) case, 127–31,
    135–7
gerunds, 135–7
*google* (verb), 117
government contracts, 61
Gowers, Sir Ernest, 21, 136–7, 187–8,
    217, 249
grammar, 87–9, 148
  future of, 246–8
  parts of speech, 95–104
  principles, 200–8
  'rules', 90–4
  tips, 212–13, 214–16
  voice, 112–13, 125–6, 205–6, 209–10
grammar checking tools, 14, 156
greengrocer's apostrophe, 182–3
GST (Goods and Services Tax), 63,
    64–5

**H**
health and safety, 68–9
home office, 67–9, 81
honesty and editing, 42–5
hourly rate for editing, 59–60, 62, 63
*however*, 170–1
hyphens, 187–8, 189

**I**
ideas, expressing, 38
*ie*, 169, 207
*if/whether*, 143
imperative (directive) mood, 110–11,
    148
*imply/infer*, 139
inclusive language, 235–8
indefinite article, 101–4, 214, 245
indefinite pronoun, 97, 136, 237

indicative (declarative) mood, 110–11, 147–8, 151
*inexpensive/cheap*, 141–2
*infer/imply*, 139
Institute of Professional Editors (IPEd), 8, 21, 22, 23, 40, 42, 56, 60; *see also* editing societies
instrumental (ablative) case, 129
insurance, 61
interjections, 100
international English, 239–41
interrogative mood, 110–11, 148
*interstate/intestate/intrastate*, 144
invoicing, 64–6, 80–1
IPEd, *see* Institute of Professional Editors (IPEd)
*irritate/aggravate*, 141
*its/it's*, 178–9; *see also* personal pronouns; possession

**J**
jargon, 25, 56, 78, 88, 117, 197, 202, 207–8, 247
joint possession, 180

**L**
*lay/lie*, 139–40
legal action, using disclaimers as protection from, 35–7
*lend/loan*, 144
*less/fewer*, 93, 143
levels of edit, 8, 10
lexical ambiguity, 217
liability, 82; *see also* disclaimers; insurance
*lie/lay*, 139–40
lists
 bullets or dot points, 16, 174
 parallel structure in, 201, 202, 204–5, 209
*loan/lend*, 144

**M**
Mackenzie, Janet, 21, 24, 44, 67, 235, 236, 249
Macquarie Dictionary, 10, 18, 19, 31, 41, 70, 88, 228, 230, 239, 249
magazine editors, 8
*may/might*, 157–9

mentoring, 10–11, 38–9
Microsoft Word
 autocorrect, 187
 em and en rules, keyboard shortcuts for, 187
 Find and Replace, 14, 15, 17, 71
 global changes, 15, 71
 grammar check, 14, 78, 156
 spellcheck, 14, 78, 95, 156
 Track Changes 6, 9, 10, 11, 13, 14, 16, 21, 22, 25, 62
*might/may*, 157–9
mood (grammar), 110–11, 147–8, 151–3
Murray, Lindley, 197–9, 208, 212–13, 247, 249

**N**
'nerbs', 116–18
newspaper editors, 8
nominalisations, 206
nominative (subjective) case, 127–30
Norfolk Island (language), 192–3
noun phrases, 103, 136, 151, 204, 214, 243
nouns, *see also* articles; case
 collective, 1, 96
 compound, 121, 179–80, 187
 countable, 93
 part of speech, as, 96
 plural, 120–1, 182–3
 possessive, 128, 135–7, 175–81
 proper, 121, 179, 183
 verbal nouns, 206
novels, 6
numbers
 numerals or words, 224–5
 punctuation in, 169–70

**O**
objective (accusative) case, 105, 127–31, 155
office organisation, 67–9, 81
omitted letters, 176, 185
on-screen editing, 14–17, 21, 40, 56, 88
*only*, 244
Oxford Dictionary, 239

## P

paperless office, 12, 77
paragraphs, 152
parallel structure, 204–5; *see also* lists
parts of speech, 95–100;
    *see also* adjectives; adverbs; articles; conjunctions; interjections; nouns; prepositions; pronouns; verbs
*passed/past*, 144
passive voice, 112–13, 125–6, 205–6, 209–10
*past/passed*, 144
perfect tense, 109, 114, 139
period, *see* full stop; punctuation
personal pronouns, 129–32, 179
  inclusive language and, 235–8
Peters, Pam, 155, 158, 250
phrases, 151
pidgins, 192–3
plagiarism, 31–3, 39–40
plain English, 5, 46, 197–9, 200–8, 209, 212–13, 247–8
  future of, 246–8
  Plain English Campaign, 226–7
planning
  for work and travel, 74–5, 81
  projects, 50–1, 62
plural possession, 180–1
plurals, 119–21, 214, 245
  apostrophes and, 182–5
pm (time), 169
possession, 128, 135–7, 175–81
possessive (genitive) case, 127–31, 135–7
predicates, 147–50
prepositional idiom, 99, 105–6, 214, 244
prepositions, 105–8, 155
  misuse of, 244
  part of speech, as, 99, 214
  'rules', 94
principles of grammar, 200–8
printing, 12
privacy, 33, 42, 43
professional development, 22
professional standards, 59;
    *see also* ethics in editing

project
  definition, 49–50, 55–8, 80
  evaluation, 53–4
  management, 49–54
  performance constraints, 52–3
  planning, 50–1, 62
pronouns, 91, 155, 211;
    *see also* case; personal pronouns
  ambiguous use, 219
  part of speech, as, 97
  possessive, 177, 216
proofreading marks, 11, 22
proper nouns, 121, 179, 183
punctuation
  changing use of in English, 171, 181
  *however*, with, 170–1
  numbers, in, 169–70
punctuation marks, 163–91
  abbreviations, in, 168–9
  apostrophe, *see* apostrophes
  colon, 166–7
  comma, 163–70
  difference between comma, semicolon and full stop, 163–7
  dashes, 170, 174, 188, 189–91
  exclamation mark, 79, 164
  full stop, 163–7, 168, 169
  hyphen, 187–8, 189
  numbers and, 169–70
  question mark, 164
  quotation marks, 170
  semicolon, 163–7

## Q

qualifications in editing, 22
question marks, 164
quotation marks, 170
quoting on editing jobs, 8, 20, 44, 59–63, 71, 80
  disclaimers, 35–7
  hourly rate, 59–60, 62, 63, 71
  task assessment, 56–7, 62

## R

redundant words, 91, 209
reference material, 20–1
research, academic, 39
restrictive clauses, 92

road signs, 82–3, 122, 160, 231
*RSVP*, 207
'rules' of grammar, 90–4, 247

**S**
Sabto, Michele, 14, 16, 249
scholarly editing, 38–40, 41–2
scrip/script, 145
scripts, editing, 35
security for documents, 68
self editing, 70–3
semicolons, 163–7
sentences, *see also* case; effective writing; voice
  ambiguous, 217–20
  attributes for perfect sentence, 198
  complex and compound, 151–3
  length and readability, 202–4, 208
  plain, 209–11
  simple, 109, 147–50
  strong, 209–11
  structure traps, 221–3
sexist language, 235–8
*shall/will*, 145, 154
shortened forms, 168–9, 176, 185
simple sentences, 109, 147–50
singular *they*, 114, 204
skills in editing, 11, 43, 44
slang, 228–30
space after full stop, 71
spell checking tools, 14, 78, 95, 156
spelling, 20–1, 70–1, 239–41
standards in editing, *see* Australian standards for editing practice; editors, professionalism
stress (work), 69
Strunk and White, 1, 21
students, editing for, 38–40, 41–2
Style manual, 6th edn, 21, 169, 171, 184, 185, 187, 237, 241, 249
styles
  different meanings of, 87
  headings, 16
  templates, 16
  writing style, 197–9; *see also* effective writing; plain English

subject (grammar)
  position in sentence, 125
  redundant, 91
  sentence components, 147–50
subject–verb agreement, 91, 114, 119–20, 121, 215
subjective (nominative) case, 127–30
subjunctive mood, 93, 110–11, 151–3
substantive editing, 57
suffixes, 71
surface structural ambiguity, 217–18
syntax, 9–10, 87, 173, 200, 201, 217–8, 241

**T**
task assessment, 56–7, 62
teaching
  editing responsibility, 9–11, 100, 215
  grammar in schools, 31, 38, 88, 95, 106, 154, 155, 173, 175, 182, 200, 239, 241
telephone etiquette, 68
tense, 109–10, 215, 243
text messages, 78, 88, 95, 122, 225, 247
*than/then*, 154–5
*thank you/thankyou*, 70
*that*, 133
*that/which*, 92
*the*, 101–4, 214, 243, 245
*then/than*, 154–5
theses, editing, 6, 26–7, 39–40, 41–42, 44, 56
*they*, 114, 132, 237
time, expressing, 169
time management, 52–3
time to edit, estimating, 62, 63
training in editing, 22
transitivity of verbs, 111, 112–3
travelling and editing, 74–6, 81
Truss, Lynn, 184, 185, 250
tutoring, 38–40

**U**
*uninterested/disinterested*, 142

## V

vagueness in writing, 220
variety in editing, 5–7, 18–19, 35–6
verbal nouns, 206
'verbicide', 116–17
verbs, 109–11, 215
   ESL writing, in, 243–4
   inventing, 116
   part of speech, as, 85
   subject–verb agreement, 91, 114, 119–20, 121, 215
   subjunctive, 93, 110–11, 151–3
   voice, 112–13, 125–6, 205–6, 209, 210
   weak, 209–10
vocative case, 128
voice (grammar), 112–13, 125–6, 205–6, 209–10
'vouns', 116–17

## W

website disclaimers, 36
*whether/if*, 143
*which/that*, 92
*who/whom*, 145–6
Wilkes, G A, 228–9, 249
*will/shall*, 145, 154
Word, *see* Microsoft Word
words
   choice of, 206–7
   classes of, 95–104
   future of, 235–48
working hours, 68
workspace, organising, 67–9, 81
writing effectively, *see* effective writing
writing standards, 70–3

## Y

years as plurals, 185

www.ingramcontent.com/pod-product-compliance
Lightning Source LLC
Chambersburg PA
CBHW050845230426
43667CB00012B/2153